OUTER RING (SADOVOYE)

INNER RING (BOULEVARD)

TVERSKAYA SQ

MYASNITSKAYA ST

7

5

4

LYUBYANSKAYA SQ.

TEATRALNAYA SQ
6

REVOLUTION SQ

NIKOLSKAYA

NEW SQ

LYUBYANSKY PROEZD

MAROSEIKA ST

MANEZH SQ

3

ILYINKA

OLD SQ

SLAVYANSKAYA SQ

ALEXANDER GARDEN

1

RED SQ

2

VARVARKA

KREMLIN

8

MOS

MOSCOW RIVER

D1052122

RUSSIAN
AT A GLANCE

PHRASE BOOK & DICTIONARY FOR TRAVELERS

BY THOMAS R. BEYER, JR.
Professor of Russian
Middlebury College, Middlebury, Vermont

Third Edition

BARRON'S

All inquiries should be addressed to:
Barron's Educational Series, Inc.
250 Wireless Boulevard
Hauppauge, New York 11788
www.barronseduc.com

ISBN-13: 978-0-7641-3767-9 (book only)
ISBN-10: 0-7641-3767-0 (book only)
ISBN-13: 978-0-7641-9370-5 (book and CD package)
ISBN-10: 0-7641-9370-8 (book and CD package)

Library of Congress Catalog Card 2007027790

Library of Congress Cataloging-in-Publication Data
Beyer, Thomas R.
    Russian at a glance / Thomas R. Beyer, Jr. — 3rd ed.
        p.   cm.
    Includes index.
    ISBN-13: 978-0-7641-3767-9 (alk. paper)
    ISBN-10: 0-7641-3767-0 (alk. paper)
    ISBN-13: 978-0-7641-9370-5 (book and CD package)
    ISBN-10: 0-7641-9370-8 (book and CD package)
1. Russian language—Conversation and phrase books—English.   I. Title.
    PG2121.B49 2008
    491.783'421—dc22   2007027790

Illustrations: Juan Suarez

PRINTED IN CHINA
9 8 7 6 5 4 3 2 1

CONTENTS

PREFACE x

■ **INTRODUCTION TO THE RUSSIAN LANGUAGE** 1

■ **QUICK PRONUNCIATION GUIDE** 2

Three Rules of Pronunciation 4

■ **THE BASICS FOR GETTING BY** 5

Most Frequently Used Expressions 5
Questions 10
Exclamations 10
Problems, Problems, Problems (Emergencies) 11
Numbers 14

■ **WHEN YOU ARRIVE** 19

Passport Control 19
Customs 23
Baggage and Porters 26
Airport Transportation 27

■ **BANKING AND MONEY MATTERS** 29

Exchanging Currency 29
Russian Money 31
Credit and Debit Cards 31
Banking 32
Business and Banking Terms 33
Tipping 34

■ **AT THE HOTEL** 35

Getting to Your Hotel 35
Checking In 36
Getting Your Key 38
Laundry and Pressing 41
Complaints 42
Hotel Services and Signs 43
Checking Out 45
Apartments 46

■ **GETTING AROUND TOWN**   **49**

The Metro   49
Trams, Trolleybuses, Buses   53
Taxis   54
Sightseeing   56
A Sightseeing Itinerary   58
Religious Services   61

■ **PLANNING A TRIP**   **63**

Air Travel   63
Shipboard Travel   66
Train Service   68

■ **DRIVING A CAR**   **70**

Road Signs   70
Car Rentals   74
On the Road   76
At the Service Station   77
Accidents, Repairs   79

■ **ENTERTAINMENT AND DIVERSIONS**   **84**

Ballet, Concerts, Movies, Opera   84
Your Ticket   89
Night Life   91
Quiet Relaxation: Cards, Chess   92
Sports   93
In the Countryside   96

■ **FOOD AND DRINK**   **98**

Eating Out   99
The Menu   104
Settling Up   111
Shopping for Food   112

■ **MEETING PEOPLE**   **117**

Greetings and Introductions   117
Socializing   121
Saying Good-bye   123

■ **SHOPPING** 124

Shops and Stores 124
Going Shopping 124
Bookstore 127
Clothing 128
Fabrics 132
Shoes and Boots 133
Electrical Appliances 135
Food and Household Items 136
Metric Weights and Measures 137
The Jewelry Store 138
Audio and Video Equipment 140
The Newsstand 141
Photographic Equipment 142
Souvenirs 144
Office Supplies 147
Tobacco 148
Toiletries 149

■ **PERSONAL CARE AND SERVICES** 152

Barber Shop 152
Beauty Parlor 154
The Bathhouse 156
Laundry and Dry Cleaning 158
Shoe Repairs 160
Watch Repairs 161
Camera Repairs 162

■ **MEDICAL CARE** 164

Pharmacy 164
Doctors 166
Parts of the Body 167
What's Wrong 169
Doctor's Instructions 170
Patient's Concerns 170
Accidents 171
Dentists 172
Opticians 174
Special Needs 175

■ COMMUNICATIONS 177

Post Office 177
Telephones 178
Faxes 181
Telegrams 182
Computers 183
Computer Mini-Dictionary 185
Internet Sites 189

■ GENERAL INFORMATION 191

Telling Time 191
Expressions of Time 193
Days 194
Months 195
Dates 196
Seasons 196
Weather 197
Temperature Conversions 197
Official Holidays 198
Russia and Its Neighbors 199
Countries and Nationalities 202
Directions 203
Important Signs 203
Abbreviations 205
Metric Conversions 206
Emergency Telephone Numbers 208
Mini-Dictionary for Business Travelers 209

■ QUICK GRAMMAR GUIDE 213

Nouns 213
Pronouns 215
Adjectives/Possessive Modifiers 216
Adverbs 217
Verbs 217
Questions 219
Negations 220
Word Order 220
Prepositions 221

■ READY REFERENCE KEY   223

ENGLISH-RUSSIAN DICTIONARY   225

RUSSIAN-ENGLISH DICTIONARY   258

INDEX   285

PREFACE

So you're taking a trip to one of the most fascinating countries in the world. That's exciting! In more ways than one, this new phrase book will prove an invaluable companion that will make your stay far more interesting and truly unforgettable.

The best way to describe the Russia of the twenty-first century is change, change, change. The fall of the Soviet Union and the benefits of gas and oil exports have succeeded in making Russia one of the most rapidly developing nations of the world. Entrepreneurs are bringing innovation and new possibilities to the transportation, tourist, and service industries. Dozens of new airlines, hundreds of restaurants, private bus and limo services are here today, and sometimes gone tomorrow. The Russian language resources of our book are up-to-date and less susceptible to change, but you will want to double-check on travel arrangements and new possibilities before you leave for an absolutely fascinating time in this enormous land!

This phrase book is part of a series published by Barron's Educational Series, Inc. In these books we present the phrases and words that a traveler most often needs for a brief visit to a foreign country, where the customs and language are often different. Each of these phrase books highlights the terms particular to that country, in situations that the tourist is most likely to encounter. With a specially developed key to pronunciation, this book will enable you to communicate quickly and confidently in colloquial terms. It is intended not only for beginners with no knowledge of the language, but also for those who have studied Russian and have some familiarity with it.

Some of the unique features and highlights of the Barron's series are:

- Easy to follow *pronunciation keys* and complete phonetic transcriptions of all words and phrases in the book.
- Compact dictionary of commonly used words and phrases—built right into the phrase book so there's no need to carry a separate dictionary.
- Useful phrases for the *tourist*, grouped together by subject matter in a logical way so that the appropriate phrase is easy to locate when you need it.
- Special phrases for the *business traveler*, including banking terms.
- Comprehensive section on *food and drink*, with food terms you will find on menus; these terms are often difficult or impossible to locate in dictionaries.

■ *Emergency phrases* and terms we hope you won't need: medical problems, theft or loss of valuables, replacement or repair of watches, cameras, and the like.
■ *Sightseeing itineraries*, shopping tips, practical travel tips to help you get off the beaten path and into the countryside, to the small towns and cities, and to neighboring areas.
■ A *reference section* providing important signs, conversion tables, holidays, time phrases, days of the week, and months of the year.
■ A brief *grammar section*, with the basic elements of the language briefly explained.

Enjoy your vacation and travel with confidence. You have a friend by your side.

ACKNOWLEDGMENTS

I would like to thank the following individuals and organizations for their assistance on this project:
Elena Kochneva of the Pushkin Russian Language Institute, Aeroflot, and Intourist. Mostly I am grateful to the dozens of friendly and courteous Russians in Moscow and St. Petersburg, including the "key ladies," my shoe shine man, the hairdressers at the St. Petersburg Hotel, the attendants at the Krasnopresnensky Baths, the lovely woman at the watch repair shop on Pushkin Street, the taxi drivers, and all who ensured that words and phrases in the book reflect the current state of the Russian language.
In preparing for this Third Edition I traveled again to St. Petersburg and Moscow to guarantee the up-to-date quality of the language and information provided in the book. Russia is still a magical place, and this time I experienced it through the eyes of my fellow traveler and companion, Dorothea. To her and Carina, Stefanie and Alexandra, I dedicate this new edition.

Travel Tips Security has become a major concern in the twenty-first century. Be prepared to spend extra time checking in for flights, passing through preflight security, and on the other end passing through passport control and customs. Be sure to bring your smile with you and a good dose of patience. Check the Internet or with your travel agent for the latest information on baggage size and weight restrictions, security regulations, and especially for carry-on limitations.

Before the flight or before connecting flights once inside Russia you may be offered an opportunity to have your luggage wrapped in plastic. It's a good idea to prevent items from falling out and anyone from getting in.

Most importantly, in this day and age, leave your valuables at home. If you can't do without a piece of jewelry or an expensive camera, then carry it with you.

Finally, always plan on the unexpected. You should carry at least an extra day or two of your medicines, some underclothes and socks in your carry-on bag, just in case your luggage is delayed.

INTRODUCTION TO THE RUSSIAN LANGUAGE

Russian is the official language of the Russian Federation (**Российская Федерация** *raSIskaya fidiRAtsiya*). There are more than 150 million ethnic Russians. Until the fall of the Soviet Union in 1991, Russian was also used in all the republics and the study of the language was mandatory in Soviet schools. Russian was frequently used as the language of communication between Russians and citizens of Eastern European countries, where Russian was a required language in most schools. There are probably as many as 250 to 300 million people who understand and can speak Russian, but for many of them it will be a second language. This is particularly true for those born before 1980.

Even as the use and knowledge of English grows, Russian still can serve as a means of communication beyond the borders of the Russian Federation. It is important, however, that you recognize and respect the difference between Russia and those independent states created when the Soviet Union dissolved. People will appreciate your awareness that not everyone in their country is Russian. Especially when traveling to the other countries, I have found it useful to learn a few courtesy phrases, such as *Hello, Thank you, Please*, and *You're welcome* in the local language.

Russian is a Slavic language, closest to Ukrainian and White Russian, but also related to Polish, Czech, Slovak, Slovenian, Croatian, Serbian, Macedonian, and Bulgarian. Its alphabet dates to the ninth century, when the monks Cyril and Methodius developed a written language for the Slavs. The Cyrillic alphabet, as it is called, has much in common with the Greek alphabet. With a little work you will be able to read the signs and texts that make most of Russia still a mystery for many Westerners. Most Russians are delighted and flattered by foreigners who attempt to speak their language. Your efforts will be greatly rewarded.

QUICK PRONUNCIATION GUIDE

The Cyrillic alphabet has thirty-three letters. Many of them will be familiar to you from English, and several others resemble Greek letters. As in English, each letter is only an approximation of how a sound is pronounced. The guide below should get you started in speaking Russian.

STRESS

Each Russian word has only one syllable that is stressed or under accent. Russians know where the stress is and do not write the accent marks. We will indicate the stressed syllable with capital letters in our transcription as an aid for your pronunciation.

VOWELS

Russian has five vowel sounds, but ten vowel letters. Five of the letters are "hard" and five are "soft." The one vowel sound in each word that is stressed receives special emphasis. As you speak Russian try, in the beginning, to exaggerate your pronunciation.

HARD VOWELS

RUSSIAN LETTER	RUSSIAN SOUND	ENGLISH SYMBOL	EXAMPLE
а	**a** as in **A**men	A*	да *DA*
э	**e** as in **e**cho	E	ехо *Ekho*
ы	**y** as in hai**r**y	Y	мы *MY*
о	**o** as in hell**o**	O	но *NO*
у	**u** as in r**u**le	U	ну *NU*

* Throughout our book any English symbol may appear either capitalized (*A*) indicating that it is stressed, or lower case (*a*) indicating that it is not stressed.

SOFT VOWELS

RUSSIAN LETTER	RUSSIAN SOUND	ENGLISH SYMBOL	EXAMPLE
я	**ya** as in **ya**hoo	YA	я *YA*
е	**ye** as in **ye**s	YE	нет *NYET*
и	**ee** as in b**ee**	I	ива *Iva*
ё	**yo** as in **yo**-yo	YO	полёт *paLYOT*
ю	**u** as in **u**nion	YU	юмор *YUmar*

The Russian letter **ё** (with the two dots above it) is rarely written or printed with the dots. Russians simply know where it occurs and always pronounce it correctly. Throughout our book we will include the dots unless the word is part of a sign.

CONSONANT LETTERS

RUSSIAN LETTER	RUSSIAN SOUND	ENGLISH SYMBOL	EXAMPLE
б	**b** as in **b**at	B	банк *BANK*
в	**v** as in **v**ote	V	вот *VOT*
г	**g** as in **g**o	G	гол *GOL*
д	**d** as in **d**og	D	да *DA*
ж	**zh** as in a**z**ure	ZH	жена *zhiNA*
з	**z** as in **z**oo	Z	за *ZA*
й	**y** as in bo**y**	Y	мой *MOY*
к	**k** as in **k**ayak	K	касса *KAsa*
л	**l** as in **l**ot	L	лампа *LAMpa*
м	**m** as in **m**all	M	муж *MUSH*
н	**n** as in **n**ote	N	нос *NOS*
п	**p** as in **p**apa	P	парк *PARK*
р	**r** as in **r**abbit	R	рот *ROT*
с	**s** as in **s**un	S	суп *SUP*
т	**t** as in **t**oe	T	такси *taKSI*
ф	**f** as in **f**und	F	фунт *FUNT*
х	**ch** as in Ba**ch**, lo**ch**	KH	ах *AKH*
ц	**ts** as in **ts**ar	TS	царь *TSAR'*
ч	**ch** as in **ch**eap	CH	читает *chiTAyit*
ш	**sh** as in **sh**ow	SH	шапка *SHAPka*
щ	**sh** as in **sh**eep	SH	щи *SHI*
ъ	hard sign		not pronounced
ь	soft sign		not pronounced

THREE RULES OF PRONUNCIATION

1. Russians pronounce the **o** sound (as in hell**o**) only when it is stressed. When some other vowel is stressed in a word, the letter **o** is pronounced as an **a**. For example, **кот** (*KOT*), but **котá** (*kaTA*). When the letters **е, я**, and sometimes **a** are not stressed, they are pronounced **i** as in the English word **it**.

2. Consonants can be hard **ну** (*NU*) or soft **нет** (*NYET*). The soft **n** is like the sound in the word o**n**ion. A consonant is hard unless it is followed by a soft vowel letter **я, е, и, ё, ю** or the soft sign **ь**.

3. At the end of a word, or before voiced consonants, **б, в, г, д, ж**, and **з** become their voiceless counterparts, **б → п, в → ф, г → к, д → т, ж → ш, з → с**. Examples: **ход** *KHOT*, **баб** *BAP*, **ног** *NOK*, **автомат** *aftaMAT*, **водка** *VOTka*.

All these changes happen automatically for the native speaker. But if you carefully repeat the examples on the cassette along with the audioscript, you too can sound like a Russian!

Travel Tips   Increasingly the airlines and hotels have placed restrictions on cancellations. Be sure that you understand completely the terms of your reservation. If you are unable to fly as planned or if you are delayed for some reason contact the airline, hotel, or travel agency immediately. You may still be eligible for a full or partial refund.

You should also consider purchasing travel insurance that would reimburse you for the full cost of your trip for unforeseen circumstances.

THE BASICS FOR GETTING BY

MOST FREQUENTLY USED EXPRESSIONS

The expressions in this section are the ones you'll use again and again—fundamental building blocks of conversation, ways to express your wants or needs, and some simple interrogative forms that you can use to construct all sorts of questions. It's a good idea to practice these phrases until you know them by heart.

Hello.	**Здравствуйте.**	*ZDRASTvuytye*
Hi.	**Привет!**	*priVYET*
Yes.	**Да.**	*DA*
No.	**Нет.**	*NYET*
Maybe.	**Может быть.**	*MOzhit BYT'*
Please.	**Пожалуйста.**	*paZHAlusta*
Thank you.	**Спасибо.**	*spaSIba*
Thank you very much.	**Большое спасибо.**	*bal'SHOye spaSIba*
Excuse me!	**Извините!**	*izviNItye*
Pardon me!	**Простите!**	*praSTItye*
I beg your pardon.	**Прошу прощения.**	*praSHU praSCHYEniya*
Make way!	**Дорогу!**	*daROgu*
Watch out! Careful!	**Осторожно!**	*astaROZHna*

Just a minute!	**Минуточку!**	*miNUtachku*
That's all right.	**Хорошо.**	*kharaSHO*
That's fine.	**Ладно.**	*LAdna*
It doesn't matter.	**Ничего.**	*nichiVO*
Good morning.	**Доброе утро.**	*DObraye Utra*
Good afternoon.	**Добрый день.**	*DObry DYEN'*
Good evening.	**Добрый вечер.**	*DObry VYEchir*
Good night.	**Спокойной ночи.** *spaKOYnay NOchi*	
Comrade	**Товарищ**	*taVArish*
Mister	**Господин**	*gaspaDIN*
Miss, Mrs.	**Госпожа**	*gaspaZHA*
Young man!	**Молодой человек!** *malaDOY chilaVYEK*	
Young lady!	**Девушка!**	*DYEvushka*
Good-bye.	**До свидания.**	*da sviDAniya*
Until tomorrow.	**До завтра.**	*da ZAFtra*
See you later.	**Пока.**	*paKA*
Do you speak English?	**Вы говорите по-английски?** *VY gavaRItye pa-anGLIYski*	
I speak a little Russian.	**Я говорю немного по-русски.** *YA gavaRYU niMNOga pa-RUski*	
Do you understand?	**Вы понимаете?**	*VY paniMAyitye*
I understand.	**Я понимаю.**	*YA paniMAyu*

I don't understand.	**Я не понимаю.**	*YA NYE paniMAyu*
I'm listening.	**Я слушаю.**	*YA SLUshayu*
Speak up!	**Говорите!**	*gavaRItye*
Speak louder.	**Говорите громче!** *gavaRItye GROMche*	
Speak slower.	**Говорите медленнее!** *gavaRItye MYEdliniye*	
What?	**Что?**	*SHTO*
What did you say?	**Что вы сказали?**	*SHTO VY skaZAli*

Russian often has distinctive forms for men and women. We will use the abbreviation (*m*) to indicate masculine and (*f*) to indicate feminine.

How do you say _____	**Как _____** *KAK*
■ in Russian?	**по-русски?** *pa-RUski*
What does that mean?	**Что это значит?** *SHTO Eta ZNAchit*
Do you know?	**Вы знаете?** *VY ZNAyitye*
Don't you know?	**Вы не знаете?** *VY NYE ZNAyitye*
Please repeat.	**Повторите, пожалуйста.** *paftaRItye paZHAlusta*
I'm an American (*m*)	**Я американец.** *YA ameriKAnits*
I'm an American (*f*)	**Я американка.** *YA ameriKANka*
I'm British. (*m*)	**Я англичанин.** *YA angliCHAnin*
I'm British. (*f*)	**Я англичанка.** *YA angliCHANka*
I'm Canadian. (*m*)	**Я канадец.** *YA kaNAdits*
I'm Canadian. (*f*)	**Я канадка.** *YA kaNATka*
My name is _____.	**Меня зовут _____.** *miNYA zaVUT*
What's your name?	**Как вас зовут?** *KAK VAS zaVUT*
How are you?	**Как поживаете?** *KAK pazhiVAyitye*
Fine.	**Хорошо.** *kharaSHO*
And you?	**А вы?** *A VY*
Where is _____?	**Где _____?** *GDYE*
■ the bathroom	**туалет** *tuaLYET*
■ the entrance	**вход** *FKHOT*
■ the exit	**выход** *VYkhat*
■ the telephone	**телефон** *tiliFON*

■ a taxi
такси   *taKSI*

■ our bus
наш автобус   *NASH aFTObus*

Which way did they go?
Куда они пошли?
kuDA aNI paSHLI

■ to the right
направо   *naPRAva*

■ to the left
налево   *naLYEva*

■ straight ahead
прямо   *PRYAma*

How much does it cost?
Сколько стоит?   *SKOL'ka STOit*

I'd like _____.
Мне хочется _____.
MNYE KHOchitsa

Please bring me _____.
Принесите мне, пожалуйста _____.
priniSItye MNYE paZHAlusta

Please show me _____.
Покажите мне, пожалуйста _____.
pakaZHYtye MNYE paZHAlusta

I'm hungry. (*m*)
Я голоден.   *YA GOladin*

I'm hungry. (*f*)
Я голодна.   *YA galaDNA*

I'm thirsty.
Мне хочется пить.
MNYEKHOchitsa PIT'

I'm tired. (*m*)
Я устал.   *YA uSTAL*

I'm tired. (*f*)
Я устала.   *YA uSTAla*

What's that?
Что это?   *SHTO Eta*

What's up?
В чём дело?   *F CHOM DYEla*

What's new?
Что нового?   *SHTO NOvava*

I know.
Я знаю.   *YA ZNAyu*

I don't know.
Я не знаю.   *YA NYE ZNAyu*

QUESTIONS

Who?	**Кто?**	*KTO*
What?	**Что?**	*SHTO*
Where?	**Где?**	*GDYE*
Where to?	**Куда?**	*kuDA*
When?	**Когда?**	*kagDA*
Why?	**Почему?**	*pachiMU*
What for?	**Зачем?**	*zaCHYEM*
How?	**Как?**	*KAK*
How much?	**Сколько?**	*SKOL'ka*

EXCLAMATIONS

Ouch!	**Ой!**	*OY*
That hurts.	**Больно.**	*BOL'na*
Okay!	**Хорошо!**	*kharaSHO*
Super!	**Классно!**	*KLAsna*
You're super!	**Молодец!**	*malaDYETS*
Darn it!	**Чёрт возьми!**	*CHORT vaz'MI*
Well!	**Ну!**	*NU*
How beautiful!	**Как красиво!**	*KAK kraSIva*
Ugh!	**Фу!**	*FU*

That's awful!	**Ужасно!**	*uZHASna*
Great! Wonderful!	**Замечательно!**	*zamiCHAtil'na*
That's the one!	**Вот это!**	*VOT Eta*
My goodness!	**Боже мой!**	*BOzhe MOY*
Cheers!	**На здоровье!**	*na zdaROvye*
Quiet!	**Тише!**	*TIshe*
Shut up!	**Молчите!**	*malCHItye*
That's enough!	**Хватит!**	*KHVAtit*
Never mind!	**Ничего!**	*nichiVO*
Of course!	**Конечно!**	*kaNYESHna*
With pleasure!	**С удовольствием!** *s udaVOL'stviyim*	
Let's go!	**Пошли!**	*paSHLI*
What a shame!	**Как жаль!**	*KAK ZHAL'*
Nonsense!	**Ерунда!**	*yirunDA*
Are you crazy?	**Вы с ума сошли?** *VY s uMA saSHLI*	
What a fool!	**Какой дурак!**	*kaKOY duRAK*
Good luck!	**Удачи!**	*uDAchi*

PROBLEMS, PROBLEMS, PROBLEMS
(EMERGENCIES)

Hurry up!	**Спешите!**	*spiSHYtye*
Look!	**Смотрите!**	*smaTRItye*

Watch out! Be careful!	**Осторожно!**	*astaROZHna*
Listen!	**Слушайте!**	*SLUshaytye*
Wait!	**Подождите!**	*padaZHDItye*
Fire!	**Пожар!**	*paZHAR*
I have lost _____.(m)	**Я потерял _____.**	*YA patiRYAL*
I have lost _____.(f)	**Я потеряла _____.**	*YA patiRYAla*
my suitcase	**мой чемодан**	*MOY chimaDAN*
my purse	**мою сумку**	*maYU SUMku*
my briefcase	**мой портфель**	*MOY partFYEL'*
my cellphone	**мой мобильник**	*MOY maBIL'nik*
my laptop	**мой ноутбук**	*MOY NOTbuk*
I am lost! (m)	**Я потерялся!**	*YA patiRYALsya*
I am lost! (f)	**Я потерялась!**	*YA patiRYAlas'*
We're lost.	**Мы потерялись.**	*MY patiRYAlis'*
What's the matter with you?	**Что с вами?**	*SHTO s VAmi*
What (the devil) do you want?	**Что вам нужно?** *SHTO VAM NUZHna*	
Leave me alone!	**Оставьте меня в покое!** *aSTAF'tye miNYA f paKOye*	
Go away!	**Пошёл вон!**	*paSHOL VON*
Help!	**Помогите**	*pamaGItye*
I'm going to call a cop!	**Я позову милиционера!** *YA pazaVU militsiaNYEra*	
Get out!	**Вон!**	*VON*

Stop him!	**Задержите его!**	*zadirZHYtye yiVO*
He's stolen ____.	**Он украл ____.**	*ON uKRAL*
She's stolen ____.	**Она украла ____.**	*aNA uKRAla*
▧ my passport	**мой паспорт**	*MOY PASpart*
▧ my ring	**моё кольцо**	*maYO kal'TSO*
▧ my wallet	**мой бумажник**	*MOY buMAZHnik*
▧ my watch	**мои часы**	*maI chiSY*
Does anyone speak English?	**Кто-нибудь говорит но-английски?**	*KTO-nibut' gavaRIT pa-anGLIYski*
I need an interpreter.	**Мне нужен переводчик.**	*MNYE NUzhin piriVOTchik*
I want to speak with____.	**Я хочу говорить с ____.**	*YA khaCHU gavaRIT s*
▧ an attorney	**адвокатом**	*advaKAtam*
▧ consular officer	**сотрудником консульства**	*saTRUDnikam KŌNsul'stva*

I want to telephone _____.	**Я хочу позвонить _____.** *YA khaCHU pazvaNIT'*	
the American Embassy	**в американское посольство** *v amiriKANskaye paSOL'stva*	
the British Embassy	**в английское посольство** *v anGLIYskaye paSOL'stva*	
the Canadian Embassy	**в канадское посольство** *v kaNADskaye paSOL'stva*	

NUMBERS

If you really want to get around in Russia you will need to know the numbers in Russian. This knowledge is essential for shopping, arranging meetings, ordering tickets, and so on. In a word, knowing the numbers is an essential part of daily communication. The following list contains the cardinal and ordinal numbers along with some other useful quantities.

CARDINAL NUMBERS

0	**нуль**	*NUL'*
1	**один**	*aDIN*
2	**два**	*DVA*
3	**три**	*TRI*
4	**четыре**	*chiTYrye*
5	**пять**	*PYAT'*
6	**шесть**	*SHEST'*
7	**семь**	*SYEM'*
8	**восемь**	*VOsim'*
9	**девять**	*DYEvit'*
10	**десять**	*DYEsit'*

11	**одиннадцать**	*aDInatsat'*
12	**двенадцать**	*dviNAtsat'*
13	**тринадцать**	*triNAtsat'*
14	**четырнадцать**	*chiTYRnatsat'*
15	**пятнадцать**	*pitNAtsat'*
16	**шестнадцать**	*shistNAtsat'*
17	**семнадцать**	*simNAtsat'*
18	**восемнадцать**	*vasimNAtsat'*
19	**девятнадцать**	*divitNAtsat'*
20	**двадцать**	*DVAtsat'*
21	**двадцать один**	*DVAtsat' aDIN*
22	**двадцать два**	*DVAtsat' DVA*
23	**двадцать три**	*DVAtsat' TRI*
24	**двадцать четыре**	*DVAtsat' chiTYrye*
25	**двадцать пять**	*DVAtsat' PYAT"*
26	**двадцать шесть**	*DVAtsat' SHEST"*
27	**двадцать семь**	*DVAtsat' SYEM'*
28	**двадцать восемь**	*DVAtsat' VOsim'*
29	**двадцать девять**	*DVAtsat' DYEvit'*
30	**тридцать**	*TRItsat'*
31	**тридцать один**	*TRItsat' aDIN*
40	**сорок**	*SOrak*
41	**сорок один**	*SOrak aDIN*
50	**пятьдесят**	*pidiSYAT*
60	**шестьдесят**	*shizdiSYAT*
70	**семьдесят**	*SYEM'disit*

80	восемьдесят	*VOsim'disit*
90	девяносто	*diviNOSta*
100	сто	*STO*
101	сто один	*STO aDIN*
110	сто десять	*STO DYEsit'*
200	двести	*DVYESti*
300	триста	*TRISta*
400	четыреста	*chiTYrista*
500	пятьсот	*pit'SOT*
600	шестьсот	*shist'SOT*
700	семьсот	*sim'SOT*
800	восемьсот	*vasim'SOT*
900	девятьсот	*divit'SOT*
1000	тысяча	*TYsicha*
2000	две тысячи	*DVYE TYsichi*
5000	пять тысяч	*PYAT' TYsich*
1,000,000	миллион	*miliON*
2,000,000	два миллиона	*DVA miliOna*
5,000,000	пять миллионов	*PYAT' miliOnaf*
1,000,000,000	миллиард	*miliART*

ORDINAL NUMBERS

first	первый	*PYERvy*
second	второй	*ftaROY*
third	третий	*TRYEti*
fourth	четвёртый	*chitVYORty*

fifth	пятый	*PYAty*
sixth	шестой	*shiSTOY*
seventh	седьмой	*sid'MOY*
eighth	восьмой	*vas'MOY*
ninth	девятый	*diVYAty*
tenth	десятый	*diSYAty*

The ordinal numbers in Russian are modifiers and agree with the noun in number, gender, and case. A complete list of those endings can be found on p. 216. You should not be confused when you see the different endings **-ый, -ая, -ое**, such as:

First floor	**Первый этаж**	*PYERvy eTASH*
Second group	**Вторая группа**	*ftaRAya GRUpa*
Fifth seat	**Пятое место**	*PYAtaye MYESta*

USEFUL QUANTITIES

a half	половина	*palaVIna*
a quarter	четверть	*CHETvirt'*
ten of a kind	десяток	*diSYAtak*
100 grams	сто грамм	*STO GRAM*
a little bit	немного	*niMNOga*
too little	слишком мало	*SLISHkam MAla*
a little less	поменьше	*paMYEN'she*
a lot	много	*MNOga*
too much	слишком много	*SLISHkam MNOga*
a little more	побольше	*paBOL'she*
a pair	пара	*PAra*

once	**один раз**	*aDIN RAS*
twice	**два раза**	*DVA RAza*
many times	**много раз**	*MNOga RAS*
one more time	**ещё раз**	*yiSHO RAS*

Travel Tips Russian law demands that all purchases and transactions be done in rubles. How and where can you get Russian money? Traveler's checks, once the preferred method, are not accepted by all local banks or exchange points. They will want cash, and some accept only new currency and almost-flawless bills. You can also use your debit card or credit card to obtain Russian cash at a number of banking machines, especially in the large cities. Be sure to check on what charges will apply before leaving home.

You might also want to inform your bank or credit card provider that you will be traveling to Russia and likely conducting transactions there. Otherwise they might suspend activity on your card until you return. It is best to take more than one card and know the PIN codes for them. Also remember there are often daily limits on cash withdrawals that consider the weekend (close of business on Friday until opening of business on Monday) as just one day!

WHEN YOU ARRIVE

Even before you arrive you will have to apply for and receive a visa for Russia. This requires completing an application (**анкета** *anKYEta*) to submit with a letter of invitation or hotel confirmation, a passport-size photograph, your passport, and the required fee. Updated information on Russian visas can be obtained from your travel agency or the Russian Consulates or Embassy (http://www.russianembassy.org). Since the visa is actually attached to your passport you should be prepared to part with your passport for a week or longer. Be sure to plan ahead!

On board your plane or ship you will likely be asked to complete a migration card (**миграционная карта** *migratsiOnaya KARta*) that you should keep with your passport. This card may or may not be registered and stamped when you arrive at your destination. When in doubt ask your hotel or your hosts. The migration card comprises a Part A (Arrival) and a Part Б (Departure) connected by a perforated line (see pages 20–21).

PASSPORT CONTROL

When you arrive in Russia you will first proceed to the Passport Control Desk (**Паспортный контроль** *PASpartny kanTROL'*). There your passport and visa will be examined, and after stamping your visa the border guard will return both passport and visa to you. You must then claim your bags on the baggage carousel and pass through customs. There are two lanes. Since Customs regulations are consistently changing, check the signs posted in the airport indicating whether you can pass through the Green Line (**Зелёный коридор** *ziLYOny kariDOR*) or the Red Line (**Красный коридор** *KRASny kariDOR*). If you have nothing to declare you may proceed through the Green Line. If you have a substantial amount of

«А» (Въезд/Arrival)

Российская Федерация Russian Federation	Республика Беларусь Republic of Belarus

| Миграционная карта
Migration Card | Серия/
Serial | 41 06 |
| | № | 1647942 |

Фамилия/Surname
(Family name)

Имя/Given name(s)

Отчество/Patronymic

Дата рождения/Date of birth

| День
Day | Месяц
Month | Год
Year | Пол/Sex
Муж./Male ☐ Жен./Female ☐ |

Гражданство/Nationality

Документ удостоверяющий личность/   Номер визы/Visa number:
Passport or other ID

Цель визита (нужное подчеркнуть):
Purpose of travel (to be underlined):
Служебный/Official, Туризм/Tourism,
Коммерческий/Business,
Учёба/Education, Работа/Employment,
Частный/Private, Транзит/Transit

Сведения о приглашающей стороне
(наименование юридического лица, фамилия,
имя, (отчество) физического лица), населенный
пункт/Name of host person or company, locality:

Срок пребывания/Duration of stay: Подпись/Signature:
С/From: До/To:

Служебные отметки/For official use only

| Въезд в Российскую Федерацию/
Республику Беларусь/
Date of arrival in the Russian
Federation/Republic of Belarus | Выезд из Российской Федерации/
Республики Беларусь/
Date of departure from the Russian
Federation/Republic of Belarus |

«Б» (Выезд/Departure)

Российская Федерация Russian Federation	Республика Беларусь Republic of Belarus

Миграционная карта Migration Card	Серия/ Serial	41 06
	№	1647942

Фамилия/Surname
(Family name)

Имя/Given name(s)

Отчество/Patronymic

Дата рождения/Date of birth

День Day	Месяц Month	Год Year

Пол/Sex
Муж./Male ☐ Жен./Female ☐

Гражданство/Nationality

Документ удостоверяющий личность/
Passport or other ID

Номер визы/Visa number:

Цель визита (нужное подчеркнуть):
Purpose of travel (to be underlined):
Служебный/Official, Туризм/Tourism,
Коммерческий/Business,
Учёба/Education, Работа/Employment,
Частный/Private, Транзит/Transit

Сведения о приглашающей стороне
(наименование юридического лица, фамилия,
имя, (отчество) физического лица, населенный
пункт/Name of host person or company, locality:

Срок пребывания/Duration of stay:

C/From: До/To:

Подпись/Signature:

Служебные отметки/For official use only

Въезд в Российскую Федерацию/ Республику Беларусь/ Date of arrival in the Russian Federation/Republic of Belarus	Выезд из Российской Федерации/ Республики Беларусь/ Date of departure from the Russian Federation/Republic of Belarus

money you will likely have to fill out a customs declaration form (**декларация** *diklaRAtsiya*) (see pages 24–25) and proceed to the Red Line. Here you will hand over your customs declaration form, which contains a list of valuables (jewelry, cameras, etc.) and of currencies and traveler's checks in your possession. The customs official may ask to examine your luggage and then will initial and stamp your declaration form and return it to you. Please keep it with you.

Here is my passport.	**Вот мой паспорт.** *VOT MOY PASpart*
Here is my visa.	**Вот моя виза.** *VOT maYA VIza*
Here is my migration card.	**Вот моя миграционная карта.** *VOT maYA migratsiOnaya KARta*
I'm a tourist.	**Я турист.** *YA tuRIST*
I'm a businessman.	**Я бизнесмен.** *YA bisnisMYEN*
I'm on a business trip.	**Я по бизнесу.** *YA pa BISnisu*
I'll be here for _____.	**Я здесь буду _____.** *YA ZDYES' BUdu*
◼ a few days	**несколько дней** *NYEskal'ka DNYEY*
◼ a few weeks	**несколько недель** *NYEskal'ka niDYEL'*
◼ a month	**один месяц** *aDIN MYEsits*
I'm alone. (*m*)	**Я один.** *YA aDIN*
I'm alone. (*f*)	**Я одна.** *YA aDNA*
I'm with my wife.	**Я с женой.** *YA z zhiNOY*

I'm with my husband.   **Я с мужем.**   *YA s MUzhim*

I'm with my family.   **Я с семьёй.**   *YA s siM'YOY*

CUSTOMS

Here is my declaration.   **Вот моя декларация.**
VOT maYA diklaRAtsiya

I have nothing to declare.   **Мне нечего декларировать.**
MNYE NYEchiva diklaRIravat'

These are my suitcases.   **Вот мои чемоданы.**   *VOT maI chimaDAny*

These are souvenirs.   **Это сувениры.**   *Eta suviNIry*

They are for my personal use.   **Это мои личные вещи.**
Eta maI LICHniye VYEshi

Do I have to pay duty?   **Мне нужно платить пошлину?**
MNYE NUZHna plaTIT' POSHlinu

May I close my bag?   **Можно закрыть чемодан?**
MOZHna zaKRYT' chimaDAN

CUSTOMS DECLARATION

- To be filled in by persons over 16.
- To answer mark a cross in the appropriate box below ☒
- Keep for the whole duration of your temporary stay abroad/in the country and submit to the Customs on your way back. Not renewable in case of loss.

☐ entry ☐ exit ☐ transit

1. Information on traveller:

family name (last name)	first name	second name

country of permanent residence	nationality	passport #

arrived from (country of departure)	leaving for (country of destination)

With me I have children under age ☐ Yes ☐ No Number _____

2. Information on luggage:

2.1. Accompanied luggage, including hand luggage ☐ Yes ☐ No _____ pieces.

2.2. Unaccompanied luggage (a/s accompanying documents) ☐ Yes ☐ No _____ pieces.

3. Information on merchandise:

With me and in my luggage I have items which are due to be declared and transportation of which across borders must be documentarily permitted by authorities:

3.1. National and other currency in cash, currency valuables, articles made of precious metals and precious stones in any form or condition. ☐ Yes ☐ No

Description of currency, valuables or items	Total sum/Quantity	
	In figures	In words

3.2. Weapons of all descriptions, ammunition, explosives ☐ Yes ☐ No

3.3. Drugs and psychotropic substances ☐ Yes ☐ No

3.4. Antiques and objects of art ☐ Yes ☐ No

3.5. Printed editions and information media ☐ Yes ☐ No

3.6. Poisonous and powerful medicines and substances ☐ Yes ☐ No

3.7. Radioactive materials ☐ Yes ☐ No

3.8. Wildlife objects, parts and products thereof ☐ Yes ☐ No

3.9. High-frequency radio-electronic devices and means of communication ☐ Yes ☐ No

3.10. Goods subject to customs duties ☐ Yes ☐ No

3.11. Temporarily admitted (exported) goods ☐ Yes ☐ No

3.12. Transportation unit ☐ Yes ☐ No

- For the purposes of Customs control goods as in 3.2.-3.12., if any, must be described in detail on the back side of the Customs Declaration in par. 4.

ПАССАЖИРСКАЯ
ТАМОЖЕННАЯ ДЕКЛАРАЦИЯ

* **Заполняется каждым лицом, достигшим 16-летнего возраста.**
* **Нужный ответ помечается в соответствующей рамке знаком** ☒
* **Сохраняется на весь период временного въезда/выезда и предъявляется таможенным органам при возвращении. При утере не возобновляется.**

	въезд ☐	выезд ☐	транзит ☐

1. Сведения о лице:

фамилия	_имя_	_отчество_

		серия №
страна постоянного проживания	_гражданство/подданство_	паспорт

из какой страны прибыл (указывается страна отправления)	_в какую страну следует (указывается страна назначения)_

Со мною следуют несовершеннолетние дети ☐ Да ☐ Нет Количество _____

2. Сведения о наличии багажа:

2.1. Сопровождаемый багаж, включая ручную кладь ☐ Да ☐ Нет	2.2. Несопровождаемый багаж (по грузосопроводительным документам) ☐ Да ☐ Нет
Количество мест	Количество мест

3. Сведения о наличии товаров:

При мне в сопровождаемом багаже имеются товары, которые требуют обязательного письменного декларирования и перемещение которых через границу производится по разрешительным документам соответствующих компетентных органов.

3.1. Национальная валюта и иная наличная валюта, ценные бумаги, изделия из драгоценных металлов и драгоценных камней в любом виде и состоянии за исключением временно ввозимых (вывозимых) ☐ Да ☐ Нет

Наименование		Сумма/Количество	
валюты, ценностей или изделий	Цифрами	Прописью	

3.2. Оружие всякое, боеприпасы, взрывчатые вещества ☐ Да ☐ Нет	3.8. Объекты флоры и фауны, их части и полученная из них продукция ☐ Да ☐ Нет
3.3. Наркотики и психотропные вещества ☐ Да ☐ Нет	3.9. Радиоэлектронные средства, высокочастотные устройства ☐ Да ☐ Нет
3.4. Культурные ценности ☐ Да ☐ Нет	3.10. Товары, подлежащие обложению таможенными платежами ☐ Да ☐ Нет
3.5. Печатные издания и другие носители информации ☐ Да ☐ Нет	3.11. Временно ввозимые (вывозимые) товары ☐ Да ☐ Нет
3.6. Ядовитые и отравляющие вещества и лекарства ☐ Да ☐ Нет	3.12. Транспортное средство ☐ Да ☐ Нет
3.7. Радиоактивные материалы ☐ Да ☐ Нет	

* **В целях таможенного контроля подробные сведения о товарах, указанных в п. п. 3.2. – 3.12, при их наличии необходимо указать на оборотной стороне декларации в п.4.**

BAGGAGE AND PORTERS

Baggage carts (**прокат тележек** *praKAT tiLEzhik*) can be rented inside the luggage area. If you haven't located your luggage, check with the Lost Luggage section (**Розыск багажа** *ROzysk bagaZHA*). If you need a porter be sure he has the appropriate identification badge. When you have cleared customs you will enter the main hall of the airport. If you are with a tourist group or have been invited by a Russian organization, your hosts will probably be waiting for you at the Meeting Point (**Место встречи** *MYESta VSTRYEchi*). If you are traveling alone you might have already prepaid for some services, such as transfer to your hotel, etc. In any case, there will be an information desk (**Информация** *infarMAtsiya*) where someone can help you arrange transportation.

Where can I find a cart?	**Где можно взять тележку?** *GDYE MOZHna VZYAT' tiLYEZHku*
Porter, please!	**Носильщик, пожалуйста!** *naSIL'shik paZHAlusta*

These are our (my) bags.	**Вот наши (мои) вещи.** *VOT NAshi (maI) VYEshi*
Be careful with this one.	**Осторожно с этим.** *astaROZHna s Etim*
I'll carry this one.	**Этот я сам понесу.** *Etat YA SAM paniSU*
Put them down here.	**Положите их сюда, пожалуйста.** *palaZHYtye IKH syuDA paZHAlusta*
Thank you very much.	**Спасибо большое.** *spaSIba bal'SHOye*
This is for you.	**Вот вам.** *VOT VAM*

AIRPORT TRANSPORTATION

If you are with a group or are being met by your hosts, transportation to your accommodations will be provided. If you are completely on your own, you can arrange for a so-called "airport transfer" with any number of travel agencies available on the Internet. You should confirm your flight number and time of departure, but pay only when you receive the services. You may want to use the ATM machine at the airport to obtain rubles for the ride. Russian airports, like many worldwide, attract any number of free agents trying to earn money by transporting passengers. It is never a wise idea to use anything other than officially sanctioned cabs or car services. Be sure you know the status of the driver who will be taking you to your hotel, apartment, or meeting place.

For those who know the language well and have experience in Russia there are less expensive ways to make it downtown in Moscow and St. Petersburg. Many local citizens choose to avoid the high prices of taxis or car services and rely on local transportation.

Where is our bus?	**Где наш автобус?** *GDYE NASH aFTObus*
Does this bus go downtown?	**Этот автобус идёт в центр?** *Etat aFTObus iDYOT f TSENTR*
I want to go to the hotel _____.	**Я хочу ехать в гостиницу _____.** *YA khaCHU YEkhat' v gaSTInitsu*
Cosmos	**Космос** *KOSmas*
Petersburg	**Петербург** *pitirBURK*
Savoy	**Савой** *saVOY*
How much is the fare?	**Сколько стоит?** *SKOL'ka STOit*
That's too expensive!	**Это слишком дорого!** *Eta SLISHkam DOraga*
That's fine. Let's go.	**Хорошо. Поехали.** *kharaSHO paYEkhali*

Travel Tips Keep it light and on wheels! Airlines seem to have more and more weight and size restrictions for checked baggage and carry-on items. Check for the latest information with your air carrier. You do yourself a favor by being prepared to carry all your luggage over substantial distances (as much as several hundred yards) in airports, at train stations, and elsewhere. Pack only what you will need, and find luggage that rolls to keep the strain on your muscles to a minimum.

BANKING AND MONEY MATTERS

In Russia you usually pay for all goods and services in Russian rubles. Consequently, you will have to exchange your own "hard" currency at an official currency exchange outlet (**Обмен валюты** *abMYEN vaLYUty*). In major cities you may obtain Russian rubles from an ATM (**банкомат** *bankaMAT*) with your bank card or credit card. Traveler's checks are not accepted everywhere.

Usually you cannot exchange Russian rubles for other currencies outside of Russia, and experienced travelers avoid accumulating too many rubles toward the end of their stay. As with many things in Russia, the rules of the game change constantly—so inquire at your own bank and credit card offices before you leave, and ask your Russian hosts for the latest information when you arrive.

> You may encounter some prices indicated as **y.e.,** which stands for conventional units (**условные единицы** *uSLOvnye yediNItsy*). This is the equivalent in euros of the price, which will eventually be converted into rubles for payment. Recently attempts have been made to eliminate the use of this device. But if you see that **y.e.,** be prepared to pay premium rates for the services.

EXCHANGING CURRENCY

I want to exchange _____.	**Я хочу обменять _____.** *YA khaCHU abmiNYAT'*
■ American dollars	**американские доллары** *amiriKANskiye DOlary*
■ British pounds	**английские фунты** *anGLIYskiye FUNty*
■ Canadian dollars	**канадские доллары** *anGLIYskiye DOlary*

■ traveler's checks

дорожные чеки
daROZHniye CHEki

What is the
exchange rate?

Какой обменный курс?
kaKOY abMYEny KURS

Where must I sign?

Где мне расписаться?
GDYE MNYE raspiSAtsa

Large bills, if
possible.

Если можно, крупными
купюрами. *YEsli MOZHna*
KRUPnymi kuPYUrami

Small bills, if
possible.

Если можно, мелькими купюрами.
YEsli MOZHna MYEL'kimi
kuPYUrami

Please give me
change for this.

Разменяйте, пожалуйста.
razmiNYAYtye paZHAlusta

Give me a receipt,
please.

Дайте мне квитанцию, позалуйста.
DAYtye MNYE kviTANtsiyu
paZHAlusta

The exchange rate and charges vary from place to place.
Your hotel might not have the most advantageous rate—but
be careful not to exchange large amounts of currency in
public view. To keep track of your expenses, you may want
to convert the following amounts of rubles to the equivalents
in your own currency.

RUSSIAN RUBLES	MY CURRENCY
25	
100	
500	
1000	
2500	

RUSSIAN MONEY

The basic format of Russian and Soviet currency, kopecks and rubles, has remained stable for hundreds of years. There are 100 kopecks in a ruble. But the value of the ruble fluctuated enormously until the turn of the century. While there are still kopeck coins, you will rarely encounter them except perhaps in a supermarket. As of 2008 the following coins and bills were in circulation. The 1 kopeck piece is silver-colored, the 10 and 50 kopeck pieces are bronze-colored. Kopeck coins (**копейка** *kaPEYka*) depict St. George slaying the dragon. There are silver colored coin denominations of 1, 2, and 5 rubles. Ruble coins (**рубль** *RUBL'*) have the distinctive two-headed eagle of the Russian coat of arms. Notes are in denominations of 10, 50, 100, 500, and 1000 rubles.

CREDIT AND DEBIT CARDS

Most American and European major credit cards are accepted at hotels and in hotel restaurants, clubs, and bars. This is often a convenient and safe way to pay for purchases. The charges in rubles will be automatically converted by your credit card company or bank into dollars or your local currency. But be sure to keep your receipts for all these transactions.

Do you accept credit cards?	**Вы принимаете кредитные карточки?** *VY priniMAyitye kriDITniye KARtachki*
I have only this credit card.	**У меня только такая кредитная карточка.** *U miNYA TOL'ka taKAya kriDITnaya KARtachka*
Must I pay in hard currency?	**Надо платить валютой?** *NAda plaTIT' vaLYUtay*
May I pay cash?	**Можно платить наличными?** *MOZHna plaTIT' naLICHnymi*

BANKING

Currently, foreign organizations and individuals may have an account with an ever increasing number of banks.

I would like to open an account.	**Я хочу открыт счёт.** *YA khaCHU atKRYT' SHOT*
I want to make a deposit.	**Я хочу выдать вклад.** *YA khaCHU VYdat' FKLAT*
I want to make a withdrawal.	**Я хочу принять вклад.** *YA khaCHU priNYAT' FKLAT*
I need a deposit slip.	**Мне нужен приходный ордер.** *MNYE NUzhin priKHODny ORdir*
I need a withdrawal slip.	**Мне нужен расходный ордер.** *MNYE NUzhin rasKHODny ORdir*

BUSINESS AND BANKING TERMS

amount	**сумма**	*SUma*
ATM machine	**банкомат**	*bankaMAT*
banker	**банкир**	*banKIR*
borrow	**брать взаймы**	*BRAT' vzayMI*
clear	**отмена**	*atMYEna*
cashier	**касса**	*KAsa*
capital	**капитал**	*kapiTAL*
cash register	**кассовой аппарат**	*kasaVOY apaRAT*
checkbook	**чековая книжка**	*CHYEkavaya KNISHka*
clear	**сброс**	*ZBROS*
enter	**ввод**	*VVOT*
gains	**доходы**	*daKHOdy*
interest rate	**процент**	*praTSENT*
investment	**инвестиция**	*inviSTItsiya*
lend	**давать взаймы**	*daVAT' vzayMI*
losses	**убытки**	*uBYTki*
make change	**разменять**	*razmiNYAT'*
money	**деньги**	*DYENgi*
mortgage	**ипотека**	*ipaTYEka*
open an account	**открыть счёт**	*otKRYT' SCHYOT*
PIN number	**код**	*KOT*
premium	**премия**	*PRYEmiya*
profit	**прибыль**	*PRYbyl'*
safe	**сейф**	*SYEYF*
signature	**подпись**	*POTpis'*
window	**окошко**	*aKOshka*

TIPPING

Russians, particularly in the major cities, expect tips similar to those in Berlin, London, New York, Paris, Rome, and Tokyo. Check your restaurant bill and other establishments for a service charge already included. Otherwise 10–20% is the expectation—especially if you are pleased with the service. Porters expect the equivalent of at least one dollar per bag. For small courtesies the equivalent of a dollar will be warmly appreciated.

AT THE HOTEL

If you are traveling with a group, your hotel arrangements will have already been made through one of the many travel organizations. If you are being met by an official organization, it will have arranged accommodations. When you arrive at the airport, go directly to the Information Desk or meet your hosts.

Individuals now have a wide array of choices. There are many travel agencies specializing in hotels for Russia. You can also consult the Internet, where you will be shown a variety of choices ranging from expensive five-star accommodations to less expensive options. You may be asked to prepay and receive a confirmation number. Many agencies or hotels will also send you the required confirmation for your visa approval. Be sure to think of location and read the reviews of recent travelers. A newly emerging and growing market for short-term rentals is provided by private apartments (**квартиры** *kvarTIry*) that may appeal to the more adventuresome.

GETTING TO YOUR HOTEL

I want to go to the hotel _____.	**Я хочу поехать в гостиницу _____.** *YA khaCHU paYEkhat' v gaSTInitsu*	
▪ Cosmos	**Космос**	*KOSmas*
▪ International	**Международная**	*mizhdunaRODnaya*
▪ Astoria	**Астория**	*aSTOriya*
▪ Nevsky	**Невский**	*NYEfski*
▪ Petersburg	**Петербург**	*pitirBURK*
▪ Metropole	**Метрополь**	*mitraPOL'*
▪ National	**Националь**	*natsiaNAL'*
▪ Baltic	**Прибалтийская**	*pribalTIYskaya*

Is it far?	**Она далеко?** *aNA daliKO*
Is it near?	**Она близко?** *aNA BLISka*
What's the number of my bus?	**Какой номер моего автобуса?** *kaKOY NOmir mayiVO aFTObusa*
What's the number of my car?	**Какой номер моей машины?** *kaKOY NOmir maYEY maSHYny*

CHECKING IN

When you arrive at the hotel, you must present your passport, which will be registered. Be sure to ask for its return. You may need your passport for identification, to exchange money, and to gain entry into many offices, including your embassy. At many hotels, you will obtain and return your key at the front desk. You will be issued a Guest Card (**Карта гостя** *KARta gaSTYA*) as identification for security personnel at the hotel entrance. Carry it with you.

Here is my voucher.	**Вот мой ваучер.** *VOT MOY VAUchir*
I reserved a single room.	**Я забронировал номер на одного.** *YA zabraNIraval NOmir na adnaVO*
We need a double room.	**Нам нужен номер на двоих.** *NAM NUzhin NOmir na dvaIKH*
I reserved a deluxe room.	**Я забронировал номер люкс.** *YA zabraNIraval NOmir LYUKS*
Does the room have _____?	**В номере есть _____?** *V NOmire YEST" _____?*
▦ air conditioning	**кондиционер** *konditsiaNYER*
▦ a bathtub	**ванна** *VAna*

■ a double bed **двуспальная кровать**
dvuSPAL'naya kraVAT'

■ two single beds **две односпальные кровати**
DVYE adnaSPAL'nye kraVAti

■ king/queen size bed **большая кровать**
bal'SHAya kraVAT'

■ cable television **кабельное телевидение**
KAbil'naye tiliVIdiniye

■ a nice view **красивый вид** *kraSIvy VIT*

■ a shower **душ** *DUSH*

May I see the room? **Можно смотреть номер?**
MOZHna smaTRYET' NOmir?

I (don't) like it. **Он мне (не) нравится.**
ON MNYE (NYE) NRAvitsa

It's very noisy. **Очень шумно.** *Ochin' SHUMna*

Do you have **У вас есть другой номер?**
another room? *U VAS YEST' druGOY NOmir*

May I leave this **Можно это оставить в сейфе?**
in the safe? *MOZHna Eta aSTAvit' v SEYfe*

Where can I get the **Где мне взять ключ?**
key? *GDYE MNYE VZYAT' KLYUCH*

When can I pick **Когда можно получить паспорт?**
up my passport? *kagDA MOZHna paluCHIT' PASpart*

On what floor is **На каком этаже мой номер?**
my room? *na kaKOM etaZHE MOY NOmir*

Where is the **Где лифт?** *GDYE LIFT*
elevator?

Where is the **Где бюро обслуживания?**
service bureau? *GDYE byuRO apSLUzhivaniya*

When is the restaurant open?	**Когда ресторан открыт?** *kagDA ristaRAN atKRYT*
Is there a snack bar on the floor?	**Есть буфет на этаже?** *YEST'buFYET na etaZHE*
Do I need a ticket for breakfast?	**Мне нужен талон на завтрак?** *MNYE NUzhin taLON na ZAFtrak*

GETTING YOUR KEY

In some Russian hotels you will be given an electronic card for the door. But you may also be given a heavy key that you pick up and leave at the reception desk whenever you come and go.

You should also feel free to call and ask the receptionists for information and express your needs and complaints to them.

Hello! My name is _____.	**Здравствуйте! Меня зовут _____.** *ZDRASTvuytye miNYA zaVUT*
My key, please.	**Мой ключ, похалуйста.** *MOY KLYUCH paZHAlusta*
Room No. 5.	**Номер пять.** *NOmir PYAT"*
Room No. 16.	**Номер шестнадцать.** *NOmir shistNAtsat'*
Room No. 102.	**Номер один нуль два.** *NOmir aDIN NUL' DVA*
Room No. 234.	**Номер два три четыре.** *NOmir DVA TRI chiTYrye*
Room No. 567.	**Номер пять шесть семь.** *NOmir PYAT" SHEST' SYEM'*
Room No. 891.	**Номер восемь девять один.** *NOmir VOsim' DYEvit' aDIN*
Room No. 1205.	**Номер двенадцать нуль пять.** *NOmir dviNAtsat' NUL' PYAT"*
Please bring me _____.	**Принесите мне, ножалуйста _____.** *priniSItye MNYE paZHAlusta*
▪ an ashtray	**пепельницу** *PYEpil'nitsu*
▪ a bar of soap	**кусок мыла** *kuSOK MYla*
▪ a blanket	**одеяло** *adiYAla*
▪ some boiling water	**кипяток** *kipiTOK*
▪ a bottle of mineral water	**бутылку минеральной воды** *buTYLku miniRAL'nay vaDY*
▪ a cot	**раскладушку** *rasklaDUSHku*
▪ some envelopes	**конверты** *kanVYERty*

■ a glass of tea	**стакан чая**	*staKAN CHAya*
■ another pillow	**ещё подушку**	*yiSHO paDUSHku*
■ some postcards	**открытки**	*atKRYTki*
■ another towel	**ещё полотенце** *yiSHO palaTYENtse*	
■ more hangers	**ещё вешалки**	*yiSHO VYEshalki*
■ some toilet paper	**туалетную бумажку** *tuaLYETnuyu buMAZHku*	
■ writing paper	**бумагу для писем** *buMAgu dlya PIsim*	

Just a minute!	**Минуточку!**	*miNUtachku*
Come in!	**Входите!**	*fkhaDItye*
Please place it there.	**Положите, пожалуйста, туда.** *palaZHYtye paZHAlusta tuDA*	

Please wake me at _____.
Разбудите меня _____.
razbuDItye miNYA

■ 6:00 AM	**в шесть часов**	*f SHEST' chiSOF*
■ 6:30 AM	**в половине седьмого** *f palaVInye sid'MOva*	
■ 7:00 AM	**в семь часов**	*f SYEM' chiSOF*
■ 7:30 AM	**в половине восьмого** *f palaVInye vas'MOva*	

Do not disturb.	**Не беспокойте.**	*NYE bispoKOYtye*
Make up the room.	**Уберите номер.**	*ubiRItye NOmir*
Please exchange towels.	**Пожалуйста, заменяйте полотенци.** *paZHAlusta zamiNYATtye palaTYENtsi*	
They can be used again.	**Будут использоваться вновь.** *Budut isPOL'zavatsa VNOF'*	

LAUNDRY AND PRESSING

Many hotels will have laundry service. Look for the price list in your room. Since this service can be costly, be sure you understand the prices. The following list should prove useful.

Laundry	**Прачечная** *PRAchichnaya*
Gentlemen	**Для мужчин** *DLYA MUSHchin*
Shirt (starched)	**рубашка (накрахмаленная)** *ruBASHka (nakrakhMAleinaya)*
Polo shirt	**футболка** *fudBOLka*
Shorts	**шорты** *SHORty*
Underwear	**нижнее бельё** *NIZHnie biL'YO*
Pajamas	**пижама** *piZHAma*
Socks	**носки** *naSKI*
Handkerchief	**носовой платок** *nasaVOY plaTOK*
Pants	**брюки** *BRYUki*
Ladies	**Для женщин** *DLYA ZHENschin*
Dress	**платье** *PLAt'ye*
Suit	**костюм** *kaSTYUM*
Blouse	**блузка** *BLUSka*
Underwear	**нижнее бельё** *NIZHnie biL'YO*
Night gown	**ночная рубашка** *nachNAya ruBASHka*

Skirt	**юбка** *YUPka*
■ pressing only	**Глажение** *GLAzhiniye*
Shirt	**рубашка** *ruBASHka*
■ folded	**сложить** *slaZHYT'*
■ on hangers	**плечики** *PLYEchiki*
Suit	**костюм** *kaSTYUM*
Jacket	**пиджак** *PIDzhak*
Pants	**брюки** *BRYUki*
Evening dress	**вечернее платье** *viCHYERniye PLAt'i*
Raincoat	**плащ** *PLAsch*
Coat	**пальто** *pal'TO*

COMPLAINTS

There is no ____.	**Нет ____.** *NYET*
■ cold water	**холодной воды** *khaLODnay vaDY*
■ hot water	**горячей воды** *gaRYAchey vaDY*

____ doesn't work.	**____ не работает.** *NYE raBOtayit*
■ The faucet	**Смеситель** *smiSItil'*
■ The lamp	**Лампа** *LAMpa*
■ The plug	**Розетка** *raZYETka*
■ The radio	**Радио** *RAdio*
■ The refrigerator	**Холодильник** *khalaDIL'nik*
■ The sink	**Умывальник** *umyVAL'nik*
■ The shower	**Душ** *DUSH*
■ The switch	**Выключатель** *vyklyuCHAtil'*

▨ The telephone	**Телефон**	*tiliFON*
▨ The television	**Телевизор**	*tiliVIzar*
▨ The toilet	**Унитаз**	*uniTAS*

It's too cold in my room.	**В номере слишком холодно.** *v NOmirye SLISHkam KHOladna*
It's too hot in my room.	**В номере слишком жарко.** *v NOmirye SLISHkam ZHARka*
The window doesn't open.	**Окно не открывается.** *akNO NYE atkryVAyitsa*
The window doesn't close.	**Окно не закрывается.** *akNO NYE zakryVAyitsa*
The room hasn't been cleaned.	**Номер не убран.** *NOmir NYE Ubran*

HOTEL SERVICES AND SIGNS

You will probably see some of the following signs in your hotel.

Administrator	**АДМИНИСТРАТОР** *adminiSTRAtar*
Bank	**БАНК** *BANK*
Bar	**БАР** *BAR*
Barber Shop/ Beauty Salon	**ПАРИКМАХЕРСКАЯ** *parikMAkhirskaya*
Cafe	**КАФЕ** *kaFYEY*
Cashier	**КАССА** *KAsa*

Checkroom	**КАМЕРА ХРАНЕНИЯ** *KAmira khraNYEniya*
Coatroom	**ГАРДЕРОБ** *gardiROP*
Currency Exchange	**ОБМЕННЫЙ ПУНКТ** *abMYEny PUNKT*
Emergency Exit	**ЗАПАСНЫЙ ВЫХОД** *zaPASny VYkhat*
Information	**ИНФОРМАЦИЯ** *infarMAtsiya*
Lunch Break	**ПЕРЕРЫВ** *piriRYF*
Newspaper Stand	**ГАЗЕТНЫЙ КИОСК** *gaZYETny kiOSK*
Nightclub	**НОЧНОЙ БАР** *nachNOY BAR*
No Vacancy	**МЕСТ НЕТ** *MYEST NYET*
Passport Desk	**ПАСПОРТНЫЙ СТОЛ** *PASpartny STOL*
Post Office	**ПОЧТА** *POCHta*
Reception Room	**ПРИЁМНАЯ** *priYOMnaya*
Restaurant	**РЕСТОРАН** *ristaRAN*
Restroom (men's)	**МУЖСКОЙ ТУАЛЕТ** *mushSKOY tuaLYET*
(ladies')	**ЖЕНСКИЙ ТУАЛЕТ** *ZHENskytuaLYET*
Sauna	**САУНА** *SAUna*
Security	**ОХРАНА** *aKHRAna*

Service Bureau	**БЮРО ОБСЛУЖИВАНИЯ** *byuRO apSLUzhivaniya*
Snack Bar	**БУФЕТ** *buFYET*
Souvenirs	**СУВЕНИРЫ** *suviNIry*
Swimming Pool	**БАССЕЙН** *baSYEYN*
Theater Desk	**ТЕАТРАЛЬНЫЙ СТОЛ** *tiaTRAL'ny STOL*

CHECKING OUT

I'm departing today.	**Я сегодня уезжаю.** *YA siVODnya uyiZHAyu*
When is checkout time?	**Когда расчётный час?** *kagDA rasSHOTny CHAS*
Please order a taxi for me.	**Закажите мне такси, пожалуйста.** *zakaZHYtye MNYE taKSI paZHAlusta*
How will you be paying?	**Как вы будете платить?** *KAK VY BUditye plaTIT'*
I'll pay with a credit card.	**Я плачу кредитной карточкой.** *YA plaCHU kriDITnay KARtachkay*
I left my suitcase in the room.	**Я оставил чемодан в номере.** *YA aSTAvil chimaDAN v NOmirye*
Let the bellboy bring it down.	**Пусть швейцар принесёт.** *PUST' shviyTSAR priniSYOT*

APARTMENTS

You might want to try renting an apartment for one or more nights. Many are very conveniently located in downtown areas and they can be considerably less expensive than tourist hotels. You can check on the Internet information regarding apartment location and size. Most agencies have maps with photos of the places. Look for something near a metro station for easy access to any point in Moscow or St. Petersburg.

If you look at the Russian announcements you'll want to understand the following.

One Room	**однокомнатная** *adnaKOMnatnaya*
Two Room	**двукомнатная** *dvuKOMnatnaya*

The apartment has a:	**В квартире есть** *f KVARtire YEST'*
▪ kitchen	**кухня** *KUKHnya*
▪ telephone	**телефон** *tiliFON*
▪ refrigerator	**холодильник** *khalaDIL'nik*
▪ washing machine	**стиральная машина** *stiRAL'naya maSHYna*
▪ coffee maker	**кофеварка** *kafeVARka*
▪ microwave oven	**микровольная печь** *mikraVOL'naya PYECH'*
▪ television	**телевизор** *tiliVIzar*
▪ computer	**компьютер** *kamPYUtir*
▪ pull-out couch	**раскладной диван** *raskladNOY diVAN*

Is there an elevator?	**Есть лифт?** *YEST' LIFT*
On what floor?	**На каком этаже?** *Na kaKOM etaZHE*

Can you fill out the reservation request below?

Заявка на размещение
Request for accommodations

Просим Вас забронировать номера в гостинице_____

We request you to reserve rooms in the hotel_____

Количество человек Number of persons	
Ф.И.О. Family name, First name, Patronymic (if you have one)	
Страна Country	
Кол-во номеров/категория номера Number of rooms/category	
Дата заезда/часы Date of arrival/time	
Дата выезда/часы Departure date/time	
Завтрак Breakfast	
Форма оплаты Form of payment	
Примечание Comments	

Контактное лицо _____
Contact person

Телефон, факс _____
Telephone, fax

Travel Tips   Touring on the cheap?
You can save on many daily expenses by avoiding the
convenient tourist outlets where high prices seem to
be the rule. Frequently, tickets for theater events can
be obtained at outdoor kiosks for prices that average
Russians can afford and are willing to pay. A meal in
a place catering to locals may cost you a fraction
of what they charge in the hotel restaurants. Be
adventuresome—when in Moscow do as the
Muscovites do. Simply observe the local customs,
use some of your newly learned Russian phrases,
and smile.

A final tip to save money: use the subway for
transportation around the city. You avoid the traffic,
save money, and treat yourself to an excursion through
the magnificent underground architecture of many
subway stations.

GETTING AROUND TOWN

If you really want to explore the country, get out and about on your own. You'll certainly want to walk along some of the busier streets, and you should also be familiar with the excellent systems of public transportation in most major cities.

THE METRO

In Moscow, St. Petersburg, and other large cities you absolutely must try out the subway (**метро** *miTRO*). The system is clean and very inexpensive, and many of the stations themselves are architectural masterpieces. You can find the metro by the big red capital **M.** The metro begins running early in the morning (5:30 A.M.) and stops at 12:30 A.M. in St. Petersburg and 1:00 A.M. in Moscow. Be sure to plan ahead if you want to ride the metro back to your hotel. The trains run with very short intervals, sometimes as little as thirty seconds during rush hour. Moscow has the

most extensive system, based on a circular main line
(**Кольцевая линия** *kal'tsiVAya LIniya*). Several lines
intersect the circle and meet at various places near the
middle of the city. Each station has a large map, and you
can find a map inside each subway car. On the wall you will
see a complete listing of the stations on your particular line.
To enter the metro you must purchase at the cashier's booth
(**Касса** *KAsa*) either a magnetic ticket (**магнитический
билет** *magniTIchiski biLYET*), a smart-card (**смарт-карта**
SMART KARta), or a token (**жетон** *zhiTON*) and insert it into
one of the automatic gates. If you will be riding frequently,
why not purchase a ticket for several trips (**проезд** *praYEST*)
at once. You normally purchase by the number of rides, and
there are discounts for multiple rides that come in 5, 10, 20 or
60 trips. You might want a smart card good for 30 days.

One trip, please.	**Одну поездку, пожалуйста.** *adNU paYEsku, paZHAlusta*
Two trips.	**Две поездки.** *DVYE paYEski*
Five trips.	**Пять поездок.** *PYAT' paYEzdak*
Ten trips.	**Десять поездок.** *DYEsit' paYEzdak*
Twenty trips.	**Двадцать поездок.** *DVAtsat' paYEzdak*
Sixty trips.	**Шестъдесят поездок.** *shizdiSYAT' paYEzdak*
A smart card for 30 days.	**Смарт-карту на тридцать дней.** *SMART KARtu na TRItsat' DNYEY*

You will certainly get a chance to use your Russian
reading skills on the metro, searching for the correct line
and destination. However, since the metro maps and the
station guides also depend on color codes and numbers
for the appropriate metro line, you should have no problem
getting from here to there.

Travel Tips You can take an excursion
of the metro all by yourself. The most ornate stations
are those on the Circle Line (**Кольцевая линия**
kal'tsiVAya Liniya). Most tourist brochures and
maps of the city will have a metro map. Just count the
number of stations to get to the Circle Line. You may
have to transfer to it (**переход** *piriKHOT*). Then ride
one station, wait for the crowds to exit and spend
a minute or two examining the artwork and taking
pictures before you get on the next train, which will
be coming in no time at all.

Where is the nearest _____?	**Где ближайшая _____?** *GDYE bliZHAYshaya*
■ subway station	**станция метро** *STANtsiya miTRO*
How can I get to _____?	**Как проехать _____?** *KAK praYEkhat'*
■ downtown	**в центр** *f TSENTR*
■ Red Square	**на Красную площадь** *na KRASnuyu PLOshat'*
■ Moscow University	**в МГУ** *v EM GA U*
How many more stops?	**Сколько ещё остановок?** *SKOL'ka yiSHO astaNOvak*
Where should I get off?	**Где мне выйти?** *GDYE MNYE VYti*
Do I have to transfer?	**Мне надо пересесть?** *MNYE NAda piriSYEST'*
Please tell me when to get off.	**Скажите, пожалуйста, когда мне выйти.** *skaZHYtye paZHAlusta kagDA MNYE VYti*

Careful, the doors are closing.	**Осторожно, двери закрываются.** *astaROZHna DVYEri zakryVAyutsa*

You will see several signs inside the metro. You should know what they mean.

Don't lean against the doors.	**Не прислоняться** *NYE prislaNYAtsa*
Entrance	**Вход** *FKHOT*
Exit to the city	**Выход в город** *VYkhat v GOrat*
No entrance	**Нет входа** *NYET FKHOda*
Reserved for	**Место для** *MYESta dlya*
■ the disabled	**инвалидов** *invaLIdaf*
■ the elderly	**лиц пожилого возраста** *LITS pazhyLOva VOZrasta*
■ and passengers with children	**и пассажиров с детьми** *i pasaZHYraf z dit' MI*
Transfer	**Переход** *piriKHOT*

МОСКОВСКИЙ МЕТРОПОЛИТЕН

ИСПОЛЬЗОВАТЬ ДО	СТОИМОСТЬ (РУБ)	№ БИЛЕТА
—	4	0007119056

Билет для проезда в метрополитене на одну поездку.

(M)

Подделка проездных документов преследуется по закону.

TRAMS, TROLLEYBUSES, BUSES

You are likely to encounter trams or trolley cars that run on tracks (**трамвай** *tramVAY*), trolleybuses that have tires but are connected overhead to electric cables (**троллейбус** *traLYEYbus*), and regular buses (**автобус** *aFTObus*). You can use a monthly pass or purchase a book of tickets (**проездные билеты** *prayizNYye biLYEty*) at most street corner kiosks. You may be able to purchase a ticket from the driver when the vehicle is stopped. In many cities the honor system is in effect, and you must stamp your ticket in a ticket punch (**компостер** *kamPOStir*) or put your coins in the cash box and tear off a ticket. Spot checks are made, and if you do not have a valid ticket you will be subject to a fine and a brief lecture on social responsibility. If you lack the correct change, you might ask your fellow passengers to help. All trams, trolleybuses, and buses are identified by a number.

There are also minivans that pick up and discharge at just a few stops, **маршрутка** *marSHRUTka* or **маршрутное такси** *marSHRUTnaya taKSI*. The fare as well as destinations are normally posted on the door.

Where is the nearest ____ stop?	**Где ближайшая остановка ____?** *GDYE bliZHAYshaya astaNOFka*
■ tram	**трамвая** *tramVAya*
■ trolleybus	**троллейбуса** *traLYEYbusa*
■ bus	**автобуса** *aFTObusa*
How much is the fare?	**Сколько стоит проезд?** *SKOL'ka STOit praYEST*
What is the next stop?	**Какая следующая остановка?** *kaKAya SLYEduyushaya astaNOFka*
Does this bus go to ____?	**Этот автобус идёт до ____?** *Etat aFTObus iDYOT da*
■ the Bolshoi Theater	**Большого театра** *bal'SHOva tiAtra*
■ the Hermitage	**Эрмитажа** *ermiTAzha*

| How many stops? | **Сколько ещё остановок?** |
| | *SKOL'ka yiSHO astaNOvak* |

| Are you getting off? | **Вы выходите?** *VY vyKHOditye* |

| A book of tickets, please. | **Абонементную книжку, пожалуйста.** *abaniMYENTnuyu KNISHku paZHAlusta* |

| Punch my ticket, please. | **Пробейте, пожалуйста.** *praBYEYtye paZHAlusta* |

| Can you give me change? | **Не разменяйте?** *NYE razmiNYAYtye* |

TAXIS

Metered taxis can also transport you at very reasonable prices, but it is not always easy to find a free one. A little green lamp in the windshield indicates that the taxi is free. You may hail a taxi on the street or seek out the nearest cab stand, marked by a capital T on a checkered background. In addition to metered taxis, many private car operators (**частники** *CHASniki*) are willing to take you to your destination for a few rubles. You will see that Russians readily make use of these private entrepreneurs, but you are advised to use caution. Never enter a car with other passengers, always agree on the price before setting off for your destination, and if you are the least bit uncomfortable, send this one on his way.

| Is there a taxi stand near by? | **Есть поблизости стоянка такси?** *YEST" paBLIzasti staYANka taKSI* |

| Are you free? | **Вы свободны?** *VY svaBODny* |

I want to go _____.	**Я хочу поехать _____.** *YA khaCHU paYEkhat'*
to the airport	**в аэропорт** *v aeraPORT*
to this address	**в этот адрес** *v Etat Adris*
to the hotel	**в гостиницу** *v gaSTInitsu*
to Kiev Station	**на Киевский вокзал** *NA KIyivski vagZAL*
to the Kremlin	**в Кремль** *F KRYEML'*
How much does it cost?	**Сколко стоит?** *SKOL'ka STOit*
Faster. I'm late.	**Быстрее. Я опаздываю.** *bySTRYEye YA aPAZdyvayu*
A little slower, please.	**Помедленее, позжалуйста.** *paMYEdliniye paZHAlusta*
Stop here.	**Остановитесь здесь.** *astanaVItyes' ZDYES'*
Go straight.	**Прямо.** *PRYAma*
To the right.	**Направо.** *naPRAva*
To the left.	**Налево.** *naLYEva*
Is it still far?	**Ещё далеко?** *yiSHO daliKO*
Please wait for me.	**Подождите меня, позжалуйста.** *padaZHDItye miNYA paZHAlusta*
How much do I owe?	**Сколько с меня?** *SKOL'ka s miNYA*
This is for you.	**Это для вас.** *Eta dlya VAS*

SIGHTSEEING

Where is the service bureau?	**Где бюро обслуживания?** *GDYE byuRO apSLUzhivaniya*
Where is the excursion office?	**Где экскурсионное бюро?** *GDYE ekskursiOnaye byuRO*
I need an interpreter.	**Мне нужен переводчик.** *MNYE NUzhin piriVOTchik*
How much does it cost _____?	**Сколько стоит _____?** *SKOL'ka STOit*
▪ for an hour	**за час** *za CHAS*
▪ for a day	**за день** *za DYEN'*
There are two (three, four) of us.	**Нас двое (трое, четверо).** *NAS DVOye (TROye, CHETvira)*
Where can I buy _____?	**Где мне купить _____?** *GDYE MNYE kuPIT'*
▪ a guide book	**путеводитель** *putivaDItil'*
▪ a map of the city	**план города** *PLAN GOrada*
▪ a phrase book	**разговорник** *razgaVORnik*
Is there a city tour?	**Есть экскурсия по городу?** *YEST' ekSKURsiya pa GOradu*
What are the main attractions?	**Какие главные достопримечательности?** *kaKIye GLAVniye dastaprimiCHAtil'nasti*
Where does it leave from?	**Откуда отправляется?** *atKUda atpravLYAyitsa*

We would like to see _____.	**Мы бы хотели смотреть _____.** *MY BY khaTYEli smaTRYET"*
the Bolshoi Theater	**Большой театр** *bal'SHOY tiATR*
Red Square	**Красную площадь** *KRASnuyu PLOshat'*
the Kremlin	**Кремль** *KRYEML'*
Christ the Saviour Cathedral	**Храм Христа Спасителя** *KHRAM khriSTA spaSItilya*
St. Basil's Cathedral	**Храм Василия Блаженного/ Покровский собор** *KHRAM vaSIliya blaZHEnava/paKROFski saBOR*
the Manezh Shopping Mall	**Торговый комплекс Манеж** *tarGOvy KOMpliks maNYESH*
the Old Arbat	**Старый Арбат** *STAry arBAT*
the Vernissage	**Вернисаж** *virniSASH*
Moscow University	**МГУ** *EM GA U*
GUM (the department store)	**ГУМ** *GUM*
Children's World	**Детский Мир** *DYETski MIR*
the Aurora	**Аврору** *avROru*
the Winter Palace	**Зимний дворец** *ZIMni dvaRYETS*
the Armory	**Оружейную палату** *aruZHEYnuyu paLAtu*
a market	**рынок** *RYnak*
the cathedral	**собор** *saBOR*
the cemetery	**кладбище** *KLADbishe*
the city hall	**городской совет** *garatSKOY saVYET*

■ a church	**церковь**	*TSERkaf'*
■ the concert hall	**концертный зал**	*kanTSERTny ZAL*
■ the fortress	**крепость**	*KRYEpast'*
■ the gardens	**сады**	*saDY*
■ the institute	**институт**	*instiTUT*
■ the library	**библиотеку**	*bibliaTYEku*
■ the monastery	**монастырь**	*manaSTYR'*
■ the monument	**памятник**	*PAmitnik*
■ the museum	**музей**	*muZYEY*
■ the palace	**дворец**	*dvaRYETS*
■ the park	**парк**	*PARK*
■ the river	**реку**	*RYEku*
■ the stadium	**стадион**	*stadiON*
■ the tower	**башню**	*BASHnyu*
■ the university	**университет**	*univirsiTYET*
■ the zoo	**зоопарк**	*zaaPARK*

Is it open?	**Открыто?**	*atKRYta*
Is it closed?	**Закрыто?**	*zaKRYta*
What is the admission price?	**Сколько стоит билет?**	*SKOL'ka STOit biLYET*
May I take photos?	**Можно фотографировать?**	*MOZHna fatagraFIravat'*

A SIGHTSEEING ITINERARY

   Russia has a rich history and culture. In addition to the major cities of Russia, Moscow and St. Petersburg, there are dozens of other cities and villages with a splendid architectural tradition. You also should not miss the opportunity to sample the great variety of cultures and cuisines of the individual republics, each of which has its own distinctive character. What follows is merely a sketch—a broad overview of some places in Moscow and St. Petersburg that you might want to see if they are not included in your tour, or if you are traveling on your own and designing your own sightseeing schedule.

MOSCOW

Begin your visit to Moscow with an excursion around the city (**экскурсия по городу** *ekSKURsiya pa GOradu*), now the capital of the Russian Federation. Here the old mixes with the new, and nowhere is the combination more apparent than on Red Square (**Красная площадь** *KRASnaya PLOshat'*) and in the Kremlin (**Кремль** *KRYEML'*). Once the stronghold of the Russian tsars and highlighted by magnificent cathedrals, including the landmark St. Basil's, the square was the center of world attention for the parades on May Day (May 1) and the Anniversary of the Revolution (November 7). Here is the famous Lenin Mausoleum (**Мавзолей Ленина** *mavzaLYEY LYEnina*). Inside the Kremlin walls is the seat of the Russian government, along with the famous Palace of Congresses (**Дворец съездов** *dvaRYETS SYEZdaf*), often open to the public for ballet and opera performances. Here too is the famous Armory (**Оружейная палата** *aruZHEYnaya paLAta*), now a museum celebrating Russia's regal past. There is also an opportunity to see the diamond collection, the Russian Crown Jewels (**Алмазный Фонд** *alMAZny FONT*). Turning to modern Moscow, the most

famous museums here are the Tretyakov Gallery
(**Третьяковская галерея** *trit'yaKOFskaya galiRYEya*)
and the Pushkin Museum, with excellent collections of
Western art. A favorite spot for photos is near Moscow
University, overlooking the Moscow River. Often you will see
newlyweds who come here for a picture-taking session. For a
change of pace and an opportunity to see and buy Russian
arts and crafts, you should plan on visiting the Moscow open
air market (**Вернисаж** *virniSASH*) that can be reached by
the metro at the Partizan metro station (**Партизанская**
partiZANskaya). Plan ahead because it is only open on
weekends (Saturdays and Sundays).

Should you wish to get out into the countryside, a day
trip can bring you to the estate of Leo Tolstoy at Yasnaya
Polyana. Another worthwhile destination is the town of
Sergiev Posad, where the Russian Orthodox Church keeps
alive century-old traditions. Here you'll find an Orthodox
seminary and working cathedrals, along with the final resting
place of Boris Godunov. For a change of pace you might want
to visit the home of the Russian cosmonauts (**космонавты**
kasmaNAFty) at Star City (**Звёздны** *ZVYOZny*).

Государственный Эрмитаж приглашает посетить:
Дворец Меншикова – Университетская наб., 15
Зимний дворец Петра I – Дворцовая наб., 32
Главный штаб – Дворцовая пл., 6/8
Музей фарфора – пр. Обуховской обороны, 151
Фондохранилище "Старая деревня" – Заусадебная ул., 37"А"

ГОСУДАРСТВЕННЫЙ
ЭРМИТАЖ
The State Hermitage Museum

Дни и часы работы: вторник – суббота 10.30-18.00
воскресенье 10.30-17.00

www.hermitagemuseum.org

ST. PETERSBURG

Created as a "window to Europe" by Peter the Great in
the first part of the eighteenth century, St. Petersburg—then
Leningrad as it was named for a good part of the twentieth
century—quickly became the capital and the architectural
showplace of the Russian empire. No expense was spared on
the palaces, ministries, and churches that adorn the center of

the city. Crisscrossed by numerous canals, it is a true "Venice of the North." The city has a wealth of attractions: the Palace Square, site of the storming of the Winter Palace (**Зимний дворец** *ZIMni dvaRYETS*), the Peter and Paul Fortress (**Петропавловская крепость** *pitraPAVlafskaya KRYEpast'*), the Russian Mint, and the Peter and Paul Cathedral, which became the resting place of the Romanov emperors. The dark side of Russian history can be seen in the fortress cells where Dostoevsky and other leading intellectuals were once imprisoned. Here at the Smolny Institute, the first school for women in Russia, Lenin planned the revolution that changed the face of the Russian Empire in the twentieth century. Do not miss the Hermitage (**Эрмитаж** *ermiTASH*), second only to the Louvre in Paris for its collection of art. You might also visit some of the other residences of the tsarist family, Peter the Great's country palace with its magnificent fountains (**Петродворец** *pitradvaRYETS*), or the stately homes at Pushkin (**Пушкин**) and Pavlovsk (**Павловск**).

To see Old Russia, you might plan a trip to Suzdal (**Суздаль**), a city preserved as a museum of Russian architecture. Here you will be treated to Russian meals baked and served in clay pots, along with a taste of Russian mead (**медовуха** *midaVUkha*).

Travel Tips You can beat the lines at the State Hermitage by purchasing your admission tickets online. If you have a credit card you can print out a voucher that will let you pick up your ticket at a special window. This way you'll have more time to spend viewing the exhibits!

RELIGIOUS SERVICES

Churches and cathedrals are everywhere! The Russian Orthodox churches are far more than architectural monuments. If you wish to attend services please be advised that women are expected to have something covering their heads (a kerchief will do). Many monasteries follow a strict dress code, and jeans or casual slacks may not be tolerated. Religious services of other denominations are held regularly. Inquire at your hotel or contact your embassy for up-to-date information on times and places.

Is there _____ nearby?	**Есть поблизости _____?** *YEST' paBLIzasti*
▪ a Catholic church	**католический костёл** *kataLIchiski kaSTYOL*
▪ a Protestant church	**протестантская церковь** *pratiSTANTskaya TSERkaf'*
▪ an Orthodox church	**православная церковь** *pravaSLAVnaya TSERkaf'*
▪ a mosque	**мечеть** *miCHET'*
▪ a synagogue	**синагога** *sinaGOga*
At what time is the service?	**Когда служба?** *kagDA SLUZHba*
I would like to speak with _____.	**Я хотел бы поговорить _____.** *YA khaTYEL BY pagavaRIT'*
▪ a priest	**со священником** *sa sviSHEnikam*
▪ an imam	**имамом** *iMAmam*
▪ a minister	**с пастором** *s PAStaram*
▪ a rabbi	**с раввином** *s raVInam*

Travel Tips Many Russians still carry a net bag (**сеточка** *SYEtachka*) or a plastic bag when they go out for the day: they call it an **авоська** *aVOS'ka*, meaning "just in case." Many Russian items are not packaged, and you still may not receive free bags in many stores.

PLANNING A TRIP

During your stay you may want to plan a trip to additional places of interest. You can travel throughout Russia by plane, train, ship, bus, or car.

> *Travel Tips* Travelers with physical challenges are advised to plan carefully for a trip to Russia. In planning your trip, be sure to contact travel agencies and organizations that have had recent experience with issues of access. You might want to check the internet for up-to-date information and practical tips. Keep in mind that Russia lags significantly behind Canada, the United States, and countries in Western Europe in providing access to basic services, from attractions to lodging and transportation. While the infrastructure is lacking, you will find many sympathetic individuals willing to try to accommodate your needs. But your expectations should be realistic and sensitive to the limitations and realities of Russian life.

AIR TRAVEL

When planning your own travel arrangements it is useful to know the three-letter airport designations in Russian. In Moscow SVO is the assigned code for Sheremetyevo (**Шереметьево**), the main international airport. VKO is for Vnukovo (**Внуково**) and DME is for Domodedovo (**Домодедово**). PUL is the designation for the international airport in St. Petersburg—Pulkovo (**Пулково**).

At the airport, learn how to decipher the signs. Arrivals are **Прибытия** *priBYtiya*. Departures are **Отправления** *atpravLYEniya*. Check whether your flight is on time, that is, according to schedule (**по расписанию** *pa raspiSAniyu*), or delayed, in which case the new expected (**ожидаемое** *azhiDAimaye*) arrival or departure time will be indicated.

Where is the check-in counter?	**Где регистрация?** *GDYE rigiSTRAtsiya*
When is there a flight to _____?	**Когда полёт в _____?** *kagDA paLYOT v*
■ St. Petersburg	**Санкт Петербург** *SANKT pitirBURK*
■ Riga	**Ригу** *RIgu*
■ Tashkent	**Ташкент** *tashKYENT*
■ Tbilisi	**Тбилиси** *tbiLIsi*
A one-way ticket to _____.	**Один билет до _____.** *aDIN biLYET da*
■ Irkutsk	**Иркутска** *irKUTska*
■ Kiev	**Киева** *KIyiva*
A round-trip ticket.	**Туда и обратно.** *tuDA I aBRATna*
A seat _____.	**Место _____.** *MYESta*
■ next to the window	**у окна** *u akNA*
■ on the aisle	**у прохода** *u praKHOda*
■ in first class	**в первом классе** *f PYERvam KLAsye*
■ in business class	**в бизнес классе** *v BIZnis KLAsye*
■ in economy (tourist) class	**в туристическом классе** *f turiSTIchiskam KLAsye*
What does the ticket cost?	**Сколько стоит билет?** *SKOL'ka STOit biLYET*
Will a meal be served?	**Кормить будут?** *karMIT' BUdut*
When does the aircraft depart?	**Когда вылетает самолёт?** *kagDA VYlitayit samaLYOT*
When does it arrive?	**Когда прибывает?** *kagDA pribyVAyit*

How long is the flight?	**Сколько времени длится полёт?** *SKOL'ka VRYEmini DLItsa palYOT*
I'll check this suitcase.	**Этот чемодан я сдаю в багаж.** *Etat chimaDAN YA ZDAyu v baGASH*
What is our flight number?	**Какой номер нашего рейса?** *kaKOY NOmir NAshiva RYEYsa*
This is your boarding pass.	**Вот посадочный талон.** *VOT paSAdachny taLON*
You have oversized/ overweight baggage.	**У вас негабаритный багаж.** *u VAS nigabaRITny baGASH*
This is your baggage claim check.	**Вот багажная бирка.** *VOT baGAZHnaya BIRka*
Please confirm my reservation.	**Потвердите моё бронирование.** *patvirDItye maYO braNIravaniya*
We are now boarding.	**Объявляется посадка.** *abyavLYAyitsa paSATka*
Please check these _____.	**Проверьте, пожалуйста, эти _____.** *praVYER'tye paZHAlusta Eti*
▪ films	**плёнки** *PLYONki*
▪ computer disks	**компьютерные диски** *kamPYUtirniye DISki*
Please do not x-ray them.	**Не просветьте, пожалуйста.** *NYE praSVYET'tye paZHAlusta*

NOTE: Airport security X-ray machines have become increasingly sensitive, and most will not damage your film or electronic media. To be on the safe side, you might have computer disks and valuable photographic memories checked by hand. You can always ask politely. If the attendant refuses, bow to his wishes.

SHIPBOARD TRAVEL

Traveling by ship, taking a river cruise (**круиз** *kruIS*), can be a leisurely way to see the country and countryside. Look at the form below and see if you could send a request for information. It is similar to many such forms on the Internet.

ЗАКАЗ ТУРА
Order a Trip

Ваше имя: (Your name) _____

Ваш e-маил: (Your e-mail) _____

Контактный телефон:
(Contact telephone) _____

Направление: (Destination) _____

Время, продолжительность: _____
(Time, length)

Текст сообщения: (Text of your message)

Travel Tips Most computers today will permit you to read and type Russian script. But if you are on a public computer you may need to be able to type in Russian. A very useful tool is a virtual on-screen Cyrillic keyboard that permits you to type in Russian on any computer and then simply paste your text wherever needed.
http://ourworld.compuserve.com/homepages/PaulGor/ screen_e.htm

Where is the dock?	**Где пристань?** *GDYE PRIstan'*
When does the next boat leave for _____?	**Когда следующий теплоход до _____?** *kagDA SLYEduyushi tiplaKHOT da*
How long does the trip take?	**Сколько времени в пути?** *SKOL'ka VRYEmini f puTI*
When do we land?	**Когда мы приплываем?** *kagDA MY priplyVAyim*
When do we sail?	**Когда мы отплываем?** *kagDA MY atplyVAyim*
A first-class ticket.	**Билет первого класса.** *biLYET PYERvava KLAsa*
A tourist-class ticket.	**Билет туристического класса.** *biLYET turiSTIchiskava KLAsa*
I would like a cabin.	**Я хотел бы каюту.** *YA khaTYEL BY kaYUtu*

I don't feel well.	**Мне плохо.** *MNYE PLOkha*

Do you have anything for sea-sickness?	**Есть у вас что-нибудь от морской болезни?** *YEST" u VAS SHTO-nibut' at marSKOY baLYEZni*

TRAIN SERVICE

Traveling by train can be a pleasant way to go between cities. The overnight trains between Moscow and St. Petersburg or other cities offer an opportunity to make acquaintances, avoid weather delays at airports, and get a good night's sleep. Moscow has several train stations, which serve different destinations. Be sure to ask from which station your train departs.

I want to get to ____.	**Мне на ____.** *MNYE na*
▪ Kazan Station	**Казанский вокзал** *kaZANski vagZAL*
▪ Kiev Station	**Киевский вокзал** *KIyifski vagZAL*
▪ Leningrad Station	**Ленинградский вокзал** *lininGRATski vagZAL*
▪ Riga Station	**Рижский вокзал** *RISHki vagZAL*
▪ Yaroslav Station	**Ярославский вокзал** *yaraSLAFski vagZAL*

A first-class ticket.	**Билет в мягком вагоне.** *biLYET v MYAkam vaGOnye*
A second-class ticket.	**Билет в купейном вагоне.** *biLYET v kuPYEYnam vaGOnye*
A round-trip ticket please.	**Обратный билет, пожалуйста.** *aBRATny biLYET paZHAlusta*

A non-smoking compartment.	**Купе для некурящих.** *kuPE dlya nikuRYAshikh*
When does the train leave?	**Когда отправляется поезд?** *kagDA atpravLYAyitsa POyist*
From what platform?	**С какой платформы?** *s kaKOY platFORmy*
Where is Car # _____?	**Где вагон номер _____?** *GDYE vaGON NOmir*
Where is my seat/berth?	**Где моё место?** *GDYE maYO MYESta*
Is there a dining car?	**Есть вагон-ресторан?** *YEST' vaGON ristaRAN*
Bring us some tea, please.	**Принесите нам чаю, пожалуйста.** *priniSItye NAM CHAyu paZHAlusta*
Where are we now?	**Где мы сейчас?** *GDYE MY siCHAS*
Will we arrive on schedule?	**Мы прибываем по расписанию?** *MY pribiVAyim pa raspiSAniyu*
Are we late?	**Мы опаздываем?** *MY aPAZdyvayim*

DRIVING A CAR

You may rent a car in Russia or drive your own car into the country. Be sure to ask about insurance and whether mileage and gas are included in the quoted rate. You should be familiar with European rules of the road and international road signs. Most major highways have signs in the Latin alphabet as well as Cyrillic, so you should have no trouble getting around. In major cities you generally are not permitted to make a left turn from major roadways unless there is a special left-turn lane. Instead, drive through the intersection, and after approximately fifty meters you can make a U-turn, after which you can turn right onto the desired street. This is called the **разворот** *razvaROT*. Russians drive with their parking lights on in cities and use the headlights only outside city limits or on unlit stretches of road. Don't be surprised if you end up in one of Moscow's nightmarish traffic jams (**пробка** *PROPka*).

ROAD SIGNS

Russia uses the international system of traffic signs. You should familiarize yourself with the important ones.

CAUTION SIGNS

Опасность	Caution
Скользкая дорога	Slippery Road
Пешеходный переход	Pedestrian Crossing
Опасный поворот	Dangerous Curve
Железнодорожный переезд	Railroad Crossing

REGULATION SIGNS

Главная дорога	Main Road
Уступите дорогу	Yield

Стоп	Stop
Преимущество встречного движения	Oncoming Traffic Has Right of Way
Въезд запрещён	No Entry
Движение запрещено	No Traffic
Разворот запрещён	No U-turn
Обгон запрещён	No Passing
Остановка запрещена	No Stopping
Стоянка запрещена	No Parking
Максимальная скорость	Maximum Speed
Конец ограничения	End of Restriction

PRESCRIPTIVE SIGNS

Минимальная скорость	Minimum Speed
Лёгковые автомобили	Cars Only
Пешеходная дорожка	Pedestrian Path

INFORMATION SIGNS

Автомойка	Car Wash
Заправка	Gas Station
Автосалон	Auto Repair
Место стоянки	Parking
Платная парковка	Paid Parking
Нажмите кнопку	Push the Button
Возьмите талон	Take Your Ticket

Caution

No U-turn

Yield

Slippery Road

No Passing

Stop

Pedestrian Crossing

No Stopping

Oncoming Traffic Has Right of Way

Dangerous Curve

No Parking

No Entry

Railroad Crossing

Maximum Speed

No Traffic

End of Restriction

Traffic Police

Parking

Minimum Speed

Main Road

U-turn Permitted

Cars Only

Dead End

Taxi Stand

Pedestrian Path

Detour

Trolley Stop

Место для разворота	U-turn Permitted
Стоянка такси	Taxi Stand
Остановка трамвая	Trolley Stop
Объезд	Detour
Тупик	Dead End
Пост ГАИ	Traffic Police

PARKING

Parking has become a major issue. There are lots of private parking lots and metered systems. Be sure you know what the rules are before you earn a pricey ticket for failing to comply. And watch for the NO PARKING signs (blue sign with a single red diagonal line), or NO STOPPING (blue with crossed red lines).

CAR RENTALS

You might want to reserve a rental car in advance through a travel agent or over the internet. You will also be able to rent a car once inside Russia. Rates can vary considerably, so be sure to compare the different rates and options. You will need a valid driver's license and may need to have a credit card or leave a sizeable deposit.

I would like to rent _____.	**Я хотел бы взять на прокат _____.** *YA khaTYEL BY VZYAT' na praKAT*
■ a car	**машину** *maSHYnu*
■ a van	**микроавтобус** *mikraaFTObus*
■ with a driver	**с водителем** *s vaDItilim*
■ without a driver	**без водителя** *byez vaDItilya*
What kinds of cars do you have?	**Какие у вас машины?** *kaKIye u VAS maSHYny*

I prefer _____.	**Я предпочитаю _____.** *YA pritpachiTAyu*
◼ a small car	**маленькую машину** *MAlin'kuyu maSHYnu*
◼ a large car	**большую машину** *bal'SHUyu maSHYnu*
◼ automatic transmission	**автоматическое переключение скоростей** *aftamaTIchiskaye piriklyuCHYEniye skaraSTYEY*

How much does it cost _____?	**Сколько она стоит _____?** *SKOL'ka aNA STOit*
◼ per hour	**за час** *za CHAS*
◼ per day	**за день** *za DYEN'*
◼ per week	**за неделю** *za niDYElyu*
◼ per month	**за месяц** *za MYEsits*
◼ per kilometer	**за километр** *za kilaMYETR*

How much is the insurance?	**Сколько стоит страхование?** *SKOL'ka STOit strakhaVAniye*
Is gas included?	**Бензин входит в стоимость?** *binZIN FKHOdit f STOimast'*
Do you accept credit cards?	**Вы принимаете кредитные карточки?** *VY priniMAyitye kriDITniye KARtachki*
◼ which?	**какие?** *kaKIye*
Here is my driver's license.	**Вот мои водителькие права.** *VOT maYI vaDItil'skiye praVA*
Must I leave a deposit?	**Мне нужно оставить залог?** *MNYE NUZHna aSTAvit' zaLOK*
What kind of gas does it take?	**На каком бензине она работает?** *na kaKOM binZInye aNA raBOtayit*

ON THE ROAD

Excuse me!	**Извините!** *izviNItye*
Can you tell me?	**Вы не скажете?** *VY NYE SKAzhitye*
Where's the road to ____?	**Где дорога в ____?** *GDYE daROga v*
Is this the road to ____?	**Эта дорога в ____?** *Eta daROga v*
Where does this road go?	**Куда идёт эта дорога?** *kuDA iDYOT Eta daROga*
How do I get to ____?	**Как мне проехать в ____?** *KAK MNYE praYEkhat' v*
How many kilometers to ____?	**Сколько километров до ____?** *SKOL'ka kilaMYEtraf da*
Do you have a road map?	**У вас есть автодорожная карта?** *u VAS YEST' aftadaROZHnaya KARta*
Can you show me on the map?	**Вы можете мне показать на карте?** *VY MOzhitye MNYE pakaZAT' na KARtye*
In which direction should I go?	**В какое направление мне ехать?** *f kaKOye napravLYEniye MNYE YEkhat'*
Straight ahead?	**Прямо?** *PYRAma*
To the right?	**Направо?** *naPRAva*

| To the left? | **Налево?** *naLYEva* |
| Where do I turn? | **Где мне повернуть?** *GDYE MNYE pavirNUT'* |

AT THE SERVICE STATION

Gasoline is sold by the liter in Russia. Check whether your car needs regular (92 octane, **Аи 92**) or super (95 octane, **Аи 95**). Most Europeans know approximately how many liters of gasoline they use per 100 kilometers. You may hear them say simply "ten liters," "eleven liters," and so on. To be safe, try to calculate your own mileage in the city and on the open road.

LIQUID MEASUREMENTS (APPROXIMATE)		
LITERS	U.S. GALLONS	IMPERIAL GALLONS
30	8	6½
40	10½	8¾
50	13¼	11
60	15¾	13
70	18½	15½
80	21	17½

DISTANCE MEASURES (APPROXIMATE)	
KILOMETERS	MILES
1	0.62
5	3
10	6
20	12
50	31
100	62

I'm running out of gas.
Бензин у меня кончается.
binZIN u miNYA kanCHAyitsa

Where is the nearest service station?
Где ближайшая бензоколонка?
GDYE bliZHAYshaya binzakaLONka

Twenty liters, please _____.
Двадцать литров, пожалуйста _____. *DVAtsat' LItraf paZHAlusta*

■ of regular (93 octane)
девяносто третьего
diviNOSta TRYEt'iva

■ of super (95 octane)
девяносто пятого
diviNOSta PYAtava

Please check _____.
Проверьте, пожалуйста _____.
praVYER'tye paZHAlusta

■ the battery
аккумулятор *akumuLYAtar*

■ the brakes
тормоза *tarmaZA*

■ the carburetor
карбюратор *karbyuRAtar*

■ the ignition system
зажигание *zazhiGAniye*

■ the lights
фары *FAry*

■ the oil
масло *MAsla*

■ the spark plugs
свечи *SVYEchi*

■ the tires
шины *SHYny*

■ the water
воду *VOdu*

Can you _____? | **Вы можете _____?** *VY MOzhitye*

- charge the battery — **зарядить аккумулятор** *zariDIT' akumuLYAtar*
- change the oil — **сменить масло** *smiNIT' MAsla*
- grease the car — **смазать машину** *SMAzat' maSHYnu*
- change the tire — **сменить колесо** *smiNIT' kaliSO*

Where are the rest rooms? | **Где туалеты?** *GDYE tuaLYEty*

ACCIDENTS, REPAIRS

It overheats. | **Она перегревается.** *aNA pirigriVAyitsa*

It doesn't start. | **Она не заводится.** *aNA NYE zaVOditsa*

It doesn't go. | **Она не идёт.** *aNA NYE iDYOT*

I have a flat tire. | **У меня спустила шина.** *u miNYA spuSTIla SHYna*

The radiator is leaking. | **Радиатор протекает.** *radiAtar pratiKAyit*

The battery is dead. | **Аккумулятор сел.** *akumuLYAtar SYEL*

The keys are locked in the car. | **Ключи остались в машине.** *klyuCHI aSTAlis' v maSHYnye*

Is there a repair shop nearby? | **Поблизости есть автосервис?** *paBLIzasti YEST' aftaSYERvis*

Can you help me? | **Вы можете мне помочь?** *VY MOzhitye MNYE paMOCH*

Can you lend me _____?	**Можете одолжить _____?** *MOzhitye adalZHYT'*
a flashlight	**фонарь** *faNAR'*
a hammer	**молоток** *malaTOK*
a jack	**домкрат** *damKRAT*
pliers	**плоскогубцы** *plaskaGUPtsy*
a screwdriver	**отвёртку** *atVYORTku*
a wrench	**гаечный ключ** *GAyichny KLYUCH*

Do you have _____?	**У вас есть _____?** *u VAS YEST'*
a bolt	**болт** *BOLT*
a bulb	**лампочка** *LAMpachka*
a filter	**фильтер** *FIL'tir*
a nut	**гайка** *GAYka*

Can you fix the car?	**Можете машину починить?** *MOzhitye maSHYnu pachiNIT'*
Do you have this spare part?	**У вас есть эта запчасть?** *u VAS YEST' Eta zapCHAST'*
There's something wrong with _____.	**Что-то не в порядке с _____.** *SHTO-ta NYE f paRYATkye s*
the directional signal	**сигнальным огнём** *sigNAL'nym agNYOM*
the door handle	**ручкой** *RUCHkay*
the electrical system	**электрической системой** *elikTRIchiskay siSTYEmay*
the fan	**вентилятором** *vintiLYAtaram*
the fan belt	**ремнём вентилятора** *rimNYOM vintiLYAtara*
the fuel pump	**бензонасосом** *binzanaSOsam*

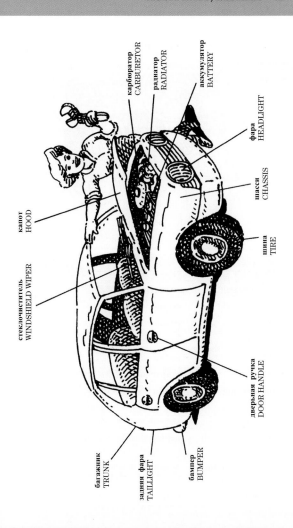

карбюратор CARBURETOR

радиатор RADIATOR

аккумулятор BATTERY

фара HEADLIGHT

шасси CHASSIS

шина TIRE

капот HOOD

стеклоочиститель WINDSHIELD WIPER

дверьная ручка DOOR HANDLE

багажник TRUNK

задняя фара TAILLIGHT

бампер BUMPER

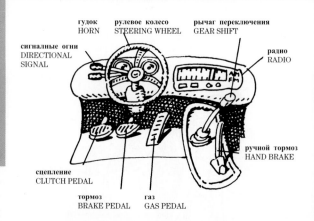

гудок
HORN

рулевое колесо
STEERING WHEEL

рычаг переключения
GEAR SHIFT

сигналные огни
DIRECTIONAL
SIGNAL

радио
RADIO

ручной тормоз
HAND BRAKE

сцепление
CLUTCH PEDAL

тормоз
BRAKE PEDAL

газ
GAS PEDAL

■ the gears	**скоростями**	*skaraSTYAmi*
■ the gear shift	**сцеплением**	*tsiPLYEniyim*
■ the headlight	**фарой**	*FAray*
■ the horn	**гудком**	*gutKOM*
■ the ignition	**зажиганием**	*zazhiGAniyim*
■ the radio	**радио**	*RAdio*
■ the starter	**стартером**	*STARtiram*
■ the steering wheel	**рулём**	*ruLYOM*
■ the taillight	**задней фарой**	*ZADnyey FAray*
■ the transmission	**переключением скоростей** *piriklyuCHENiyim skaraSTYEY*	
■ the water pump	**водяным насосам** *vadiNYM naSOsam*	
■ the windshield	**ветровым стеклом** *vitraVYM stiKLOM*	

Please look at _____.	Посмотрите, пожалуйста _____. *pasmaTRItye paZHAlusta*
■ the brakes	тормоза *tarmaZA*
■ the bumper	бампер *BAMpir*
■ the exhaust	выхлопную трубку *vykhlapNUyu TRUPku*
■ the fender	решётку *riSHYOTku*
■ the gas tank	бензобак *binzaBAK*
■ the hood	капот *kaPOT*
■ the trunk	багажник *baGAZHnik*

What's the matter?	В чём дело? *F CHOM DYEla*
Can you do it today?	Можете сделать это сегодня? *MOzhitye ZDYElat' Eta siVODnya*
How long (will it take)?	Как долго? *KAK DOLga*
Is everything O.K.?	Всё в порядке? *FSYO f paRYATkye*
How much do I owe you?	Сколько с меня? *SKOL'ka s miNYA*

ENTERTAINMENT AND DIVERSIONS

BALLET, CONCERTS, MOVIES, OPERA

No trip to Russia is complete without a visit to the theater. If you are with a group, a theater visit is probably included in your schedule. If you are on your own, you can order tickets through the theater desk in your hotel. You may also find a ticket at one of the many theater kiosks throughout the city. If you suddenly find that your evening is free, you might try to purchase a cancellation ticket by going to the theater about an hour before the performance. The most famous of Moscow's theaters is, of course, the Bolshoi (**Большой театр** *bal'SHOY tiATR*)—home to an opera and a ballet company. The Bolshoi Ballet often performs in the Palace of Congresses (**Дворец съездов** *dvaRYETS SYEZdaf*) in the Kremlin. You can also see opera and ballet in Moscow at the Stanislavsky Musical Theater (**Музыкальный театр имени Станиславского** *muzyKAL'ny tiATR Imini staniSLAFskava*). An opportunity overlooked by some tourists is the Operetta Theater (**Театр оперетты** *tiATR apiRYEty*), which performs Russian and foreign musicals and is one of the loveliest theaters in Moscow. Music lovers will not want to miss the Chaykovsky Concert Hall (**Концертный зал имени Чайковского** *kanTSERTny ZAL Imini chayKOFskava*). Visitors to St. Petersburg will surely want to see a performance at the Mariinsky Theater (**Мариинский театр** *maRIinskiy tiATR*), in Soviet times the world-renowned Kirov ballet and opera, or the Mussorgsky Opera and Ballet Theater (**Театр оперы и балета Мусоргского** *tiATR Opiry i baLYEta MUsorgskava*), in Soviet times the Maly Theater.

If you want to be sure to see your ballet or opera, order your tickets online at either the Bolshoi (http://www.bolshoi.ru/) or the Mariinsky (http://www.mariinsky.ru/). You might pay a premium, but you will be assured of good seats.

Travel Tips   If you are on a budget, discount tickets for theaters, museums, and excursions may be available. Foreigners should be prepared to pay full price, which may be comparable to the cost of such services at home. But for most Russian citizens and students there may be tickets with a discount **со скидкой** *sa SKITkay*, **со льготом** *sa L'GOtam*, or **Льготный билет** *L'GOTny biLYET*. These can be much cheaper and sometimes, if you speak Russian, you might be able to obtain one. Be careful when buying a ticket from unauthorized persons or outlets that you don't receive a discounted ticket to which you are not entitled. You may be turned away at the door! The big advantage to speaking even a few words of Russian is the chance to meet Russian citizens and to appreciate their lives from their perspective.

Other special events in Moscow are the world famous Circus (**Цирк** *TSYRK*), sporting events, including spectacular hockey and soccer matches, the Russian version of the ice-capades (**Балет на льду** *baLYET na L'DU*), and song-and-dance ensembles, including the Red Army Chorus, Beriozka, the Pyatnitsky Choir, and individual artists. Ask your friends, hosts, and hotel personnel for their recommendations.

I would like to see _____.	**Я хотел бы смотреть _____.** *YA khaTYEL BY smaTRYET'*
▣ a ballet	**балет** *baLYET*
▣ the circus	**цирк** *TSYRK*
▣ a concert	**концерт** *kanTSERT*
▣ a drama	**драма** *DRAma*
▣ a hockey match	**хоккей** *khaKYEY*
▣ a movie	**фильм** *FIL'M*
▣ a musical	**мюзикл** *MYUzikl*
▣ an opera	**оперу** *Opiru*

■ a soccer match   **футбол**   *fudBOL*

■ a show   **шоу**   *SHO*

What is playing?   **Что идёт?**   *SHTO iDYOT*

Who is playing?   **Кто играет?**   *KTO iGRAyit*

Is it an opera or a ballet?   **Это опера или балет?** *Eta Opira Ili baLYET*

    Learn how to read the advertisements for upcoming shows. Here are the names of some of Russia's most famous ballets and operas.

Boris Godunov   **Борис Годунов**   *baRIS gaduNOF*

Cinderella   **Золушка**   *ZOlushka*

Eugene Onegin   **Евгений Онегин** *yivGYEni aNYEgin*

The Nutcracker   **Щелкунчик**   *schilKUNchik*

The Queen of Spades   **Пиковая дама**   *PIkavaya DAma*

Sleeping Beauty	**Спящая красавица** *SPYAschaya kraSAvitsa*
Swan Lake	**Лебединое озеро** *libiDInaye Ozira*
I like _____.	**Я люблю _____.** *YA lyuBLYU*
◼ classical music	**классическую музыку** *klaSIchiskuyu MUzyku*
◼ modern music	**современную музыку** *savriMYEnuyu MUzyku*
◼ folk music	**народную музыку** *naRODnuyu MUzyku*
◼ jazz and blues	**джаз и блюз** *DZHAS i BLYUS*
◼ pop and rock	**поп и рок** *POP i ROK*
What kind of film is it?	**Что ето за фильм?** *SHTO Eta za FIL'M*
A comedy?	**Комедия?** *kaMYEdiya*
A drama?	**Трагедия?** *traGYEdiya*
A love story?	**Любовная история?** *lyuBOVnaya iSTOriya*
A musical?	**Музыкальный фильм?** *muzyKAL'ny FIL'M*
A mystery film?	**Детектив?** *ditikTIF*
A science fiction film?	**Научно-популярный фильм?** *naUCHna-papuLYARny FIL'M*
A war film?	**Фильм о войне?** *FIL'M a vayNYE*
Are there seats for tonight's performance?	**Есть билеты на сегодня вечером?** *YEST' biLYEty na siVODnya VYEchiram*

What kind of seats do you have?	**Какие у вас места?** *kaKIye u VAS miSTA*
One orchestra seat, please.	**Один в партере, пожалуйста.** *aDIN f parTYErye paZHAlusta*
Two balcony seats.	**Два в балконе.** *DVA v balKOnye*
Three in the first ring.	**Три в первом ярусе.** *TRI f PYERvam YArusye*
What are the least expensive seats?	**Какие самые дешёвые места?** *kaKIye SAmiye diSHOviye miSTA*
When does the performance begin?	**Когда спектакль начинается?** *kagDA spikTAKL' nachiNAyitsa*
When is the performance over?	**Когда спектакль кончается?** *kagDA spikTAKL' kanCHAyitsa*
Who has an extra ticket?	**У кого лишний билет?** *u kaVOLISHny biLYET*
Are they letting people in?	**Уже пускают?** *uZHE pusKAyut*
Please go in.	**Проходите, пожалуйста.** *prakhaDItye paZHAlusta*

When you arrive at the theater you should show your ticket, then proceed to the coat check racks (**Гардероб** *gardiROP*). You must leave your coat and hat, and you may leave your briefcase or packages. Many women change from boots into more comfortable and attractive shoes.

Travel Tips There is no charge for cloakroom service, but a modest fee is charged for rental of opera glasses. The few rubles that the attendants earn this way substitute for tips. In addition, custom permits those returning opera glasses to go to the head of the line after the performance.

Opera glasses, please.	**Бинокль, пожалуйста.** *biNOKL' paZHAlusta*
I'll take a program.	**Я возьму программку.** *YA vaz'MU praGRAMku*
Where are our seats?	**Где наши места?** *GDYE NAshi miSTA*
Who is the conductor?	**Кто дирижёр?** *KTO diriZHOR*
Who's singing?	**Кто поёт?** *KTO paYOT*
Who's dancing?	**Кто танцует?** *KTO tanTSUyit*
Will there be an intermission?	**Будет антракт?** *BUdit anTRAKT*

YOUR TICKET

Your theater ticket will contain much valuable information. Examine it carefully. On the front will be printed the name and symbol of your theater, the starting time of the performance, the location of your seats, including row and seat number, and the date of the performance. The back of the ticket will give the title of the performance and may provide information on public transportation to the theater.

The theater	**Большой Театр** *Bolshoi*
	Кремлёвский Дворец съездов *Palace of Congresses*
	Мариинский театр *Mariinsky Theater*
	Театр Мусоргского *Mussorgsky Theater*
Starting time	**Начало в 12 часов** *Noon*
	Начало в 19 часов *7:00 PM*
	Начало в 20 часов *8:00 PM*
Location	**Партер** *Orchestra*
	Амфитеатр *Rear Orchestra*
	Бельэтаж *Mezzanine*
	Балкон *Balcony*
	Ложа *Box*
	1 Ярус *First Ring*
	Правая сторона *Right*
	Левая сторона *Left*
	Середина *Center*
	Ряд *Row*
	Место *Seat*
	Цена *Price*

ФЕДЕРАЛЬНОЕ АГЕНТСТВО ПО КУЛЬТУРЕ И КИНЕМАТОГРАФИИ РОССИЙСКОЙ ФЕДЕРАЦИИ

МАРИИНСКИЙ ТЕАТР

САНКТ-ПЕТЕРБУРГ, ТЕАТРАЛЬНАЯ ПЛ., 1
тел. 326-4141 · www.mariinsky.ru

NIGHT LIFE

For late evening entertainment there are more than ample opportunities, from nightclubs (**ночной клуб** *nachNOY KLUP*) to casinos (**казино** *kaziNO*). A note of caution: Many of these establishments are expensive in the extreme. If you are on a budget, check the price list.

Let's go to a nightclub.	**Пойдём в ночной бар.** *payDYOM v nachNOY BAR*
Are reservations necessary?	**Надо заказать заранее?** *NAda zakaZAT' zaRAniye*
I feel like dancing.	**Мне хочется танцевать.** *MNYE KHOchitsa tantsiVAT'*
Is there a discotheque here?	**Здесь есть дискотека?** *ZDYES'YEST' diskaTYEka*
What is the cover charge?	**Сколько стоит входной билет?** *SKOL'ka STOit fkhadNOY biLYET*
A table close to the stage.	**Столик поближе к сцене.** *STOlik paBLIzhe k TSEnye*
When does the show begin?	**Когда варьете начинается?** *kagDA var'yiTYE nachiNAyitsa*

QUIET RELAXATION:
CARDS, CHESS

Do you have a deck of cards?	**Нет ли у вас колода карт?** *NYET LI u VAS kaLOda KART*
Would you like to play cards?	**Не хотите играть в карты?** *NYE khaTItye iGRAT' f KARty*
Do you want to shuffle?	**Перетасуете?** *piriTAsuyitye*
Cut the deck!	**Снимите!** *sniMItye*
hearts, diamonds, clubs, spades	**черви, бубны, трефы, пики** *CHERvi, BUBny, TRYEfy, PIki*
ace, king, queen, jack	**туз, король, дама, валет** *TUS, kaROL', DAma, vaLYET*
Whose turn is it?	**Кому ходить?** *kaMU khaDIT'*
It's your deal.	**Вам сдавать.** *VAM zdaVAT'*
What's the score?	**Какой счёт?** *kaKOY SHOT*
You win.	**Вы выиграли.** *VY VYigrali*
I lose.	**Я проиграл.** *YA praiGRAL*
Do you want to play _____?	**Хотите играть _____?** *khaTItye iGRAT'*
▨ checkers	**в шашки** *f SHASHki*
▨ chess	**в шахматы** *f SHAKHmaty*
We need a board.	**Нам нужна доска.** *NAM nuzhNA daSKA*

We need the pieces.	**Нам нужны фигуры.** *NAM nuzhNY fiGUry*
■ the king	**король** *kaROL'*
■ the queen	**королева** *karaLYEva*
■ the rook	**ладья** *laD'YA*
■ the bishop	**слон** *SLON*
■ the knight	**офицер** *ofiTSER*
■ the pawn	**пешка** *PYESHka*
Check.	**Шах.** *SHAKH*
Checkmate.	**Мат.** *MAT*

SPORTS

SPORTING EVENTS

Don't miss out on the opportunity to see a hockey game or a tennis match, or one of the other popular sporting events.

Basketball	**баскетбол** *baskitBOL*
Boxing	**бокс** *BOKS*
Gymnastics	**гимнастика** *gimNAstika*
Hockey	**хоккей** *khaKYEY*
Soccer	**футбол** *futBOL*
Tennis	**теннис** *TYEnis*

In addition to watching the popular spectator sports, Russians love to spend time outdoors. You might spend the afternoon in one of the major parks or go swimming in one of the outdoor pools open all year. Winter sports include skating, sledding, and cross country skiing near Sparrow Hills. You can also play tennis and golf.

BEACH OR POOL

Oh! It's hot!	**Ой! Как жарко!** *OY KAK ZHARka*
Let's go swimming.	**Пойдём купаться.** *payDYOM kuPAtsa*
Let's go to the beach.	**Пойдём на пляж.** *payDYOM na PLYASH*
Let's go to the pool.	**Пойдём в бассейн.** *payDYOM vbaSYEYN*
How do you get there?	**Как туда проехать?** *KAK tuDA praYEkhat'*
What's the admission charge?	**Сколько стоит билет?** *SKOL'ka STOit biLYET*
What's the water temperature?	**Сколько градусов воды?** *SKOL'ka GRAdusaf vaDY*
I (don't) know how to swim.	**Я (не) умею плавать.** *YA (NYE) uMYEyu PLAvat'*
Is there a lifeguard?	**Есть спасатель?** *YEST spaSAtil'*
Where is the locker room?	**Где камера хранения?** *GDYE KAmira khraNYEniya*
Can I rent _____?	**Можно взять на прокат _____?** *MOZHna VZYAT" na praKAT*
■ an air mattress	**надувной матрац** *naduvNOY maTRATS*
■ a beach ball	**мяч** *MYACH*
■ a boat	**лодку** *LOTku*
■ a chaise longue	**шезлонг** *shizLONG*
■ a beach towel	**полотенце** *palaTYENtse*
■ an umbrella	**зонт** *ZONT*

■ water skis	**водные лыжи**	*vadNIye LYzhi*
I need to buy ____.	**Мне надо купить ____.**	*MNYE NAda kuPIT'*
■ a bathing cap	**шапочку**	*SHApachku*
■ a bathing suit	**купальник**	*kuPAL'nik*
■ bathing trunks	**плавки**	*PLAFki*
■ sunglasses	**солнечные очки**	*SOL'nichniye achKI*
■ suntan lotion	**крем от загара**	*KRYEM at zaGAra*

WINTER SPORTS

I want to go ____.	**Я хочу кататься ____.**	*YA khaCHU kaTAtsa*
■ ice skating	**на коньках**	*na kan'KAKH*
■ skiing	**на лыжах**	*na LYzhakh*

■ sledding	**на санках**	*na SANkakh*
Where can I buy _____?	**Где купить _____?** *GDYE kuPIT"*	
■ bindings	**крепления**	*kriPLYEniya*
■ boots	**ботинки/сапоги**	*baTINki/sapaGI*
■ cross country skis	**беговые лыжи**	*bigaVIye LYzhi*
■ downhill skis	**горные лыжи**	*GORniye LYzhi*
■ poles	**палки**	*PALki*
■ figure skates	**фигурные коньки** *fiGURniye kan'KI*	
■ hockey skates	**хоккейные коньки** *khaKYEYniye kan'KI*	

IN THE COUNTRYSIDE

Let's go to the country.	**Поедем в деревню.** *paYEdim v diRYEVnyu*
Do you have a dacha in the country?	**У вас есть дача в деревне?** *u VAS YEST" DAcha v diRYEVnye*
How long does it take to get there?	**Сколко времени туда ехать?** *SKOL'ka VRYEmini tuDA YEkhat'*
How beautiful!	**Как красиво!** *KAK kraSIva*
Look at the _____.	**Посмотрите на _____.** *pasmaTRItye na*
■ birds	**птиц** *PTITS*
■ bridge	**мост** *MOST*
■ brook	**ручей** *ruCHYEY*

■ fields	поля	*paLYA*
■ flowers	цветы	*tsviTY*
■ forest	лес	*LYES*
■ hills	холмы	*khalMY*
■ lake	озеро	*Ozira*
■ mountains	горы	*GOry*
■ plants	растения	*raSTYEniya*
■ pond	пруд	*PRUT*
■ river	реку	*RYEku*
■ sea	море	*MOrye*
■ trees	деревья	*diRYEv'ya*
■ village	село	*siLO*
■ valley	долину	*daLInu*

I'm lost.	**Я потерялся.**	*YA patiRYALsya*

Where does _____ lead?	**Куда идёт _____?**	*kuDA iDYOT*
■ this road	эта дорога	*Eta daROga*
■ this path	эта тропинка	*Eta traPINka*

Can you show me the way?	**Вы можете мне показать дорогу?** *VY MOzhitye MNYE pakaZAT" daROgu*

FOOD AND DRINK

A restaurant meal in Russia is an event to be enjoyed and savored for the better part of an evening. For a quick bite to eat, visit one of the local **Пельменная** *pil'MYEnaya* (Siberian dumpling), **Шашлычная** *shaSHLYCHnaya* (shish-kabob), or **Гриль** *GRIL'* (grill) establishments. Moscow even has a food court (**Ресторанный дворик** *ristaRAny DVOrik*). When dining out you will have the choice not only of Russian cuisine, but also of exceptional national cuisines such as Armenian, Georgian, and Uzbek. The Russian breakfast tends to be simple, but hearty. You might have a pastry or the famous Russian dark bread with butter and marmalade. You can also have **каша** *KAsha* (a warm cereal), **сосиски** *saSISki* (hot dogs), or **яйца** *YAYtsa* (eggs), accompanied by a glass of **русский чай** *RUski CHAY* (Russian tea) with plenty of **сахар** *SAkhar* (sugar). Because lunch tends to be the main meal of the day, Russians typically will have a **салат** *saLAT* (salad), **суп** *SUP* (soup), a main course, and a light dessert, accompanied by more **чёрный хлеб** *CHORny KHLYEP* (black bread). An excellent selection for lunch is offered at the major hotels, which often feature a smorgasbord (**Шведский стол** *SHVYETski STOL*) for lunch at reasonable prices. Thus, you can sample a variety of dishes. In the evening you might have a light snack of **бутерброды** *butirBROdy* (open-faced sandwiches), with **икра** *iKRA* (caviar), **сыр** *SYR* (cheese), **рыба** *RYba* (fish), or **мясо** *MYAsa* (meat), and a **пирожное** *piROZHnaye* (sweet pastry) at one of the theater buffets. If you go to a restaurant, there will likely be elaborate **закуски** *zaKUSki* (hors d'œuvres) including assorted meats, fish, patés, and cucumbers and tomatoes with sour cream, with ample amounts of vodka, wine, or champagne for the numerous toasts normally accompanying such a feast.

Most restaurants now accept reservations and you should call ahead, or have your hosts or someone at the hotel make those arrangements. Moscow and St. Petersburg are now very cosmopolitan and you will have your choice of cuisine, decor, and price category including a growing number of familiar Western-style fast food chains.

EATING OUT

Before you select your restaurant you might want to check the Internet or one of the local printed guides for more complete information. And if you want to eat in, you can always order by phone and have it delivered. Take note of the following services.

Business lunch	**Бизнес-ланч**	*BIZnis LANCH*
Home delivery	**Доставка на дом** *daSTAFka na DOM*	
Take out food	**Еда на вынос**	*yiDA na VYnas*
Wine list	**Карта вин**	*KARta VIN*
Vegetarian menu	**Вегетарианское меню** *vigitariANskaya miNYU*	
Meat menu	**Мясное меню**	*misNOyi miNYU*
Fish menu	**Рыбное меню**	*RYBnaya miNYU*
Beer on tap	**Разливное пиво**	*razLIVnaye PIva*
Average cost of the bill	**Средняя стоимость счёта** *SRYEDnyaya STOimast' SCHOta*	
Live music	**Живая музыка**	*ZHIvaya MUzyka*

In major cities such as Moscow and St. Petersburg you are likely to have a choice of international cuisine. Find your own favorites:

foreign cuisine	**иностранная кухня** *inaSTRAnaya KUKHnya*	
Chinese	**китайская**	*kiTAYskaya*
Georgian	**грузинская**	*gruZINskaya*

Italian	**итальянская** *itaLYANskaya*
Russian	**русская** *RUSkaya*
Thai	**тайская** *TAYskaya*
Uzbek	**узбекская** *uzBYEKskaya*

The main Russian meals are

breakfast	**завтрак** *ZAFtrak*
lunch	**обед** *aBYET*
supper	**ужин** *Uzhin*

You will probably come across the following establishments serving food.

buffet	**буфет** *buFYET*
cafe	**кафе** *kaFYEY*
cafeteria	**столовая** *staLOvaya*
grill	**гриль** *GRIL'*
ice cream parlor	**кафе мороженое** *kaFYEY maROzhinaye*
pancake house	**блинная** *BLInaya*
pelmennaya (Siberian dumpling shop)	**пельменная** *pil'MYEnaya*
restaurant	**ресторан** *ristaRAN*
shashlychnaya (shish-kabob)	**шашлычная** *shaSHLYCHnaya*
snack bar	**закусочная** *zaKUsachnaya*
Do you know a good restaurant?	**Вы знаете хороший ресторан?** *VY ZNAyitye khaROshi ristaRAN*

Is it very expensive?	**Он очень дорогой?** *ON Ochin' daraGOY*
Can I sample Russian cuisine there?	**Там можно попробовать русскую кухню?** *TAM MOZHna paPRObavat' RUskuyu KUKHnyu*
I'd like to reserve a table _____.	**Я хочу заказать стол _____.** *YA khaCHU zakaZAT" STOL*
■ for tonight	**на сегодня** *na siVODnya*
■ for tomorrow evening	**на завтра** *na ZAFtra*
■ for two (three, four) persons	**на двоих (троих, четверых)** *na dvaIKH (traIKH, chitviRYKH)*
■ at 8:00 PM (20:00)	**в двадцать часов** *v DVAtsat' chiSOF*

The customs surrounding a Russian restaurant meal deserve a minute of your attention. You should be attentive to signs posted on the front door. **Перерыв** *piriRYF* indicates that the restaurant is closed for a break between meals. **Свободных мест нет** *svaBODnykh MYEST NYET* means no free places at the moment. You might want to wait, but in the evening most Russians will stay until closing time. When you get past the doorman, check your coat and hat at the **Гардероб** *gardiROP*. From there you proceed to the *maitre d'hotel* (**метрдотель** *mitrdaTYEL'*), who will escort you to a table. Unless your party is large enough to fill an entire table, strangers may be seated next to you. If you are alone, there will be a wait until all the seats at the table are occupied; thus it is in your interest to pick a place at a partially occupied table that has not yet been served. When the waiter (**официант** *afitsiANT*) or waitress (**официантка** *afitsiANTka*) approaches, you will hear "**Я вас слушаю** *YA VAS SLUshayu*," literally, "I am listening," which means, "I am ready to take your order." Normally you will order the entire meal at that time, including dessert (**сладкое** *SLATkaye*) and coffee or tea.

Waiter!	**Молодой человек!** *malaDOY chilaVYEK*
Miss!	**Девушка!** *DYEvushka*
Is this table being served?	**Этот стол обслуживается?** *Etat STOL apSLUzhivayitsa*
Please bring the menu.	**Меню, пожалуйста.** *miNYU paZHAlusta*
What is your specialty?	**Какое у вас фирменное блюдо?** *kaKOye u VAS FIRminaye BLYUda*
I'm (not) very hungry. (*m*)	**Я (не) очень голоден.** *YA (NYE) Ochin' GOladin*
I'm (not) very hungry. (*f*)	**Я (не) очень голодна.** *YA (NYE) Ochin' galadNA*
To begin with, bring us _____.	**Для начала, принесите нам _____.** *dlya naCHAla priniSItye NAM*
■ some vodka (100 grams)	**сто грамм водки** *STO GRAM VOTki*
■ some cognac (100 grams)	**сто грамм коньяка** *STO GRAM kan'yaKA*
■ a bottle of red wine	**бутылку красного вина** *buTYLku KRASnava viNA*
■ a bottle of white wine	**бутылку белого вина** *buTYLku BYElava viNA*
■ a bottle of beer	**бутылку пива** *buTYLku PIva*
■ a bottle of mineral water	**бутылку минеральной воды** *buTYLku miniRAL'nay vaDY*
■ a bottle of soft drink	**бутылку лимонада** *buTYLku limaNAda*
I'm ready to order now.	**Я готов заказать.** *YA gaTOF zakaZAT'*

What do you recommend?	**Что вы рекомендуете?** *SHTO VY rikaminDUyitye*

Please, also bring us _____.	**Принесите, пожалуйста _____.** *priniSItye paZHAlusta*

■ some bread	**хлеба** *KHLYEba*
■ some butter	**масла** *MAsla*
■ some more _____	**ещё _____** *yiSHO*
■ an ashtray	**пепельницу** *PYEpil'nitsu*
■ a knife	**нож** *NOSH*
■ a fork	**вилку** *VILku*
■ a spoon	**ложку** *LOSHku*
■ a glass	**стакан** *staKAN*
■ a vodka glass	**рюмку** *RYUMku*
■ a plate	**тарелку** *taRYELku*
■ a napkin	**салфетку** *salFYETku*

I'll have the _____.	**Я возьму _____.** *YA vaz'MU*

Travel Tips If you are traveling on your own, finding a restaurant and ordering a meal can be time consuming. You can probably get a cup of coffee, juice, and rolls or pastries for breakfast at your hotel buffet. For a delicious lunch without a wait, try the smorgasbord (**Шведский стол** *SHVETski STOL*) at one of the hotels for foreigners. If the hotel fare is a bit pricey you can certainly visit any of the fast food outlets or kiosks that can be found wherever visitors gather. In the evening you might do as Russians do and eat at the theater buffet. You should go early (at least forty-five minutes before the performance) to avoid the rush and the lines. It might result in a new acquaintance and a conversation.

THE MENU

Russian menus are pre-printed and are often several pages long. Only those selections with a price indicated are available. Even so, you might ask whether your favorite dish can be ordered.

APPETIZERS (ЗАКУСКИ)
COLD (ХОЛОДНЫЕ) AND WARM (ЖАРКИЕ)

At banquets and formal dinners great care, attention, and expense are devoted to appetizers (закуски *zaKUSki*), which accompany the obligatory toasts with Russian vodka. It is important to dig in and help yourself. Russians recommend black bread spread with lots of butter and cucumbers sprinkled with salt as a way to compensate for the alcohol. You will be delighted by the variety of items, which can range from elaborate fish trays to exquisite caviar. But if you are on a tight budget, be sure to ask in advance what all this costs.

assorted fish	**ассорти рыбное**	*asarTI RYBnaye*
assorted meats	**ассорти мясное**	*asarTI misNOye*
caviar	**икра**	*iKRA*
■ black caviar	**зернистая икра**	*zirNIStaya iKRA*
■ red caviar	**кетовая икра**	*KYEtavaya iKRA*
mushrooms	**грибы**	*griBY*
mushrooms julienne	**жульен из грибов**	*zhuL'YEN iz griBOF*
pancakes/bliny	**блины**	*bliNY*
pastries	**пирожки**	*pirashKI*
■ with cabbage	**с капустой**	*s kaPUstay*
■ with mushrooms	**с грибами**	*z griBAmi*

- with meat   с мясом   *s MYAsam*
- with onion   с луком   *s LUkam*
- with potatoes   с картошкой   *s karTOshkay*

sandwich   бутерброд   *butirBROT*

THE EGG (ЯЙЦО)

hard-boiled eggs   яйца вкрутую   *YAYtsa frkuTUyu*

soft-boiled eggs   яйца всмятку   *YAYtsa FSMYATku*

fried eggs   яичница-глазунья
yaICHnitsa glaZUn'ya

scrambled eggs   яичница-болтунья
yaICHnitsa balTUn'ya

THE SALAD (САЛАТ)

In addition to the standard salad dishes, almost every restaurant has its house specialty salad (салат *saLAT*). Ask the waiter about the ingredients, and wait to be pleasantly surprised, visually and gastronomically.

fresh vegetable salad   салат из свежих овощей
saLAT is SVYEzikh avaSCHYEY

crab salad   салат из крабов   *saLAT is KRAbof*

tomato salad   салат из помидоров
saLAT is pamiDOraf

cucumber salad   салат из огурцов
saLAT iz agurTSOF

THE SOUP (СУП)
THE FIRST COURSE (ПЕРВОЕ)

Soup (суп *SUP*) is an absolute must in the winter, but even in the summer months Russians enjoy their soups. The most frequently encountered soups are борщ *BORSH*, made of beets, щи *SHI*, made from cabbage, and солянка *saLYANka*, made from fish or meat.

beet soup	**борщ** *BORSH*
bouillon	**бульон** *buL'YON*
cabbage soup	**щи** *SHI*
fish soup	**рыбный суп** *RYBny SUP*
kidney soup	**рассольник** *raSOL'nik*
mushroom soup	**грибной суп** *gribNOY SUP*
noodle soup	**суп-лапша** *SUP-lapSHA*
solyanka	**солянка** *saLYANka*

THE MAIN (SECOND) COURSE (ВТОРОЕ)

For the main course, much will depend upon the availability of different fish (**рыба** *RYba*) and meat (**мясо** *MYAsa*) dishes. Here too, you might inquire about the **фирменные блюда** *FIRminiye BLYUda* (house specialties).

FISH (РЫБА)

carp	**карп** *KARP*
cod	**треска** *triSKA*
fish pelmeni (dumplings)	**пельмени рыбные** *pil'MYEni RYBnye*
herring	**селёдка** *siLYOTka*
lobster	**омар** *aMAR*
pike, perch	**судак** *suDAK*
salmon	**сёмга** *SYOMga*
sturgeon	**осетрина** *asiTRIna*
filet of sturgeon	**балык** *baLYK*
trout	**форель** *faRYEL'*
tuna	**тунец** *tuNYETS*

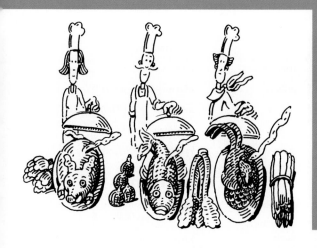

MEAT (МЯСО)

beef Stroganoff	**беф-строганов**	*bif-STROganaf*
steak	**бифштекс**	*bifSHTYEKS*
cutlets	**котлеты**	*katLYEty*
golubtsy (stuffed cabbage)	**голубцы**	*galupTSY*
roast beef	**ростбиф**	*ROSTbif*
lamb	**баранина**	*baRAnina*
liver	**печень**	*PYEchin'*
pelmeni (Siberian dumplings)	**пельмени**	*pil'MYEni*
pork chops	**свиные отбивные котлеты** *sviNIye atbivNIye katLYEty*	
ragout	**рагу**	*raGU*
schnitzel	**шницель**	*SHNItsil'*

shish kebab	**шашлык**	*shaSHLYK*
veal	**телятина**	*tiLYAtina*
fried	**жареный**	*ZHAriny*
grilled	**обжаренный**	*abZHAriny*
baked	**печёный**	*piCHOny*
boiled	**варёный**	*vaRYOny*
stewed	**тушёный**	*tuSHOny*

POULTRY (ПТИЦА)

chicken	**курица / цыплёнок**	*KUritsa / tsyPLYOnak*
duck	**утка**	*UTka*
goose	**гусь**	*GUS'*
pheasant	**фасан**	*faSAN*
poultry	**птица**	*PTItsa*
turkey	**индейка**	*inDYEYka*

DESSERTS (СЛАДКОЕ)
THE THIRD COURSE (ТРЕТЬЕ)

stewed fruit	**компот**	*kamPOT*
ice cream	**мороженое**	*maROzhinaye*
fresh fruits	**свежие фрукты**	*SVYEzhiye FRUKty*
whipped cream	**взбитые сливки**	*VZBItiye SLIFki*
cake	**торт**	*TORT*
pie	**пирог**	*piROK*

BEVERAGES (НАПИТКИ)

A word should be said about beverages (**напитки** *naPITki*), especially alcoholic ones. Whether at a restaurant, an official function, or just being hosted in someone's home, vodka, wine, champagne, and cognac may be available in liberal quantities. Drinking for Russians is surrounded with ceremony, including the obligation for the host to raise a toast, after which most Russians empty their glasses by drinking **до дна** *da DNA* (bottoms up, literally "to the bottom"). You should not feel compelled after the first toast to keep pace with your hosts. Remember to eat something for every glass and to follow the lead of the Russians and drink liberal amounts of **минеральная вода** *miniRAL'naya vaDA* (mineral water) between toasts.

Alcohol can be purchased almost anywhere—in grocery stores, supermarkets, and even kiosks on the street. To be safe, purchase only at legitimate outlets, and beware of bargains. If it looks too good (or inexpensive) to be real, then it probably isn't.

beer	**пиво**	*PIva*
■ bottled beer	**пиво бутылочное**	
	PIva buTYlachnaya	
■ draught beer	**пиво разливное**	*PIva razLIVNaya*

Travel Tips Russians have turned their eyes to the West since the fall of the Soviet Union. Along the way they have adopted Western banking, cuisine, computer technology, etc. Many of the words that Russian use are now internationally recognized, but because Russians tend to transliterate words (write them in Cyrillic) you will be better off by pronouncing unknown words aloud. The results may surprise you.

champagne	**шампанское**	*shamPANskaye*
■ very dry	**сухое**	*suKHOye*
■ semi-dry	**полусухое**	*palusuKHOye*
■ sweet	**сладкое**	*SLATkaye*
cocoa (hot chocolate)	**какао**	*kaKAo*
cognac	**коньяк**	*kaN'YAK*
coffee	**кофе**	*KOfye*
■ with milk	**с молоком**	*s malaKOM*
■ cappuccino	**капочино**	*kapaCHEEna*
■ latte	**латте**	*LAte*
■ mocha	**мокка**	*MOka*
_____ juice	**_____ сок**	*SOK*
■ apple	**яблочный**	*YAblachny*
■ grape	**виноградный**	*vinaGRADny*
■ orange	**апельсиновый**	*apil'SInavy*
kvass	**квас**	*KVAS*
milk	**молоко**	*malaKO*
mineral water	**минеральная вода**	*miniRAL'naya vaDA*
soft drink	**лимонад**	*limaNAT*
■ Coca-Cola®	**Кока-кола**	*KOka-KOla*
■ Pepsi®	**Пепси**	*PEPsi*
■ Seven-Up®	**Севен-ап**	*SYEvin-AP*
tea	**чай**	*CHAY*
■ with lemon	**с лимоном**	*s liMOnam*
■ with sugar	**с сахаром**	*s SAkaharam*
black tea	**чай чёрный**	*CHAY CHORny*

| | green | зелёный | *ziLEny* |
| | white | белый | *BYEly* |

| wines by the glass | вина бокалами | *viNA baKAlami* |

| _____ wine | _____ вино | *viNO* |

	Armenian	армянское	*arMYANskaya*
	Georgian	грузинское	*gruZINskaye*
	dry	сухое	*suKHOye*
	red	красное	*KRASnaye*
	sweet	сладкое	*SLATkaye*
	white	белое	*BYElaye*

| cocktails | коктейли | *kakTEYli* |

| gin | джин | *DZHIN* |

| Irish coffee | Айриш-кофе | *AYrish-KOfye* |

| liqueurs | ликёры | *liKYOry* |

| rum | ром | *ROM* |

| tequila | текила | *tiKIla* |

| vodka | водка | *VOTka* |

| whiskey | виски | *VIski* |

SETTLING UP

Your bill, especially in major cities, will probably include a service charge. Be sure to look for it or ask the waiter. Beyond that charge, be guided by your satisfaction with the service. Something between 10 and 20 percent of the bill total is appropriate.

The check, please.	**Счёт, пожалуйста.** *SHOT paZHAlusta*
Separate checks, please.	**Посчитайте отдельно, пожалуйста.** *pashiTAYtye aDYEL'na paZHAlusta*
Is service included?	**Обслуживание входит в счёт?** *apSLUzhivaniye FKHOdit f SHOT*
I didn't order this.	**Я этого не заказывал.** *YA Etava NYE zaKAzyval*
Please check the bill.	**Проверьте счёт, пожалуйста.** *praVYER'tye SHOT paZHAlusta*
It appears you've made an error.	**Кажется, что вы ошиблись.** *KAzhitsa SHTO VY aSHYblis'*
We are in a hurry.	**Мы спешим.** *MY spiSHYM*
Will it take long?	**Нам долго ждать?** *NAM DOLga ZHDAT'*
This is for you.	**Это для вас.** *Eta dlya VAS*

SHOPPING FOR FOOD

Sometime during your stay you'll probably want to purchase something for a midnight snack or an early morning start. You might visit a bakery (**булочная** *BUlachnaya*) or a pastry shop (**кондитерская** *kanDItirskaya*), try out a Russian style supermarket (**гастроном** *gastraNOM*), or buy something at an outdoor market (**рынок** *RYnak*) or the stands on the street corners. Most items are sold by weight, and you'll purchase many things by the hundred grams (about one quarter of a pound) or by the kilogram (two and one quarter American pounds).

BREADS (ХЛЕБ)
THE BAKERY (БУЛОЧНАЯ)

a loaf of white bread	**батон белого хлеба** *baTON BYElava KHLYEba*
dark bread	**чёрный хлеб** *CHORny KHLYEP*
rye bread	**ржаной хлеб** *rzhaNOY KHLYEP*
a roll	**булочка** *BUlachka*

DAIRY PRODUCTS
MILK AND CHEESE (МОЛОКО и СЫР)

Russian cheese	**российский сыр** *raSIYski SYR*
Dutch cheese	**голландский сыр** *gaLANTski SYR*
creamy butter	**сливочное масло** *SLIvachnaye MAsla*
chocolate butter	**шоколадное масло** *shakaLADnaye MAsla*
cream cheese	**творог** *tvaROK*
sour cream	**сметана** *smiTAna*
kefir (a yogurt-like beverage)	**кефир** *kiFIR*

CAKES (ТОРТЫ)
THE PASTRY SHOP (КОНДИТЕРСКАЯ)

jelly	**варенье** *vaRYEn'ye*
muffins/cupcakes	**кекс** *KYEKS*
a round cookie	**кольцо** *kal'TSO*
oatmeal cookies	**овсянное печенье** *afSYAnaye piCHEn'ye*
a cake	**торт** *TORT*
a pie	**пирог** *piROK*
pastry	**пирожное** *piROZHnaye*

SEASONINGS (ПРИПРАВА)

saccharin	**сахарин** *sakhaRIN*
sugar	**сахар** *SAkhar*
salt	**соль** *SOL'*
pepper	**перец** *PYErits*
horseradish	**хрен** *KHRYEN*
mayonnaise	**майонез** *mayaNYES*
mustard	**горчица** *garCHItsa*
mint	**мята** *MYAta*
paprika	**паприка** *PAprika*
garlic	**чеснок** *chiSNOK*
vegetable oil	**растительное масло** *raSTItil'naye MAsla*
vinegar	**уксус** *UKsus*

COLD CUTS

ham	**ветчина** *vichiNA*
salami	**колбаса** *kalbaSA*

FRUITS (ФРУКТЫ)

apple	**яблоко** *YAblaka*
apricot	**абрикос** *abriKOS*
banana	**банан** *baNAN*
cherry	**вишня** *VISHnya*
currants	**смородина** *smaROdina*
date	**финик** *FInik*
fig	**фига** *FIga*
grapefruit	**грейпфрут** *GRYEYPfrut*
grapes	**виноград** *vinaGRAT*

kiwi	**киви**	*KIvi*
lemon	**лимон**	*liMON*
melon	**дыня**	*DYnya*
orange	**апельсин**	*apil'SIN*
pear	**груша**	*GRUsha*
peach	**персик**	*PYERsik*
pineapple	**ананас**	*anaNAS*
plum	**слива**	*SLIva*
pomegranate	**гранат**	*graNAT*
raspberries	**малина**	*maLIna*
strawberries	**клубник**	*klubNIK*
tangerine	**мандарин**	*mandaRIN*
watermelon	**арбуз**	*arBUS*
almonds	**миндаль**	*minDAL'*
chestnuts	**каштан**	*kaSHTAN*
nuts	**орехи**	*aRYEkhi*

GRAINS (КРУПЫ)

buckwheat	**гречка**	*GRECHka*
oats	**овёс**	*aVYOS*
rice	**рис**	*RIS*
rye	**рожь**	*ROSH*
wheat	**пшеница**	*pshiNItsa*

ICE CREAM (МОРОЖЕНОЕ)

_____ ice cream	**_____ мороженое**	*maROzhinaye*
■ chocolate	**шоколадное**	*shakaLADnaye*
■ vanilla	**сливочное**	*SLIvachnaye*

VEGETABLES (ОВОЩИ)

artichoke	**артишок** *artiSHOK*
asparagus	**спаржа** *SPARzha*
beets	**свёкла** *SVYOkla*
cabbage	**капуста** *kaPUSta*
carrots	**морковь** *marKOF"*
cauliflower	**цветная капуста** *tsvitNAya kaPUSta*
cucumbers	**огурцы** *agurTSY*
eggplant	**баклажан** *baklaZHAN*
hot pepper	**перец острый** *PYErits Ostry*
lettuce	**салат** *saLAT*
mushrooms	**грибы** *griBY*
noodles	**лапша** *lapSHA*
onions	**лук** *LUK*
peas	**горох** *gaROKH*
potatoes	**картофель** *karTOfil'*
pumpkin	**тыква** *TYKva*
radishes	**редиска** *riDISka*
rice	**рис** *RIS*
sauerkraut	**квашенная капуста** *KVAshinaya kaPUSta*
spinach	**шпинат** *shpiNAT*
string beans	**стручковая фасоль** *struchKOvaya faSOL'*
sweet pepper	**перец сладкий** *PYRrits SLATki*
tomatoes	**помидоры** *pamiDOry*
turnips	**репька** *RYEP'ka*

MEETING PEOPLE

GREETINGS AND INTRODUCTIONS

Hello!	**Здравствуйте!**	*ZDRASTvuytye*
My name is ____.	**Меня зовут ____.**	*miNYA zaVUT*
What is your name?	**Как вас зовут?**	*KAK VAS zaVUT*

> Russians have three names, a first name (**имя** *Imya*), a patronymic derived from one's father's name (**отчество** *Ochistva*), and a family name (**фамилия** *faMIliya*). It is polite to refer to recent acquaintances with the name and patronymic. Thus one would address even the president of the country as **Владимир Владимирович** *vlahDEEmeer vlahDEEmeerovich*. Russians are likely to have a nickname. For example, Ivan—**Иван** *iVAN* becomes Vanya—**Ваня** *Vanya*, Aleksandr—**Александр** *alikSANDR* becomes Sasha—**Саша** *Sasha*.

Traditionally Russians used a combination of these three names and you will still encounter them in literature, films, and in formal settings. You are never wrong by erring on the side of courtesy. At the time of introductions ask for the person's first name and then the patronymic.

What is	**Как**	*KAK*
■ your first name?	**ваше имя?**	*VAshe Imya*
■ your patronymic?	**ваше отчество?**	*VAshe Ochistva*
■ your family (last) name/surname?	**ваша фамилия?**	*VAsha faMIliya*

Be aware that there is a growing tendency toward informality, so many Russians are accustomed to hearing and responding to their first names only.

Pleased to meet you.	**Очень приятно.** *Ochin' priYATna*

I am from ____.	**Я из ____.** *YA iz*
■ Australia	**Австралии** *afSTRAlii*
■ Canada	**Канады** *kaNAdy*
■ England	**Англии** *ANglii*
■ the USA	**США** *SA SHA A*

I like ____ very much.	**Мне очень нравится ____.** *MNYE Ochin' NRAvitsa*
■ Moscow	**Москва** *maskVA*
■ St. Petersburg	**Санкт Петербург** *SANKT pitirBURK*
■ your country	**ваша страна** *VAsha straNA*
■ your republic	**ваша республика** *VAsha riSPUblika*

May I introduce myself.	**Разрешите мне представиться.** *razriSHYtye MNYE pritSTAvitsa*
May I introduce my _____.	**Разрешите мне представить _____.** *razriSHYtye MNYE pritSTAvit'*
■ brother	**брата** *BRAta*
■ colleague	**коллегу** *kaLYEgu*
■ daughter	**дочь** *DOCH*
■ father	**отца** *aTSA*
■ friend	**друга** *DRUga*
■ husband	**мужа** *MUzha*
■ mother	**мать** *MAT'*
■ sister	**сестру** *siSTRU*
■ wife	**жену** *zhiNU*
■ son	**сына** *SYna*
I am _____.	**Я _____.** *YA*
■ an artist	**художник** *khuDOZHnik*
■ a builder	**строитель** *straItel'*
■ a businessman	**бизнесмен** *biznisMYEN*
■ a correspondent	**корреспондент** *karispanDYENT*
■ a diplomat	**дипломат** *diplaMAT*
■ a doctor	**врач** *VRACH*
■ a dentist	**зубной врач** *zubNOY VRACH*
■ a lawyer	**адвокат** *advaKAT*
■ a teacher	**преподаватель** *pripadaVAtil'*
■ a student	**студент** *stuDYENT*
■ a nurse	**медсестра** *medsiSTRA*
■ a writer	**писатель** *piSAtil'*
Where are you from?	**Откуда вы?** *atKUda VY*

Where do you work?	**Где вы работаете?** *GDYE VY raBOtayitye*
What is your profession?	**Кто вы по профессии?** *KTO VY pa praFYEsii*
I will be staying ____.	**Я здесь буду ____.** *YA ZDYES' BUdu*
■ a few days	**несколько дней** *NYEskal'ka DNYEY*
■ a week	**неделю** *niDYElyu*
■ a month	**месяц** *MYEsits*
Would you like a picture?	**Хотите фотографию?** *khaTItye fataGRAfiyu*
Stand there.	**Стойте там.** *STOYtye TAM*
Smile!	**Улыбайтесь!** *ulyBAYtis'*
Say "cheese"! ("raisin")	**Скажите "изюм"!** *skaZHYtye iZYUM*
I want a photo of you.	**Я хочу фотографию вас.** *YA khaCHU fataGRAfiyu VAS*
■ as a remembrance	**на память** *na PAmit'*

Travel Tips The Russian kitchen is the place to be for good conversations over hot tea. The formal living room is normally reserved for honored guests, but if they invite you to the kitchen table, then be sure to accept the invitation, for it means that at least for the evening you will be one of the family.

SOCIALIZING

May I have this dance? (May I invite you?)	**Разрешите вас пригласить?** *razriSHYtye VAS priglaSIT'*
All right. With pleasure.	**Хорошо. С удовольствием.** *kharaSHO s udaVOL'STviyim*
Would you like a cigarette?	**Закурите?** *zaKUritye*
Would you like a drink?	**Что-нибудь выпьете?** *SHTO-nibut' VYpitye*
Do you mind if I smoke?	**Ничего если я закурю?** *nichiVOYEsli YA zakuRYU*
May I take you home?	**Можно вас домой проводить?** *MOZHna VAS daMOY pravaDIT'*
May I call you?	**Можно вам позвонить?** *MOZHna VAM pazvaNIT'*
What is your telephone number?	**Какой ваш номер телефона?** *kaKOY VASH NOmir tiliFOna*
Here is my telephone number.	**Вот мой номер телефона.** *VOT MOY NOmir tiliFOna*
Here is my address.	**Вот мой адрес.** *VOT MOY Adris*
Will you write to me?	**Вы мне напишете?** *VY MNYE naPIshitye*
Are you married? (of a man)	**Вы женаты?** *VY zhiNAty*

Are you married? (of a woman)	**Вы замужем?** *VY ZAmuzhim*
Are you alone? (of a man)	**Вы один?** *VY aDIN*
Are you alone? (of a woman)	**Вы одна?** *VY adNA*
Is your husband here?	**Ваш муж здесь?** *VASH MUSH ZDYES'*
Is your wife here?	**Ваша жена здесь?** *VAsha zhiNA ZDYES'*
I'm here with my family.	**Я здесь с семьёй.** *YA ZDYES' s siM'YOY*
Do you have children?	**У вас есть дети?** *u VAS YEST" DYEti*
How many?	**Сколько?** *SKOL'ka*
How old are they?	**Сколько им лет?** *SKOL'ka IM LYET*
What are you doing tomorrow?	**Какие у вас планы на завтра?** *kaKIye u VAS PLAny na ZAFtra*
Are you free this evening?	**Вы свободны сегодня вечером?** *VY svaBODny siVODnya VYEchiram*
Would you like to go together?	**Хотите пойти вместе?** *khaTItye payTI VMYEStye*
I'll wait for you in front of the hotel.	**Я вас жду у входа гостиницы.** *YA VAS ZHDU u FKHOda gaSTInitsy*
I'll pick you up.	**Я за вами заеду.** *YA za VAmi zaYEdu*

SAYING GOOD-BYE

Thank you for your hospitality.	**Спасибо за гостеприимство.** *spaSIba za gastipriIMstva*
Nice to have met you.	**Очень приятно с вами познакомиться.** *Ochin' priYATna s VAmi paznaKOmitsa*
Regards to _____.	**Привет _____.** *priVYET*
Until tomorrow.	**До завтра.** *da ZAFtra*
Until later.	**Пока.** *paKA*
Until this evening.	**До вечера.** *da VYEchira*
Good-bye.	**До свидания.** *da sviDAniya*
Goodnight.	**Спокойной ночи.** *spaKOYnay NOchi*
Farewell.	**Прощайте.** *praSHAYtye*
I wish you _____.	**Я желаю вам _____.** *YA zhiLAyu VAM*
■ all the best	**всего доброго** *fsiVO DObrava*
■ bon voyage	**счастливого пути** *shastLIvava puTI*
■ good luck	**удачи** *uDAchi*

SHOPPING

SHOPS AND STORES

▬▬▬▬

To sample the wide variety of consumer items, you might begin with a visit to one of the large department stores in Moscow. Located on Red Square, the most famous store is GUM (**ГУМ**), the State Department Store. Just a few blocks away you can visit TSUM (**ЦУМ**), the Central Department Store, and Children's World (**Детский мир** *DYETski MIR*). As with any major city, Moscow and St. Petersburg offer a variety of shops, many of them aimed at visitors, and where prices might be higher than in stores frequented by the local citizens. Russian stores open around 9:00 AM and remain open until about 8:00 PM. Many close for an hour during the lunch period. Signs posted on the door indicate the opening and closing times as well as the lunch break (**перерыв на обед** *piriRYF na aBYET*), but they will be listed according to the twenty-four hour clock. Thus 1:00 PM is 13:00 and 7:30 PM is 19:30. In addition to the stores you might try the farmers' market (**рынок** *RYnak*). Don't miss the fashionable shops in Moscow on Novy Arbat and Tverskaya Street, or Russia's premier shopping mall on Manezhnaya Square. In St. Petersburg you must stroll and shop on Nevsky Prospect.

GOING SHOPPING

▬▬▬▬

I'd like to go shopping today.	**Сегодня я хочу пойти по магазинам.** *siVODnya YA khaCHUpayTI pa magaZInam*
Where is a nearby _____?	**Где поблизости _____?** *GDYE paBLIzasti*
■ antique shop	**комиссионый магазин** *kamisiOny magaZIN*
■ bakery	**булочная** *BUlachnaya*

■ barber shop	**парикмахерская** *parikMAkhirskaya*	
■ beauty parlor	**женский салон** *ZHENski saLON*	
■ bookstore	**книжный магазин** *KNIZHny magaZIN*	
■ butcher shop	**магазин "Мясо"** *magaZIN MYAsa*	
■ camera shop	**магазин "Фототовары"** *magaZIN fotataVARY*	
■ candy store	**магазин "Конфеты"** *magaZIN kanFYEty*	
■ clothing store	**магазин "Одежда"** *magaZIN aDYEZHda*	
■ department store	**универмаг** *univirMAK*	
■ drugstore	**аптека** *apTYEka*	
■ dry cleaner's	**химчистка** *khimCHISTka*	
■ fabric store	**магазин "Ткани"** *magaZIN TKAni*	
■ florist	**магазин "Цветы"** *magaZIN tsviTY*	
■ fruit and vegetable store	**магазин "Овощи и Фрукты"** *magaZIN Ovashi I FRUKty*	
■ furrier	**магазин "Меха"** *magaZIN miKHA*	
■ gift (souvenir) store	**магазин "Подарки"** *magaZIN paDARki*	
■ hardware store	**хозяйственный магазин** *khaZYAYSTviny magaZIN*	
■ health-food store	**магазин "Диета"** *magaZIN diYEta*	
■ jewelry store	**ювелирный магазин** *yuviLIRny magaZIN*	
■ laundry	**прачечная** *PRAchichnaya*	
■ liquor store	**магазин "Вино"** *magaZIN viNO*	
■ newsstand	**газетный киоск** *gaZYETny kiOSK*	
■ optician	**оптика** *OPtika*	
■ pastry shop	**кондитерская** *kanDItirskaya*	
■ shoe store	**магазин "Обувь"** *magaZIN Obuf'*	

■	shoe repair shop	**ремонт обуви** *riMONT Obuvi*
■	sporting goods store	**магазин "Спорттовары"** *magaZIN sparttaVAry*
■	stationery store	**канцелярские товары** *kantsiLYARskiye taVAry*
■	supermarket	**гастроном** *gastraNOM*
■	tailor	**ателье мод** *atiL'YE mot*
■	tobacco shop	**магазин "Табак"** *magaZIN taBAK*
■	toiletries shop	**парфюмерия** *parfyuMYEriya*
■	toy store	**магазин "Игрушки"** *magaZIN iGRUSHki*
■	travel agent	**бюро путешествий** *byuRO putiSHESTvi*
■	watchmaker	**ремонт часов** *riMONT chiSOF*

Young man! **Молодой человек!** *malaDOY chilaVYEK*

Young lady! **Девушка!** *DYEvushka*

Can you help me? **Вы можете мне помочь ____?** *VY MOzhitye MNYE paMOCH'*

In many Russian shops you first examine the articles with the help of the salesperson behind the counter. When you decide on your purchase, you need to find out the price. Then you go to the cashier and tell him or her the total cost and the department. After paying you receive a receipt (**чек** *CHEK*), which you bring back to the original counter, where your purchase will be waiting for you. If you feel unsure of the Russian number system, you might have the salesperson write down the price. The personnel are scrupulously honest, and if you smile and show courtesy and good humor you are likely to be helped through the process.

BOOKSTORE (КНИЖНЫЙ МАГАЗИН)

Where is the biggest (best) bookstore?	**Где самый большой (лучший) книжный магазин?** *GDYE SAmy bal'SHOY (LUCHshi) KNIZHny magaZIN*
How may I help you?	**Как вам помочь?** *KAK VAM paMOCH*
Go ahead! I'm listening.	**Говорите! Я вас слушаю.** *gavaRItye YA VAS SLUshayu*
Do you have books in English?	**У вас есть книги на английском языке?** *u VAS YEST" KNIgi na anGLIYskam yizyKYE*
The title of the book is _____.	**Название книги _____.** *naZVAniye KNIgi*
The author of the book is _____.	**Автор книги _____.** *AFtar KNIgi*
I don't know the title.	**Я не знаю названия.** *YA NYE ZNAyu naZVAniya*
I don't know the author.	**Я не знаю автора.** *YA NYE ZNAyu AFtara*
I'm just looking.	**Я только смотрю.** *YA TOL'ka smaTRYU*
I would like to buy _____.	**Я хотел бы купить _____.** *YA khaTYEL BY kuPIT"*
■ a guide book	**путеводитель** *putivaDItil'*
■ a map of this city	**план города** *PLAN GOrada*
■ a pocket dictionary	**карманный словарь** *karMAny slaVAR'*

■ a Russian-English dictionary	**русско-английский словарь** *Ruska-anGLIYski slaVAR'*
Where can I find _____?	**Где можно наити _____?** *GDYE MOZHna nayTI*
■ children's books	**детские книги** *DYETskiye KNIgi*
■ art books	**книги по искусству** *KNIgi pa iSKUSTvu*
■ a collection of stories	**сборник рассказов** *ZBORnik raSKAzaf*
■ a collection of poetry	**сборник стихотворений** *ZBORnik stikhatvaRYEni*
■ a history book	**книгу по истории** *KNIgu pa iSTOrii*
■ a novel in translation	**роман в переводе** *raMAN f piriVOdye*
I'll take these books.	**Я возьму эти книги.** *YA vaz'MU Eti KNIgi*
How much do they cost?	**Сколько они стоят?** *SKOL'ka aNI STOyit*
Could you write it down, please.	**Запишите мне это, пожалуйста.** *zapiSHYtye MNYE Eta paZHAlusta*
Wrap them up, please.	**Заверните их, пожалуйста.** *zavirNItye IKH paZHAlusta*

CLOTHING (ОДЕЖДА)

Would you please show me _____.	**Покажите мне, пожалуйста _____.** *pakaZHYtye MNYE paZHAlusta*
■ a belt	**пояс (ремень)** *POyas (riMYEN')*
■ a blouse	**блузку** *BLUSku*
■ a bra	**бюстгальтер** *byustGAL'tir*
■ a dress	**платье** *PLAt'ye*

- a coat   **пальто**   *pal'TO*
- a fur coat   **шубу**   *SHUbu*
- a fur hat   **меховую шапку** *mikhaVUyu SHAPku*
- gloves   **перчатки**   *pirCHATki*
- a handkerchief   **носовой платок**   *nasaVOY plaTOK*
- a jacket   **пиджак**   *pidZHAK*
- jeans   **джинсы**   *DZHYNsy*
- mittens   **рукавицы**   *rukaVItsy*
- panties (ladies')   **трусики**   *TRUsiki*
- pants   **брюки**   *BRYUki*
- pantyhose   **колготки**   *kalGOTki*
- a raincoat   **плащ**   *PLASH*
- a robe   **халат**   *khaLAT*
- a scarf   **шарф**   *SHARF*
- a shirt   **сорочку (рубашку)** *saROCHku (ruBASHku)*
- (a pair of) shoes   **обувь**   *Obuf'*
- a skirt   **юбку**   *YUPku*

- shorts (men's briefs)   **трусы**   *truSY*

- a slip   **комбинацию**   *kambiNAtsiyu*

- a half-slip   **нижнюю юбку** *NIZHnyuyu YUPku*

- slippers   **тапочки**   *TApachki*

- socks   **носки**   *naSKI*

- stockings   **чулки**   *chulKI*

- a suit   **костюм**   *kaSTYUM*

- a sweater   **свитер**   *SVItir*

- a tie   **галстук**   *GALstuk*

- an undershirt   **майку**   *MAYku*

- a wallet   **бумажник**   *buMAZHnik*

Do you have anything _____?   **У вас есть что-нибудь _____?** *u VAS YEST' SHTO-nibut'*

- with long sleeves   **с длинными рукавами** *z DLInymi rukaVAmi*

- with short sleeves   **с короткими рукавами** *s kaROTkimi rukaVAmi*

- cheaper   **подешевле**   *padiSHEvlye*

- else   **ещё**   *yiSHO*

- larger   **побольше**   *paBOL'she*

- more expensive   **подороже**   *padaROzhe*

- longer   **подлиннее**   *padliNYEye*

- of better quality   **лучшего качества** *LUCHshiva KAchistva*

- shorter   **покороче**   *pakaROche*

- smaller   **поменьше**   *paMYEN'she*

Where are the sale items?   **Где товары по сниженным ценам?** *GDYE taVAry pa SNIzhinym tsiNAM*

I don't like the color.   **Мне не нравится цвет.** *MNYE NYE NRAvitsa TSVYET*

Do you have it in _____?	У вас есть _____? *u VAS YEST'*
■ black	**чёрный** *CHORny*
■ dark blue	**синий** *SIni*
■ light blue	**голубой** *galuBOY*
■ brown	**коричневый** *kaRICHnivy*
■ gray	**серый** *SYEry*
■ green	**зелёный** *ziLYOny*
■ pink	**розовый** *ROzavy*
■ red	**красный** *KRASny*
■ white	**белый** *BYEly*
■ yellow	**жёлтый** *ZHOLty*

It doesn't fit me.	**Это не мой размер.** *Eta NYE MOY razMYER*
It fits me well.	**Это на меня сидит хорошо.** *Eta na miNYA siDIT kharaSHO*
I take size _____.	**Мой размер _____.** *MOY razMYER*
May I try it on?	**Можно примерить?** *MOZHna priMYErit'*
Where are the changing rooms?	**Где примерочные кабины?** *GDYE priMYErachniye kaBIny*
I need a _____.	**Мне нужен _____.** *MNYE NUzhin*
■ small	**маленький размер** *MAlin'ki razMYER*
■ medium	**средний размер** *SRYEDni razMYER*
■ large	**большой размер** *bal'SHOY razMYER*
I'll take it.	**Я возьму.** *YA vaz'MU*

FABRICS (ТКАНИ)

chiffon	**шифон** *shiFON*
corduroy	**рубчатый вельвет** *RUPchaty vil'VYET*
cotton	**хлопчатобумажная ткань** *khlapchatabuMAZHnaya TKAN'*
felt	**войлок** *VOYlak*
flannel	**фланель** *flaNYEL'*
fur	**мех** *MYEKH*
■ fox	**лиса** *liSA*
■ rabbit	**кролик** *KROlik*
■ mink	**норка** *NORka*
■ sheepskin	**овчина** *afCHIna*
■ marmot	**сурок** *suROK*
■ sable	**соболь** *SObal'*
■ wolf	**волк** *VOLK*
gabardine	**габардин** *gabarDIN*
lace	**кружева** *kruzhiVA*
leather	**кожа** *KOzha*
linen	**полотно** *palatNO*
nylon	**нейлон** *niyLON*
permanent press	**плиссированная ткань** *plisiROvanaya TKAN'*
polyester	**полиэфир** *palieFIR*
poplin	**поплин** *paPLIN*

rayon	**вискоза** *viSKOza*
sateen	**сатин** *saTIN*
satin	**атлас** *atLAS*
silk	**шёлк** *SHOLK*
suede	**замша** *ZAMsha*
terrycloth	**махровая ткань** *maKHROvaya TKAN'*
velvet	**бархат** *BARkhat*
velveteen	**вельвет** *vil'VYET*
wash-and-wear	**немнущаяся ткань** *niMNUshayasya TKAN'*
wool	**шерсть** *SHERST'*
Show me something _____.	**Покажите мне что-нибудь _____.** *pakaZHYtye MNYE SHTO-nibut'*
◼ in a solid color	**однотонное** *adnaTOnaye*
◼ with stripes	**в полоску** *f paLOSku*
◼ with polka dots	**в горошек** *v gaROshik*
◼ in plaid	**в клетку** *f KLYETku*
◼ in herringbone	**в ёлочку** *v YOlachku*
◼ checked	**в шашечку** *f SHAshichku*

SHOES AND BOOTS (ОБУВЬ)

I want to look at (men's) shoes.	**Я хочу смотреть ботинки.** *YA khaCHU smaTRYET' baTINki*
I want to look at (women's) shoes.	**Я хочу смотреть туфли.** *YA khaCHU smaTRYET' TUfli*

I want to buy a pair of boots.	**Я хочу купить пару сапог.** *YA khaCHU kuPIT' PAru saPOK*
I don't know my size.	**Я не знаю какой размер.** *YA NYE ZNAyu kaKOY razMYER*
These are too big.	**Они мне велики.** *aNI MNYE viliKI*
These are too narrow.	**Они мне тесны.** *aNI MNYE tiSNY*
These are too small	**Они мне малы.** *aNI MNYE maLY*
These are too wide.	**Они мне широки.** *aNI MNYE shiraKI*
They pinch me.	**Они меня жмут.** *aNI miNYA ZHMUT*
They fit me.	**Они мне как раз.** *aNI MNYE KAK RAS*
I'll take them.	**Я их возьму.** *YA IKH vaz'MU*
I also need shoelaces.	**Мне также нужны шнурки.** *MNYE TAGzhe nuzhNY shnurKI*

When you shop for clothes in Russia you must be aware that there are great variations in sizes. It is helpful if you know your height (**рост** *ROST*) and chest (**обхват груди** *apKHVAT GRUdi*) and waist (**обхват талии** *apKHVAT TAlii*) measurements in centimeters in order to use the conversion charts found in many department and clothing stores. In any case, you should try on the item. Ask for the changing booths—**примерочные кабины** *priMYErachniye kaBIny*. Conversion charts are at best approximations, and frequently differ from one place to another. When in doubt, be sure to try the item on for a good fit.

ELECTRICAL APPLIANCES
(ЭЛЕКТРОТОВАРЫ)

Russian electrical appliances operate on 220-volt current, except for some outlets for electric shavers and hair dryers in hotel rooms. To use 110-volt electrical appliances you will need a converter, and you will also need an adapter plug to enable European or American plugs to fit Russian sockets. Alternatively, you might purchase a hair dryer or electric shaver with dual voltage.

I want to buy _____.　　**Я хочу купить _____.**
　　　　　　　　　　　YA khaCHU kuPIT'

- an adapter — **адаптер** *aDAPtir*
- a battery — **батарею** *bataRYEyu*
- a blender — **сокавыжиматель** *sakavyzhiMAtil'*
- an electric shaver — **электрическую бритву** *elikTRIchiskuyu BRITvu*
- an extension cord — **шнур-удлинитель** *SHNUR-udliNItil'*
- a hair dryer — **фен** *FYEN*
- a plug — **вилку** *VILku*
- a radio — **радио** *RAdio*
- a cassette recorder — **магнитофон** *magnitaFON*
- a television set — **телевизор** *tiliVIzar*
- a VCR — **видео-магнитофон** *VIdio-magnitaFON*
- a toaster — **тостер** *TOStir*
- a transformer — **трансформатор** *transfarMAtar*

It doesn't work.　　**Он не работает.** *ON NYE raBOtayit*

Can you repair this?　　**Вы можете это починить?**
　　　　　　　　　　VY MOzhitye Eta pachiNIT'

Travel Tips Many electrical appliances, such as hair dryers, may have a dial that needs to be set to either 110 or 220 volts. Computers and other electronic equipment may come with power cords that clearly indicate they are capable of being used with either power input. The more important consideration is whether the prongs on your plug will fit into an adapter, and whether that adapter will in fact work in foreign outlets. Be aware that many American devices, especially those for personal grooming, have a special polarized plug with one of the prongs being much wider at its tip. If you have purchased an adapter at home be sure to check it with all of the appliances you intend to bring.

FOOD (ГАСТРОНОМ) AND HOUSEHOLD ITEMS (ХОЗЯЙСТВЕННЫЕ ТОВАРЫ)

When you set out for the stores, bring along a plastic bag or, even better, a net bag. Russians have a name for this bag—**авоська** *aVOS'ka* (just in case). Some items will be wrapped in plain gray or brown paper, but you'll find it more convenient to carry them in the bag. Many food stores are self-service, but in others you'll need to determine the price of what you want, then tell the cashier and pay. Only after you have a receipt can you line up to obtain the item.

Please give me _____.	**Дайте мне, пожалуйста, _____.** *DAYtye MNYE paZHAlusta*
■ a bar of soap	**кусок мыла** *kuSOK MYla*
■ a bottle of juice	**бутылку сока** *buTYLku SOka*
■ a box of cereal	**пакет крупы** *paKYET kruPY*
■ a can of tomato sauce	**банку томатного соуса** *BANku taMATnava SOUsa*

METRIC WEIGHTS AND MEASURES

	Solid Measures (approximate measurements only)		
OUNCES	GRAMS (Грамм)	GRAMS (Грамм)	OUNCES
¼	7	10	⅓
½	14	100	3½
¾	21	300	10½
1	28	450	16 (1 lb.)
POUNDS	KILOGRAMS (Килограмм)	KILOGRAMS (Килограмм)	POUNDS
1	½	1	2¼
5	2¼	3	6½
10	4½	5	11
20	9	10	22
50	23	50	110
100	45	100	220

	Liquid Measures (approximate measurements only)		
OUNCES	MILLILITERS (Грамм)	MILLILITERS (Грамм)	OUNCES
1	30	10	⅓
6	175	50	1½
12	350	100	3½
16	475	150	5
32	900	250	8½
GALLONS	LITERS (Литр)	LITERS (Литр)	GALLONS
1	3¾	1	¼ (1 quart)
5	19	5	1⅓
10	38	10	2½

NOTE: Common measurements for purchasing food are one kilo (one kilogram = one thousand grams) or some multiple of one hundred grams: **сто грамм, двести грамм.** Russians also use grams instead of milliliters for liquid measurement. A common measure of vodka is 100 grams.

- ten eggs — **десяток яиц** *diSYAtak yaITS*
- a jar of coffee — **банку кофе** *BANku KOfye*
- a kilo of potatoes — **кило картошки** *kiLO karTOSHki*
- a half-kilo of cherries — **пол-кило вишни** *POL-kiLO VISHni*
- a liter of milk — **литр молока** *LITR malaKA*
- a box of candy — **коробку конфет** *kaROPku kanFYET*
- 100 grams of cheese — **сто грамм сыра** *STO GRAM SYra*
- 200 grams of salami — **двести грамм колбасы** *DVYESti GRAM kalbaSY*
- a roll of toilet paper — **рулон туалетной бумаги** *ruLON tuaLYETnay buMAgi*

THE JEWELRY STORE
(ЮВЕЛИРНЫЙ МАГАЗИН)

We would like to see _____. — **Мы хотели бы посмотреть _____.** *MY khaTYEli BY pasmaTRYET"*

- some beads — **бусы** *BUsy*
- a bracelet — **браслет** *braSLYET*
- a brooch — **брошь** *BROSH*
- a chain — **цепочку** *tsiPOCHku*
- a charm — **брелок** *briLOK*
- some earrings — **серьги** *SYER'gi*
- a necklace — **ожерелье** *azhiRYEl'ye*
- a pin — **булавку** *buLAFku*
- a ring — **кольцо** *kal'TSO*
- a wedding/ engagement ring — **обручальное кольцо** *abruCHAL'naye kal'TSO*

■ a watch	**часы**	*chiSY*
■ a digital watch	**электронные часы** *elikTROniye chiSY*	

Is this _____?	**Это _____?**	*Eta*
■ gold	**золото**	*ZOlata*
■ platinum	**платина**	*PLAtina*
■ silver	**серебро**	*siriBRO*
■ stainless steel	**нержавейка**	*nirzhaVYEka*

Is it solid gold or gold plated?	**Это золото или позолоченое?** *Eta ZOlata Ili pazaLOchinaye*

How many carats?	**Сколько каратов?** *SKOL'ka kaRAtaf*

What is this stone?	**Что это за камень?** *SHTO Eta za KAmin'*

I like _____.	**Я люблю _____.**	*YA lyuBLYU*
■ amber	**янтарь**	*yanTAR'*
■ amethyst	**аметист**	*amiTIST*
■ aquamarine	**аквамарин**	*akvamaRIN*
■ diamond	**бриллиант**	*briliANT*
■ emerald	**изумруд**	*izumRUT*
■ ivory	**слоновую кость** *SLOnavuyu KOST"*	
■ jade	**нефрит**	*niFRIT*
■ jasper	**яшму**	*YASHmu*
■ malachite	**малахит**	*malaKHIT*
■ onyx	**оникс**	*Oniks*
■ pearls	**жемчуг**	*zhimCHUK*
■ sapphire	**сапфир**	*sapFIR*
■ topaz	**топаз**	*taPAS*

■ tourmaline	**турмалин** *turmaLIN*
■ turquoise	**бирюзу** *biRYUzu*

I like this ring.	**Мне нравится это кольцо.** *MNYE NRAvitsa Eta kal'TSO*
How much does it cost?	**Сколько оно стоит?** *SKOL'ka aNO STOit*

AUDIO AND VIDEO EQUIPMENT (АУДИО-ВИДЕО ТОВАРЫ)

Is there an audio-video store nearby?	**Есть поблизости магазин аудио-видео?** *YEST' paBLIzasti magaZIN AUdio-VIdio*
Do you have _____?	**У вас есть _____?** *U VAS YEST'*
■ a camcorder	**видеокамера** *vidioKAmera*
■ a digital camcorder	**цифровая видеокамера** *tsifraVAya vidioKAmera*
■ a CD player	**CD-плеер** *SI-DI PLYEyer*
■ a CD recorder	**CD-магнитофон** *SI-DI magnitaFON*
■ CDs	**компактдиски** *kampakDISki*
■ DAT cassettes	**DAT-кассеты** *DI-AY-TI kaSYEty*
■ DVD movies	**DVD-видеофильмы** *DI-VI-DI vidioFIL'M*
■ a DVD player	**DVD-плеер** *DI-VI-DI PLEyer*
■ digital videofilm	**пленка для цифрового видео** *PLYONka DLYA tsifraVOva VIdio*
■ a minidisk player	**плеер для миникассет** *PLEyer DLYA minikaSYET*
■ minidisks	**миникассеты** *minikaSYEty*
■ an MP3 player	**МП3 плеер** *EM PI TRI PLYEir*

- recordable CDs

  чистые компактдиски
  CHIStye kampakDISki

- a small cassette player

  маленький аудиоплеер
  MAlen'ki audioPLEyer

- VCR movies

  видеофильмы *vidioFIL'my*

- blank VCR tape

  чистая видеокассета
  CHIStaya vidiokaSYEta

- films with English subtitles

  фильмы с английскими титрами
  FIL'my s anGLIYskimi TItrami

Where is the _____ section?

Где отдел _____? *GDYE aDYEL*

- "Rock"

  Рок *ROK*

- "Russian Music"

  Русская музыка
  RUskaya MUzyka

- "Classical Music"

  Классическая музыка
  klaSIchiskaya MUzyka

- "Folk Music"

  Народная музыка
  naRODnaya MUzyka

- "Latest Hits"

  Популярная (современная) музыка *papuLYARnaya (savriMYEnaya) MUzyka*

- "Opera and Ballet"

  Опера и балет *Opira I baLYET*

THE NEWSSTAND

Do you have any newspapers in English?

У вас есть газеты на английском?
U VAS YEST' gaZYEty na anGLIYskam

Show me some magazines in English.

Покажите мне журналы на английском. *pakaZHYtye MNYE zhurNAly na anGLIYskam*

These postcards, please.	**Эти открытки, пожалуйста.** *Eti atKRYTki paZHAlusta*
Do you have stamps?	**У вас есть марки?** *u VAS YEST' MARki*
How much do I owe?	**Сколько с меня?** *SKOL'ka s miNYA*

Russian kiosks are little booths that sell everything from postcards and stamps to computer programs and videotapes. Most cassettes and CDs will work fine when you return home. But be advised that Russian television and videocassettes use a different standard than American television. Don't purchase videocassettes unless they are clearly marked for use with the NTSC standard.

DVD standards are different in Europe and in North America. After playing several DVDs your computer may lock onto one of the systems. This may make it impossible to watch DVDs of the other system. In the ever-changing world of technology you should always ask the right questions before you buy.

PHOTOGRAPHIC EQUIPMENT
(ФОТОГРАФИЧЕСКИЕ ТОВАРЫ)

Where is a camera shop?	**Где здесь фототовары?** *GDYE ZDYES' fotataVAry*
Do you develop film?	**Вы проявляете плёнку?** *VY prayaVLYAyitye PLYONku*
Do you have _____?	**У вас есть _____?** *U VAS YEST'*
■ a digital camera	**цифровая камера** *tsifroVAya KAmera*
■ memory card	**карта памяти** *KARta PAmiti*

■ a flash   **вспышка**   *FSPYSHka*

■ compact camera   **компактный фотоаппарат**
                     kamPAKTny fotoapaRAT

■ different lenses   **разные объективы**
                     RAZnye abyekTIvy

■ an SLR camera   **зеркальный фотоаппарат**
                     Z'ERkal'ny fotoapaRAT

■ a tripod   **треножник**   *triNOZHnik*

■ a zoom lens   **объектив зум**   *abyekTIF ZOOM*

■ case   **кейс, чекол**   *KYEYS, chiKOL*

If you want to purchase a digital camera (**цифровой
фотоаппарат** *tsifraVOY fotaapaRAT*) you will want to
know such words as pixel (**пиксел** *PIKsel*), megapixel
(**мегапиксельный** *migaPIKsel'ny*), and display (**дисплей**
diSPLEY). Note that many of the words for electronic
equipment are derived from English, but you will want to
try to pronounce them like a Russian!

I have two rolls.   **У меня две плёнки.**
                   U miNYA DVYE PLYONki

Please print them   **Напечатайте все!**
all!   *napiCHAtaytye FSYE*

Can you enlarge   **Вы можете эту увеличить?**
this one?   *VY MOzhitye Etu uviLIchit'*

glossy finish   **гланц**   *GLANTS*

matte finish   **матовый**   *MAtavy*

color film, 20   **цветную плёнку, двадцать кадров**
exposures   *tsvitNUyu PLYONku, DVAtsat'*
                 KAdraf

black and white film, 36 exposures	**черно-белую плёнку, тридцать шесть кадров** ≈ *RUskaya BYEluyu PLYONku, TRItsat' SHEST' KAdraf*
for slides	**на слайды** *na SLAYdy*
ASA 100	**ГОСТ 100** *GOST STO*

If you forget to bring enough film, don't be too concerned. In major cities there are numerous outlets selling film that will develop your pictures overnight or within the hour. It may be a bit more expensive, but you will be able to know if that once-in-a-lifetime shot on Red Square has really been captured.

Before you run out of memory on your memory card you can always have the photos printed or transferred to a disk. Then you can erase those photos on your camera and begin again to document your adventure.

Do you repair cameras?	**Вы чините фотоаппараты?** *VY chiNItye fotoapaRAty*
I need a battery for my flash.	**Мне нужна батарея для вспышки.** *MNYE nuzhNA bataRYEya dlya FSPYSHki*

SOUVENIRS

For fine Russian souvenirs, check the specialty shops, and don't forget the one at the airport before you depart. Some of the traditional Russian handicrafts are painted wooden dishes from the city of Khokhloma and exquisite lacquered boxes from Palekh and Mstyora. You may also want to buy some of the fine linen items or filigree work, and you certainly don't want to forget caviar and vodka for friends back home. The quality of goods at the airport duty-free shops is excellent, but prices may be higher than in town.

Travel Tips   Three of the most famous Russian souvenirs are the matryoshka nested dolls, Palekh boxes, and Khokhloma wooden dishes. The originals can be very expensive, because they represent individual works of art. Be wary of cheap imitations. If the price seems too good to be true, the item probably isn't authentic.

The matryoshka (**матрешка** *maTRYOSHka*) was actually brought to Russia from Japan in the 1890s. But since then these nested dolls, originally one increasingly smaller lady in peasant dress inside of another, have become treasured souvenirs. Today one can have a set of political figures or sports teams. The more the merrier, but most sets come in at least three with as many as seven dolls that fit one inside the other.

The famous Russian lacquer boxes, often named after the town of Palekh (**палехская шкатулка** *PAlikhskaya shkaTULka*) actually describe an art that exists in primarily four towns: Palekh, Mstyora, Fedoskino, and Kholui. These papier-mâché boxes are covered with layers of black tempera over which an artist creates an original scene. Most often the artist signs or initials her or his work and indicates the city. A final coat of lacquer makes for a gleaming souvenir.

In the town of Khokhloma they have been making wooden dishes and utensils (**хохломская посуда** *khakhlamSKAya paSUda*) for hundreds of years. Linden wood is dipped into a tin or aluminum powder, and then ornate black and red designs are painted on it by hand. When the product is fired in an oven, the silvery aluminum turns a golden color, giving the finished bowl or utensil its distinctive golden background.

I want to purchase a _____.	Я хочу купить _____. *YA khaCHU kuPIT'*
■ special gift	**особый подарок** *aSOby paDArak*
■ small souvenir	**маленький сувенир** *MAlin'ki suviNIR*

It's for _____.	Он для _____. *ON dlya*
■ my daughter	**моей дочки** *maYEY DOCHki*
■ my father	**моего отца** *mayiVO aTSA*
■ my husband	**моего мужа** *mayiVO MUzha*
■ my mother	**моей матери** *maYEY MAtiri*
■ my son	**моего сына** *mayiVO SYna*
■ my wife	**моей жены** *maYEY zhiNY*

Would you show me some _____.	Покажите мне _____. *pakaZHYtye MNYE*
■ blown glass	**художественное стекло** *khuDOzhistvinaye stiKLO*
■ carved objects	**резьбу** *riz'BU*
■ crystal	**хрусталь** *khruSTAL'*
■ nested dolls	**матрёшки** *maTRYOSHki*
■ Palekh boxes	**палехские шкатулки** *PAlikhskiye shkaTULki*
■ Khokhloma tableware	**хохломскую посуду** *khakhlamSKUyu paSUdu*
■ ceramics	**керамику** *kiRAmiku*
■ fans	**веера** *viyiRA*
■ jewelry	**ювелирные изделия** *yuviLIRniye izDEYliya*
■ lace	**кружева** *kruzhiVA*
■ leather goods	**изделия из кожи** *izDYEliya is KOzhi*
■ liqueurs	**ликёры** *liKYOry*

- musical instruments — **музыкальные инструменты** *muzyKAL'niye instruMYENty*
- perfumes — **духи** *duKHI*
- pictures — **картины** *karTIny*
- posters — **плакаты** *plaKAty*

How do you want to pay? — **Чем вы будете платить?** *CHEM VY BUditye plaTIT'*

With cash. — **Наличными.** *naLICHnymi*

With a credit card. — **Кредитной карточкой.** *kriDITnay KARtachkay*

OFFICE SUPPLIES
(КАНЦЕЛЯРСКИЕ ТОВАРЫ)

I want to buy _____. — **Я хочу купить _____.** *YA khaCHU kuPIT'*

- a ball-point pen — **ручку** *RUCHku*
- a deck of cards — **колоду карт** *kaLOdu KART*
- drawing paper — **бумагу для рисования** *buMAgu dlya rasaVAniya*
- an envelope — **конверт** *kanVYERT*
- an eraser — **ластик** *LAStik*
- glue — **клей** *KLYEY*
- a notebook — **тетрадь** *tiTRAT'*
- a pencil — **карандаш** *karanDASH*
- a pencil sharpener — **точилку** *taCHILku*
- a ruler — **линейку** *liNYEYku*
- Scotch tape — **скотч (клеющую ленту)** *SKOTCH (KLYEyushuyu LYENtu)*

- string **шпагат** *shpaGAT*
- typing paper **бумагу для пишущей машинки** *buMAgu dlya PIshushey maSHYNki*
- a writing pad **блокнот** *blakNOT*
- writing paper **бумагу для писем** *buMAgu dlya PIsim*
- thumbtacks **кнопки** *KNOPki*
- paperclips **скрепки** *SKRYEPki*
- rubber bands **резинки** *riZINki*

TOBACCO (ТАБАК)

In Russia as elsewhere the use of tobacco products in public places has been severely limited. Be sure to observe the local signs and customs. When in doubt, it is always polite to ask.

Is smoking permitted?	**Можно курить?** *MOZHna kuRIT'*
No smoking area.	**Место для некурящих.** *MYEsta dlya nikuRYAschix.*
A pack of cigarettes, please.	**Пачку сигарет, пожалуйста.** *PACHku sigaRYET paZHAlusta*
filtered	**с фильтром** *s FIL'tram*
unfiltered	**без фильтра** *byes FIL'tra*
menthol	**с ментолом** *s minTOlam*
king-size (long)	**кинг-сайз (длинные)** *KING-SAYS (DLIniye)*
Are these cigarettes strong?	**Эти сигареты крепкие?** *Eti sigaRYEty KRYEPkiye*
Are they mild?	**Они слабые?** *aNI SLAbiye*

Do you have American cigarettes?	**У вас есть американские сигареты?** *u VAS YEST' amiriKANskiye sigaRYEty*
What brands?	**Какие марки?** *kaKIye MARki*
And a pack of matches, please.	**И спички, пожалуйста.** *I SPICHki paZHAlusta*

Do you carry _____?	**У вас есть _____?** *u VAS YEST'*
■ butane gas	**газ** *GAS*
■ chewing tobacco	**махорка** *maKHORka*
■ cigarette holders	**мундштуки** *muntSHTUki*
■ cigars	**сигары** *siGAry*
■ flints	**кремни** *krimNI*
■ lighters	**зажигалки** *zazhiGALki*
■ pipes	**трубки** *TRUPki*
■ pipe tobacco	**трубочный табак** *TRUbachny taBAK*

TOILETRIES
(ПАРФЮМЕРИЯ)

Do you have _____?	**У вас есть _____?** *u VAS YEST'*
■ aftershave	**лосьон после бритья** *laS'YON POslye briT'YA*
■ bobby pins	**шпильки заколки** *SHPILki zaKOLki*
■ a brush	**щётка** *SHOTka*
■ cleansing cream	**крем для очистки кожи** *KRYEM dlya aCHISTki KOzhi*
■ nourishing cream	**питательный крем** *piTAtil'ny KRYEM*

■ cologne	**одеколон**	*adikaLON*
■ a comb	**расчёска**	*rasCHOSka*
■ condoms	**презервативы**	*prizirvaTIvy*
■ a deodorant	**дезодорант**	*dizadaRANT*
■ disposable diapers	**бумажные пелёнки** *buMAZHniye piLYONki*	
■ eye liner	**карандаш для бровей** *karanDASH dlya braVVEY*	
■ eyebrow pencil	**карандаш для век** *karanDASH dlya VYEK*	
■ eye shadow	**тени**	*TYEni*
■ face lotion	**лосьон**	*laS'YON*
■ hair spray	**лак для волос** *LAK dlya vaLOS*	
■ lip gloss	**блеск для губ** *BLYESK dlya GUP*	
■ lipstick	**губная помада** *gubNAya paMAda*	
■ make-up	**крем-пудра (мэйк-ап)** *KRYEM-PUdra (meyk-AP)*	
■ mascara	**тушь для ресниц** *TUSH dlya riSNITS*	
■ a mirror	**зеркало**	*ZYERkala*
■ mouthwash	**зубной эликсир** *zubNOY elikSIR*	
■ nail clippers	**кусачки**	*kuSACHki*
■ a nail file	**пилка**	*PILka*
■ nail polish	**лак для ногтей** *LAK dlya nakTYEY*	
■ nail polish remover	**ацетон**	*atsiTON*
■ a razor	**бритва**	*BRITva*
■ razor blades	**лезвия**	*LYEZviya*

■ rouge	**румяна**	*ruMYAna*
■ sanitary napkins	**гигиенические салфетки**	
	gigiyiNIchiskiye salFYETki	
■ (cuticle) scissors	**маникюрные ножницы**	
	maniKYURniye NOZHnitsy	
■ shampoo	**шампунь**	*shamPUN'*
■ a sponge	**губка**	*GUPka*
■ talcum powder	**тальк**	*TAL'K*
■ tampons	**тампоны (марлевые салфетки)**	
	tamPOny (MARliviye salFYETki)	
■ tissues	**салфетки**	*salFYETki*
■ toilet paper	**туалетная бумага**	
	tuaLYETnaya buMAga	
■ a toothbrush	**зубная щётка**	*zubNAya SHOTka*
■ toothpaste	**зубная паста**	*zubNAya PASta*
■ tweezers	**щипчики**	*SHIPchiki*

Travel Tips Be on the lookout for the signs indicating a big sale (**распродажа** *raspraDAzha*) or a discount (**скидка** *SKITka*). If you don't know what to purchase as a gift, you can always ask for a gift certificate (**подарочный сертификат** *paDArachny sertifiKAT*). If you plan on staying and shopping at a favorite store be sure to ask for your discount card (**скитная карта** *SKITnaya KARta*). Don't forget to look for the Gift Wrapping sign (**Упаковка подарков** *upaKOFka paDArok*).

PERSONAL CARE AND SERVICES

If your hotel doesn't offer these services, ask the desk clerk to recommend a place nearby.

BARBER SHOP (ПАРИКМАХЕРСКАЯ)

Where is a good barber shop?	**Где хорошая парикмахерскияя?** *GDYE khaROshaya parikMAkhirskaya*
Does the hotel have a barber shop?	**В гостинице есть парикмахерская?** *v gaSTInitse YEST" parikMAkhirskaya*
Do I have to wait long?	**Надо долго ждать?** *NAda DOLga ZHDAT"*
Whose turn is it?	**Чья очередь?** *CH'YA Ochirit'*
I want a shave.	**Я хочу побриться.** *YA khaCHU paBRItsa*
I want a haircut.	**Я хочу постричься.** *YA khaCHU paSTRICHsa*
A shampoo, please.	**Помойте, пожалуйста, голову.** *paMOYtye paZHAlusta GOlavu*
Short in back, long in front.	**Сзади коротко, спереди длинно.** *ZAdi KOratka SPYEridi DLIna*
Leave it long.	**Оставьте эту длину.** *aSTAF"tye Etu dliNU*
I want it (very) short.	**(Очень) коротко.** *(Ochin') KOratka*

You can cut a little _____.	**Можно покороче _____.** *MOZHna pakaROche*
■ in back	**сзади** *ZAdi*
■ in front	**спереди** *SPYEridi*
■ off the top	**сверху** *SFYERkhu*
I have a part _____.	**У меня пробор _____.** *u miNYA praBOR*
■ on the left	**слева** *SLYEva*
■ on the right	**справа** *SPRAva*
■ in the middle	**прямой** *priMOY*
I comb my hair _____.	**Я зачёсываю волосы _____.** *YA zaCHOsyvayu VOlasy*
■ straight back	**прямо назад** *PRYAma naZAT*
■ without a part	**без пробора** *byes praBOra*
Cut a little bit more here.	**Здесь чуть-чуть покороче.** *ZDYES' CHUT'-CHUT' pakaROche*
That's fine.	**Так хорошо.** *TAK kharaSHO*
I don't want _____.	**Не надо _____.** *NYE NAda*
■ a wash	**мытья** *myT'YA*
■ eau de cologne	**одеколона** *adikaLOna*
Use the scissors only.	**Только ножницами.** *TOL'ka NOZHnitsami*
A razor cut.	**Бритвой, пожалуйста.** *BRITvay paZHAlusta*
You can use the electric razor.	**Можно электрической бритвой.** *MOZHna elikTRIchiskay BRITvay*
Please trim _____.	**Подстригите _____.** *padstriGItye*

Please even out _____.	**Подравняйте _____.** *padravNYAYtye*
■ my beard	**бороду** *BOradu*
■ my moustache	**усы** *uSY*
■ my sideburns	**височки** *viSOCHki*
Please shave the back of	**Побрейте шею.** *paBRYEYtye SHEyu*
Where is a mirror?	**Где здесь зеркало?** *GDYE ZDYES' ZYERkala*
I want to look at myself.	**Хочу на себя взглянуть.** *khaCHU na siBYA vzgliNUT'*
How much do I owe you?	**Сколько я вам должен?** *SKOL'ka YA VAM DOLzhin*

BEAUTY PARLOR (ЖЕНСКАЯ ПАРИКМАХЕРСКАЯ)

Is there a beauty parlor near here?	**Поблизости есть женская парикмахерская?** *paBLIzasti YEST'* *ZHENskaya parikMAkhirskaya*
Can I make an appointment _____?	**Можно записаться _____?** *MOZHna zapiSAtsa*
■ for today	**на севодня** *na siVODnya*
■ after lunch	**после обеда** *POslye aBYEda*
■ tomorrow	**на завтра** *na ZAFtra*
What would you like to have done?	**Что вам сделать?** *SHTO VAM ZDYElat'*
A color rinse?	**Окраску волос?** *aKRASku vaLOS*
A facial massage?	**массаж лица?** *maSASH liTSA*
A haircut?	**Стрижку?** *STRISHku*

A manicure?	**Маникюр?**	*maniKYUR*
A pedicure?	**Педикюр?**	*pidiKYUR*
A permanent?	**Химическую завивку?** *khiMIchiskuyu zaVIFku*	
A shampoo?	**Мытьё?**	*myT'YO*
A tint?	**Тон?**	*TON*
A touch up?	**Поправку?**	*paPRAFku*
A wash and set?	**Мытьё и укладку?** *myT'YO I uKLATku*	
No, don't cut it.	**Нет, стричь не надо.** *NYET STRICH NYE NAda*	
What color?	**Какого цвета?**	*kaKOva TSYEta*
■ auburn	**каштановый**	*kashTAnavy*
■ blond	**белокурый**	*bilaKUry*
■ brunette	**брюнетка**	*bryuNYETka*

■ a darker color	**потемнее**	*patimNYEye*
■ a lighter color	**посветлее**	*pasvitLYEye*
■ the same color	**такой же цвет**	
	taKOY zhe TSVYET	

Don't use any hair spray.	**Без лака, пожалуйста.** *byez LAka paZHAlusta*
Just a little.	**Совсем мало.** *safSYEM MAla*
A little more.	**Побольше.** *paBOL'she*
Give me a new (stylish) hairdo.	**Сделайте мне модную причёску.** *ZDYElaytye MNYE MODnuyu priCHOSku*
Something striking _____.	**Что-нибудь экстравагантное _____.** *SHTO-nibut' ekstravaGANTnaye*

■ with curls	**с кудрями**	*s KUdryami*
■ with waves	**с волнами**	*s valNAmi*
■ with bangs	**с чёлкой**	*s CHOLkay*

In a bun on top.	**Пучок.** *puCHOK*
A pony tail?	**Хвост?** *KHVOST*

THE BATHHOUSE (БАНЯ)

 One of the true pleasures in Russia is a visit to the bathhouse, or **баня** *BAnya*. Bathhouses range from the super-luxurious and expensive to the old-fashioned and more reasonable. Prices can range from 25 rubles an hour to thousands of rubles an hour—so be sure to ask what the cost will be. You might want to rent out a luxurious private bath house for a small group of friends. Before you set out on your own, ask your host or the hotel concierge for his or her recommendations and any concerns or reservations he or she might have. Take shampoo, soap, a change of underwear, and a towel with you. Be prepared to spend a few hours spoiling yourself. At the entrance to the bathhouse you'll see vendors selling bunches of oak or birch twigs (**веник** *VYEnik*). These are a must, so buy a bunch. Inside, you purchase a ticket, then proceed to the changing rooms, where you can leave your clothes in a locker. Find a wash-basin (**тазик** *TAzik*), and you are ready to begin. Wet yourself down, then go into the steam room (**парильня** *paRIL'nya*). It is hottest at the top, so move up gradually. After a few minutes of sweating, go outside and take a cool dip in the pool, then return to the steam room. Russians suggest that this ritual be performed three times. Finally, you'll bathe and shampoo your hair. Then the old-timers recommend that you sit a while (maybe have a cool drink) so your body can adjust to normal room temperature. Oh, yes! Smack the twigs against your skin to improve the circulation. For hard-to-reach places, it is acceptable to ask your neighbor for assistance. The baths can also provide a number of services, such as pressing clothes and doing minor repairs. Some may offer a barber shop and beauty parlor with manicures and pedicures.

I'll take some twigs.	**Веник, пожалуйста.** *VYEnik paZHAlusta*
One ticket, please.	**Один билет, пожалуйста.** *aDIN biLYET paZHAlusta*
Can I leave my valuables?	**Можно сдавать ценные вещи?** *MOZHna zdaVAT' TSEniye VYEshi*
Please bring me _____.	**Принесите мне, пожалуйста _____.** *priniSItye MNYE paZHAlusta*

- some slippers   тапочки   *TApachki*
- a bar of soap   кусок мыла   *kuSOK MYla*
- a linen towel   простыню   *praSTYnyu*
- a sponge   мочалку   *maCHALku*
- some shampoo   шампунь   *shamPUN'*
- a wrap-around   накидку   *naKITku*

May I take this washbasin?	**Можно взять этот тазик?** *MOZHna VZYAT' Etat TAzik*
Where is the steam room?	**Где парильня?** *GDYE paRIL'nya*
It's too hot for me up there.	**Там мне слишком жарко.** *TAM MNYE SLISHkam ZHARka*
Where is the swimming pool?	**Где бассейн?** *GDYE baSYEYN*
Where are the showers?	**Где душ?** *GDYE DUSH*
Is there a sauna here?	**Здесь есть сауна?** *ZDYES' YEST' SAUna*
Do you have a buffet?	**У вас есть буфет?** *u VAS YEST' buFYET*

LAUNDRY AND DRY CLEANING (ПРАЧЕЧНАЯ И ХИМЧИСТКА)

You may be able to have shirts, blouses, and underwear washed at the hotel. Check the price list before you decide on the service. You may be able to borrow an iron for a quick touch-up. Ask at the reception desk. Otherwise you can use the laundromat and dry cleaner's.

Where is the nearest laundry?	**Где ближайшая прачечная?** *GDYE bliZHAYshaya PRAchichnaya*
Where is a laundromat?	**Где прачечная самообслуживания?** *GDYE PRAchichnaya samaapSLUzhivaniya*

I have a lot of clothes to be _____.

У меня набралась большая _____.
U miNYA nabraLAS' bal'SHAya

- dry cleaned — **чистка** *CHISTka*
- washed — **стирка** *STIRka*
- ironed — **глажка** *GLASHka*

Here's the list:

Вот список: *VOT SPIsak*

- three shirts — **три рубашки** *TRI ruBASHki*
- ten handkerchiefs — **десять носовых платков** *DYEsit' nasaVYKH platKOF*
- six pairs of socks — **шесть пар носков** *SHEST' PAR naSKOF*
- one blouse — **одна блузка** *aDNA BLUSka*
- panties — **трусики** *TRUsiki*
- three pajamas — **три пижамы** *TRI piZHAmy*
- one suit — **один костюм** *aDIN kaSTYUM*
- five ties — **пять галстуков** *PYAT' GALstukaf*
- two dresses — **два платья** *DVA PLAt'ya*
- one sweater — **один свитер** *aDIN SVItir*
- a pair of gloves — **перчатки** *pirCHATki*

I need them _____.

Мне нужно _____. *MNYE NUZHna*

- tonight — **к вечеру** *k VYEchiru*
- tomorrow — **завтра** *ZAFtra*
- the day after tomorrow — **послезавтра** *pasliZAFtra*

When will you bring them back?

Когда вы их принесёте?
kagDA VY IKH priniSYOtye

When will it be ready?

Когда будет готово?
kagDA BUdit gaTOva

There is a spot on the blouse.

На блузке есть пятно.
na BLUSkye YEST' pitNO

There's a button missing.	**Здесь нет пуговицы.** *ZDYES' NYET PUgavitsy*
Can you sew it back on?	**Не могли бы вы пришить?** *NYE maGLI BY VY priSHYT'*
These aren't my things.	**Это не мои вещи.** *Eta NYE maYI VYEshi*
Where can I press _____?	**Где можно гладить _____?** *GDYE MOZHna GLAdit'*
Can you repair _____?	**Вы можете чинить _____?** *VY MOzhitye chiNIT'*
Can you wash _____?	**Вы можете стирать _____?** *VY MOzhitye stiRAT'*

- my dress   **моё платье**   *maYO PLAt'ye*
- my jacket   **мой пиджак**   *MOY pidZHAK*
- my shirts   **мои рубашки**   *maI ruBASHki*
- my slacks   **мои штаны**   *maI shtaNY*
- my socks   **мои носки**   *maI naSKI*
- my suit   **мой костюм**   *MOY kaSTYUM*

SHOE REPAIRS (РЕМОНТ ОБУВИ)

All around town you are likely to see tiny shoe shine and repair booths. Why not step inside and treat yourself to a shine? At the booths you can have minor repairs performed. For major repairs, bring your shoes or boots to the shoe repair shops.

A shoe shine please.	**Почистите, пожалуйста.** *paCHIStitye paZHAlusta*
Can you fix these _____?	**Вы можете починить _____?** *VY MOzhitye pachiNIT'*

■ ladies' shoes	**туфли**	*TUfli*
■ shoes	**ботинки**	*baTINki*
■ boots	**сапоги**	*sapaGI*

Just soles.
Только подмётки.
TOL'ka padMYOTki

Heels, please.
Каблуки, пожалуйста.
kabluKI paZHAlusta

Can you do it now?
Вы можете сейчас?
VY MOzhitye siyCHAS

A pair of shoelaces.
Шнурки. *shnurKI*

A pair of insoles.
Стельки. *STYEL'ki*

WATCH REPAIRS (РЕМОНТ ЧАСОВ)

Can you repair
this _____?
Вы можете починить _____?
VY MOzhitye pachiNIT"

■ clock/watch	**часы**	*chiSY*
■ alarm clock	**будильник**	*buDIL'nik*
■ digital watch	**электронные часы**	*elikTROniye chiSY*
■ quartz watch	**кварцовые часы**	*KVARtsaviye chiSY*
■ wristwatch	**наручные часы**	*naRUCHniye chiSY*

There's something
wrong with
the _____.
Проблема с _____. *praBLYEma s*

■ glass	**стеклом**	*stiKLOM*
■ hour hand	**часовой стрелкой**	*chisaVOY STRYELkay*

■ minute hand	**минутной стрелкой** *miNUTnay STRYELkay*
■ second hand	**секундной стрелкой** *siKUNDnay STRYELkay*
■ stem (screw)	**головкой** *gaLOFkay*

Could you look at it?	**Вы могли бы посмотреть?** *VY maGLI BY pasmaTRYET"*
Can you replace the battery?	**Можно поставить новую батарейку?** *MOZHna paSTAvit' NOvuyu bataRYEYku*
Can you clean it?	**Можно их почистить?** *MOZHna IKH paCHIStit'*
I dropped it.	**Я их уронил.** *YA IKH uraNIL*
It doesn't run well.	**Они плохо идут.** *aNI PLOkha iDUT*
It's fast.	**Они спешат.** *aNI spiSHAT*
It's slow.	**Они отстают.** *aNI atstaYUT*
It's stopped running.	**Они стоят.** *aNI staYAT*
I wind it every day.	**Я завожу их каждый день.** *YA zavaZHU IKH KAZHdy DYEN'*

CAMERA REPAIRS (РЕМОНТ ФОТОАППАРАТОВ)

Can you fix this camera?	**Вы можете починить этот фотоаппарат?** *VY MOzhitye pachiNIT" Etat fotaapaRAT*

| It doesn't work well. | **Он плохо работает.** |
| | *ON PLOkha raBOtayit* |

| How much will it cost? | **Сколько стоит ремонт?** |
| | *SKOL'ka STOit riMONT* |

| When can I come and get it? | **Когда за ним прийти?** |
| | *kagDA za NIM priyTI* |

| I need it as soon as possible. | **Мне нужно как можно скорее.** |
| | *MNYE NUZHna KAK MOZHna skaRYEye* |

Travel Tips A good rule of thumb about purchases is "If you see it, buy it!" You can never be certain in Russia that an item will be there the next day or that a store will be open. A variety of things— a lunch break (**перерыв на обед** *piriRYF na aBYET*), closure for inventory (**закрыт на учёт** *zaKRYT na uCHOT*), or the periodical cleaning day (**санитарный день** *saniTARny DYEN'*)—may interfere with your intentions.

MEDICAL CARE

If you are given a prescription you will need to go to a pharmacy—**аптека** *apTYEka*. Here you can also find nonprescription remedies for what ails you. Most medicines are very inexpensive. In major cities several pharmacies provide round-the-clock emergency services.

In major cities you may be able to obtain Western brands of your favorite medicines. But do not be afraid to ask for the Russian remedy. In many cases they work just as well for minor ailments and are considerably less expensive.

PHARMACY

Where is the nearest pharmacy?	**Где ближайшая аптека?** *GDYE bliZHAYshaya apTYEka*
When does the pharmacy _____?	**Когда аптека _____?** *kagDA apTYEka*
◼ open	**открывается** *atkryVAyitsa*
◼ close	**закрывается** *zakryVAyitsa*
Where is the prescription section?	**Где рецептный отдел?** *GDYE riTSEPTny aDYEL*
Where are the nonprescription medicines?	**Где безрецептные лекарства?** *GDYE byezriTSEPTniye liKARSTva*
I need something for _____.	**Мне нужно что-нибудь от _____.** *MNYE NUZHna SHTO-nibut' at*
◼ a cold	**насморка** *NASmarka*
◼ constipation	**запора** *zaPOra*
◼ a cough	**кашля** *KASHlya*

◼ diarrhea	**поноса** *paNOsa*
◼ a fever	**жара** *ZHAra*
◼ hay fever	**сенной лихорадки** *SYEnay likhaRATki*
◼ a headache	**головной боли** *galavNOY BOli*
◼ insomnia	**бессоницы** *biSOnitsy*
◼ nausea	**тошноты** *tashnaTY*
◼ sunburn	**солнечного ожога** *SOLnichnava aZHOga*
◼ a toothache	**зубной боли** *zubNOY BOli*
◼ an upset stomach	**желудочного расстройства** *zhiLUdachnava raSTROYSTva*

Is a prescription necessary?	**Нужен рецепт?** *Nuzhin riTSEPT*
Can you fill this prescription for me?	**У вас есть лекарство по этому рецепту?** *u VAS YEST" liKARSTva pa Etamu riTSEPtu*
It's an emergency.	**Это срочно.** *Eta SROCHna*
Should I wait for it?	**Мне подождать?** *MNYE padaZHDAT"*
How long will it take?	**Сколько ждать?** *SKOL'ka ZHDAT"*
When can I come for it?	**Когда мне прийти?** *kagDA MNYE priyTI*
When should I come back?	**Когда мне вернуться?** *kagDA MNYE virNUtsa*
Do you have _____?	**У вас есть _____?** *u VAS YEST"*
◼ adhesive tape	**пластырь** *plaSTYR'*
◼ alcohol	**спирт** *SPIRT*

■ an antacid	**щёлочь**	*SHOlach*
■ an antiseptic	**антисептик**	*antiSYEPtik*
■ aspirin	**аспирин**	*aspiRIN*
■ bandages	**бинт**	*BINT*
■ cotton	**вата**	*VAta*
■ cough drops	**таблетки от кашля**	
	taBLYETki at KASHlya	
■ cough syrup	**микстура от кашля**	
	mikSTUra at KASHlya	
■ ear drops	**ушные капли**	*ushNIye KApli*
■ eye drops	**глазные капли**	*glazNIye KApli*
■ iodine	**йод**	*YOT*
■ a mild laxative	**(лёгкое) слабительное**	
	(LYOkaye) slaBItil'naye	
■ magnesia	**магнезия**	*magNYEziya*
■ mustard plaster	**горчичник**	*garCHICHnik*
■ an ointment	**мазь**	*MAS'*
■ a sedative	**успокаивающее**	
	uspaKAivayushiye	
■ sleeping pills	**снотворное**	*snaTVORnaye*
■ suppositories	**свечи**	*SVEchi*
■ a thermometer	**термометр**	*tirMOmitr*
■ vitamins	**витамины**	*vitaMIny*

DOCTORS

In an emergency call the number for immediate care—**Скорая помощь** *SKOraya POmash*. The number in Moscow and St. Petersburg is **03**. The international number in Europe for emergencies is **112,** and Russia has been adopting it in the major cities. Identify yourself as a foreigner and describe the problem, and within minutes a physician will be at your hotel. Western-style medical and dental centers have also appeared in large cities. Check at the hotel reception desk.

I don't feel well.	**Я чувствую себя плохо.** *YA CHUSTvuyu siBYA PLOkha*
I feel sick. (*m*)	**Я заболел.** *YA zabaLYEL*
I feel sick. (*f*)	**Я заболела.** *YA zabaLYEla*
Please call a doctor.	**Вызовите, пожалуйста, врача.** *VYzavitye paZHAlusta vraCHA*
Is there a doctor who speaks English?	**Есть врач, который говорит по-английски?** *YEST" VRACH kaTOry gavaRIT pa-anGLIYski*
I'm dizzy. (My head is spinning.)	**Голова кружится.** *galaVA KRUzhitsa*
I feel weak.	**Я чувствую слабость.** *YA CHUSTvuyu SLAbast'*
I want to sit down for a while.	**Мне нужно посидеть.** *MNYE NUZHna pasiDYET"*
My temperature is normal.	**У меня нормальная температура.** *u miNYA narMAL'naya timpiraTUra*
I have a high temperature.	**У меня высокая температура.** *u miNYA vySOkaya timpiraTUra*

PARTS OF THE BODY

| It hurts here. | **Болит здесь.** *baLIT ZDYES'* |
| My _____ hurts. | **У меня болит _____.**
 u miNYA baLIT |

abdomen	живот	*zhiVOT*
arm	рука	*ruKA*
back	спина	*spiNA*
breast	грудь	*GRUT'*
cheek	щека	*shiKA*
ear	ухо	*Ukha*
elbow	локоть	*LOkat'*
eye	глаз	*GLAS*
face	лицо	*liTSO*
finger	палец	*PAlits*
foot	ступня	*stupNYA*
hand	кисть	*KIST'*
head	голова	*galaVA*
heart	сердце	*SYERtse*
hip	бедро	*biDRO*
knee	колено	*kaLYEna*
leg	нога	*naGA*
lip	губа	*GUba*
mouth	рот	*ROT*
neck	шея	*SHEya*
nose	нос	*NOS*
rib	ребро	*riBRO*
shoulder	плечо	*pliCHO*
skin	кожа	*KOzha*
stomach	желудок	*zhiLUdak*
throat	горло	*GORla*
tooth	зуб	*ZUP*
wrist	запястье	*zaPYASt'ye*

WHAT'S WRONG

I have _____.	У меня _____. *u miNYA*
an abscess	нарыв *naRYV*
a broken bone	перелом *piriLOM*
a bruise	ушиб *uSHYP*
a burn	ожог *aZHOK*
something in my eye	что-нибудь в глазу *SHTO-nibut' v glaZU*
the chills	озноб *aZNOP*
a chest cold	бронхит *branKHIT*
a head cold	насморк *NASmark*
a cough	кашель *KAshil'*
cramps	судороги *SUdaragi*
a cut	порез *paRYES*
diarrhea	понос *paNOS*
a fever	температура *timpiraTUra*
a headache	головная боль *galavNAya BOL'*
an infection	инфекция *inFYEKtsiya*
a lump/swelling	опухоль *Opukhal'*
a sore throat	ангина *anGIna*
a wound	рана *RAna*

I'm allergic to _____.	У меня аллергия от _____. *U miNYA alirGIya at*
penicillin	пеницилина *pinitsiLIna*

I am taking this medicine.	Я принимаю это лекарство. *YA priniMAyu Eta liKARSTva*
I feel better.	Я чувствую себя лучше. *YA CHUSTvuyu siBYA LUCHshe*

I feel worse.	**Я чувствую себя хуже.** *YA CHUSTvuyu siBYA KHUzhe*

DOCTOR'S INSTRUCTIONS

Open your mouth!	**Откройте рот!** *atKROYtye ROT*
Stick out your tongue!	**Покажите язык!** *pakaZHYtye yiZYK*
Cough!	**Покашляйте!** *paKASHlyaytye*
Breathe deeply!	**Дышите глубоко!** *dySHYtye glubaKO*
Breathe normally!	**Дышите нормально!** *dySHYtye narMAL'na*
Undress (to the waist)!	**Разденьтесь (до пояса)!** *razDYEN'tis' (da POyasa)*
Lie down!	**Ложитесь!** *laZHYtis'*
Stand up!	**Вставайте!** *fstaVAYtye*
You may get dressed!	**Одевайтесь** *adiVAYtis'*

PATIENT'S CONCERNS

Is it serious?	**Это серьёзно?** *Eta siR'YOZna*
Do I have to go to the hospital?	**Мне нужно лечь в больницу?** *MNYE NUZHna LYECH v bal'NItsu*

Are you giving me a prescription?	**Вы мне выпишете лекарство?** *VY MNYE VYpishitye liKARSTva*
How often should I take the medicine?	**Как часто принимать лекарство?** *KAK CHASta priniMAT" liKARSTva*
How long must I stay in bed?	**Сколько времени мне лежать?** *SKOL'ka VRYEmini MNYE liZHAT"*
Thank you for everything.	**Спасибо за всё.** *spaSIba za FSYO*

ACCIDENTS

Help!	**Помогите!** *pamaGItye*
Call a doctor!	**Вызовите врача!** *VYzavitye vraCHA*
Call an ambulance!	**Вызовите скорую помощь!** *VYzavitye SKOruyu POmash*

Take me to a hospital!	**Отвезите меня в больницу!** *atviZItye miNYA v bal'NItsu*
I fell.	**Я упал.** *YA uPAL*
I was knocked over.	**Меня сбили с ног.** *miNYA ZBIli s NOK*
I was hit by a car.	**Меня сбила машина.** *miNYA zbiLA maSHYna*
I'm having a heart attack.	**У меня сердечный приступ.** *u miNYA sirDYECHny PRIstup*
I burned myself.	**Я обварился.** *YA abvaRILsya*
I cut myself.	**Я порезался.** *YA paRYEzalsya*
I'm bleeding.	**У меня кровотечение.** *u miNYA kravatiCHEniye*
I've lost a lot of blood.	**Я потерял много крови.** *YA patiRYAL MNOga KROvi*
I think the bone is broken.	**Я думаю, у меня перелом.** *YA DUmayu u miNYA piriLOM*
The leg is swollen.	**Нога вздута.** *naGA VZDUta*
The wrist is twisted.	**Запястье растянуто.** *zaPYASt'ye raSTYAnuta*
My ankle is dislocated.	**Лодыжка вывыхнута.** *laDYSHka VYvykhnuta*

DENTISTS

I have a terrible toothache.	**У меня страшно болит зуб.** *u miNYA STRASHna baLIT ZUP*

Where is the nearest dental clinic?	**Где ближайшая зубная поликлиника?** *GDYE bliZHAYshaya zubNAya paliKLInika*
I've lost a filling.	**Я потерял пломбу.** *YA patiRYAL PLOMbu*
I've broken a tooth.	**Я сломал зуб.** *YA slaMAL ZUP*
I can't chew.	**Я не могу жевать.** *YA NYE maGU zhiVAT'*
My gums hurt.	**Болят дёсны.** *baLYAT DYOSny*
Is there an infection?	**Это инфекция?** *Eta inFYEKtsiya*
Do you have to pull the tooth?	**Вам надо зуб удалить?** *VAM NAda ZUP udaLIT'*
Can you put in a filling?	**Можете поставить пломбу?** *MOzhitye paSTAvit' PLOMbu*
◾ an amalgam one	**амальгаму** *amal'GAmu*
◾ a gold one	**золотую** *zalaTUyu*
◾ a porcelain one	**фарфоровую** *farFOravuyu*
◾ a silver one	**серебряную** *siRYEbryanuyu*
◾ a temporary one	**временную** *VRYEminuyu*
Can you fix _____?	**Вы можете починить _____?** *VY MOzhitye pachiNIT'*
◾ this bridge	**этот мост** *Etat MOST*
◾ this crown	**эту коронку** *Etu kaRONku*
◾ my denture	**зубной протез** *zubNOY praTYES*
◾ this false tooth	**этот вставной зуб** *Etat fstavNOY ZUP*
When should I return?	**Когда мне вернуться?** *kagDA MNYE virNUtsa*

| How much will it cost? | **Сколько это стоит?**
 SKOL'ka Eta STOit |

OPTICIANS

Can you repair these glasses?	**Вы можете починить эти очки?** *VY MOzhitye pachiNIT' Eti achKI*
I've broken a lens.	**Я разбил стекло.** *YA razBIL stiKLO*
The frame broke.	**Разбилась оправа.** *razBIlas' aPRAva*
The arm is broken.	**Сломан заушник.** *SLOman zaUSHnik*
Can you put in a new lens?	**Можно вставить новое стекло?** *MOZHna FSTAvit' NOvaye stiKLO*
Can you tighten the screw?	**Можно подвернуть винтик?** *MOZHna padvirNUT' VINtik*
I need them urgently.	**Мне нужно срочно.** *MNYE NUZHna SROCHna*
I don't have an extra pair.	**У меня нет запасных.** *u miNYA NYET zapasNYKH*
Do you have contact lenses?	**У вас есть контактные линзы?** *u VAS YEST' kanTAKTniye LINzy*
Can you replace it immediately?	**Можете заменить сейчас?** *MOZHitye zamiNIT' siyCHAS*
Do you sell sunglasses?	**У вас продаются солнечные очки?** *u VAS pradaYUtsa SOLnichninye achKI*

SPECIAL NEEDS

What's the Russian for ____?	**Как по-русски ____?** *KAK pa-RUSki*
■ cane	**палка** *PALka*
■ crutches	**костыли** *kostyLI*
■ glasses	**очки** *achKI*
■ hearing aid	**слуховой аппарат** *slukhaVOY apaRAT*
■ sign language	**немая азбука** *nyeMAya AZbuka*
■ walker	**ходунки** *khadunKI*
■ wheelchair	**инвалидное кресло** *invaLIDnaye KRESla*

Disabled Accessibility

Persons with physical challenges will find many individuals willing to help, but, as previously mentioned, the basic infrastructure for disabled accessibility is still lacking in most places in Russia. You will find signs setting seats aside in busses, trolleys, and on the metro (**Места для инвалидов** *myeSTA GLYA invaLIdaf*). You will find Russians generally solicitous to your needs in theaters, hotels, museums, and so on, but you should expect to have yourself and your wheelchair carried up and down stairs and onto public transportation. Remember also that you must be able to cover long distances on foot even to reach public transportation or to transfer from one station or stop to another. Elevators are not available in the metro systems.

NOTE: The contemporary Russian language has not developed a vocabulary sensitive to people with physical challenges. Expressions increasingly common in English such as "visually impaired," "hearing impaired," and even "physically challenged" are simply not in current usage. The following basic phrases are provided to communicate your needs and situation to your Russian hosts.

I am blind. (*f*)	**Я слепая.**	*YA slyePAya*
I am blind. (*m*)	**Я слепой.**	*YA slyePOY*
He is deaf.	**Он глухой.**	*ON gluKHOY*
She is deaf.	**Она глухая.**	*aNA gluKHAya*
She is lame.	**Она хромая.**	*aNA khraMAya*
He is lame.	**Он хормой.**	*ON khraMOY*

Travel Tips Experienced travelers to Russia always carry a packet of tissues with them to use as napkins and to wipe their glasses, which fog up when going from the outdoor chill into the warmth of the metro stations. In an emergency the tissues can substitute for toilet paper, sometimes in short supply. Other useful items are a pocket knife with screwdriver and corkscrew, plastic bags for wet clothes or shoes, a tube of spot remover, rubber bands, small packets of laundry detergent, a travel clothesline, and a sink stopper.

COMMUNICATIONS

Most post offices are open from 9:00 AM to 6:00 PM with a one-hour break for lunch. The main post, telegraph, and telephone office on Tverskaya Street is open around the clock. Mail boxes are painted bright blue. Stamps are also available at many newsstands and kiosks. You might consider mailing home books that you purchase as gifts: the cost is minimal, and you will be less burdened on the way home. In addition, you'll delight your friends with colorful, varied stamps from Russia. They make great collector's items.

POST OFFICE (ПОЧТА)

I want to mail a letter.	**Я хочу послать письмо.** *YA khaCHU paSLAT" piS'MO*
Where's a post office?	**Где почта?** *GDYE POCHta*
Where's the mailbox?	**Где почтовый ящик?** *GDYE pachTOvy YAshik*
What is the postage on _____?	**Сколько стоит _____?** *SKOL'ka STOit*
▪ a letter	**письмо** *piS'MO*
▪ an airmail letter	**авиаписьмо** *aviapiS'MO*
▪ an insured/ certified letter	**ценное письмо** *TSEnaye piS'MO*
▪ a registered letter	**заказное письмо** *zakazNOye piS'MO*
▪ a special delivery letter	**письмо с доставкой** *piS'MO z daSTAFkay*
▪ a package	**посылка** *paSYLka*
▪ a postcard	**открытка** *atKRYTka*

■ printed matter	**бандероль**	*bandiROL'*
to the USA	**в США**	*f SA SHA A*
to Canada	**в Канаду**	*f kaNAdu*
to Australia	**в Австралию**	*v afSTRAliyu*
to England	**в Англию**	*v ANgliyu*

When will it arrive?
(be received)

Когда получат?
kagDA paLUchat

Which window is
for _____?

Какое окно за _____?
kaKOye akNO za

■ general delivery

до востребования
da vasTREYbavaniya

■ money order

денежный перевод
DYEnizhny piriVOT

■ stamps

марки *MARki*

■ collector's
stamps

коллекционные марки
kaliktsiOniye MARki

Are there any
letters for me?

Есть письма для меня?
YEST" PIS'ma dlya miNYA

My name is _____.

Меня зовут _____. *miNYA zaVUT*

Please give
me _____.

Дайте мне, пожалуйста _____.
DAYte MNYE paZHAlusta

■ ten postcards

десять открыток
DYEsit' atKYRtak

■ five 20-kopeck
stamps

пять марок по двадцать
PYAT" MArak pa DVAtsat'

TELEPHONES (ТЕЛЕФОНЫ)

You usually can place local calls from your hotel room,
either by dialing directly or by first dialing a single number
for an outside line. For most calls within Russia you can also
dial direct.

For international calls it may be less expensive to use your credit card and one of the major carriers, such as ATT, MCI, Sprint, that have local access lines in Moscow and St. Petersburg. Call your credit card company before leaving for Russia to obtain those local numbers, or have your relatives and friends call you. Send them your local number using e-mail!

Telephone booths (sometimes marked **ТАКСОФОН**) are likely to require tokens that can be obtained at many kiosks around town or telephone cards. Cellular phones (**сотовый телефон** *SO-tavy tiliFON*) or mobile phones (**мобильные телефоны** *maBIL'niye tiliFOny*) are increasingly popular and yours might even work there. If you plan on staying for a while, you may be able to rent or purchase one inexpensively.

You won't always have a telephone book at hand, so be sure to have your own private paper or electronic notebook to record the numbers of friends, colleagues, and new business acquaintances.

Where is _____?	**Где _____?**	*GDYE*
■ a pay telephone	**телефон-автомат**	*tiliFON-aftaMAT*
■ a telephone booth	**телефонная кабина** *tiliFOnaya kaBIna*	

I need a telephone card.
Мне нужна телефонная карта.
MNYE nuzhNA tiliFOnaya KARta

Can I use your phone?
Можно от вас позвонить?
MOZHna at VAS pazvaNIT'

Here is the number.
Вот номер. *VOT NOmir*

Can you help me?
Вы можете мне помочь?
VY MOzhitye MNYE paMOCH

I want to order _____.
Я хочу заказть _____.
YA khaCHU zakaZAT'

■ a long-distance call
междугородный разговор
mizhdugaRODny razgaVOR

■ an international call
мездународный разговор
mizhdunaRODny razgaVOR

■ a person-to-person call
на человека *na chilaVYEka*

■ a station-to-station call
на номер *na NOmir*

What is your telephone number?
Какой у вас номер телефона?
kaKOY u VAS NOmir tiliFOna

And the area code?
И код города? *I KOT GOrada*

Operator, please dial this number for me.
Девушка, набирайте, пожалуйста, этот номер. *DYEvushka, nabiRAYtye paZHAlusta Etat NOmir*

I've been disconnected.
Меня разъединили.
miNYA razyidiNIli

May I speak with _____?
Можно говорить с _____?
MOZHna gavaRIT' s

I can barely hear you.	**Плохо слышно.** *PLOkha SLYSHna*
Speak louder!	**Говорите громче!** *gavaRItye GROMche*
Speak slowly!	**Говорите медленно!** *gavaRItye MYEDlina*
Who is speaking?	**Кто говорит?** *KTO gavaRIT*
Who is calling?	**Кто спрашивает?** *KTO SPRAshivayit*
Don't hang up!	**Не кладите трубку!** *NYE klaDItye TRUPku*
The line is busy.	**Занято.** *ZAnyata*
No one answers.	**Никто не подойдёт.** *niKTO NYE padaDYOT*
You've reached a wrong number.	**Вы не туда попали.** *VY NYE tuDA paPAli*
Call back later.	**Перезвоните позже.** *pirizvaNItye POzhe*
Please give him a message.	**Передайте ему, пожалуйста.** *piriDAYtye yiMU paZHAlusta*

FAXES (ТЕЛЕФАКСЫ)

Do you have a fax machine?	**У вас есть телефакс?** *U VAS YEST' tiliFAKS*
What is your fax number?	**Какой у вас номер факса?** *kaKOY U VAS NOmir FAKsa*

I'd like to send you a fax.	**Я хотел бы послать вам факс.** *YA khaTYEL BY paSLAT' VAM FAKS*
May I fax this please?	**Можно послать этот факс?** *MOZHna poSLAT' Etat FAKS*
Fax it to me.	**Пошлите мне факсом.** *paSHLIti MNYE FAKsam*
I didn't get your fax.	**Я не получил ваш факс.** *YA NYE paluCHIL VASH FAKS*
Did you receive my fax?	**Вы получили мой факс?** *VY paluCHIli MOY FAKS*
I can't read your fax.	**Я не могу читать ваш факс.** *YA NYE maGU chiTAT' VASH FAKS*
Send it again.	**Пошлите его еще раз.** *paSHLIti yiVO yiSHO RAS*

TELEGRAMS (ТЕЛЕГРАММЫ)

For many, telegrams are a remnant of the past, akin to records and record players or tape recorders with reel-to-reel tapes. Nonetheless, you may need to send a telegram or transfer money this way. So here are some useful expressions just in case.

Where do they accept telegrams?	**Где принимают телеграммы?** *GDYE priniMAyut tiliGRAmy*
I want to send _____.	**Я хочу послать _____.** *YA khaCHU paSLAT'*
■ a fax	**телефакс** *tiliFAKS*
■ a telegram	**срочную телеграмму** *SROCHnuyu tiliGRAmu*

■ an international telegram	**международную телеграмму** *mizhdunaRODnuyu tiliGRAmu*
■ a telex	**телекс** *TYEliks*
How much per word?	**Сколько стоит слово?** *SKOL'ka STOit SLOva*
Where are the forms?	**Где бланки?** *GDYE BLANki*
Can I send it collect?	**Можно послать доплатно?** *MOZHna paSLAT' daPLATna*
How long does a telegram take?	**Сколько времени идёт телеграмма?** *SKOL'ka VRYEmini iDYOT tiliGRAma*

COMPUTERS (КОМПЬЮТЕРЫ)

Personal computers (**персональные компьютеры** *persaNAL'niye kamPYUtery*) and cellular telephones (**сотовые телефоны** *SOtavye teleFOny*) have helped to redefine the world of communication in the twenty-first century. Russians, like people everywhere, want access to the internet (**интернет**) and depend more and more on e-mail (**электронная почта** *elikTROnaya POCHta*). You'll certainly want to know the words and phrases connected with the new technologies.

Where can I buy _____?	**Где можно купить _____?** *GDYE MOZHna kuPIT'*
■ a desktop computer	**настольный компьютер** *naSTOL'ny kamPYUter*
■ a portable computer	**переносный компьютер** *piriNOSny kamPYUter*
■ a laptop	**ноутбук** *NOTbuk*

I need a new ____.	**Мне нужен новый ____.**
	MNYE NUzhen NOvy
■ printer	**принтер** *PRINter*
■ modem	**модем** *MOdem*
■ scanner	**сканер** *SKAner*
■ hard disk	**жесткий диск** *ZHOski DISK*
■ monitor	**монитор** *MOnitar*
■ CPU	**системный блок** *siSTYEMny BLOK*
■ laptop	**ноутбук** *NOTbuk*

What's the Russian for ____?	**Как по-русски ____?**
	KAK pa-RUski
■ turn on	**включить** *fklyuCHIT'*
■ turn off	**выключить, отключить** *VYklyuchit', atklyuCHIT'*
■ mouse	**мышь** *MYSH*
■ keyboard	**клавиатура** *klaviaTUra*
■ desktop	**рабочий стол** *raBOchi STOL*
■ file	**файл** *FAIL*
■ folder	**папка** *PAPka*
■ enter text	**водить текст** *vaDIT' TYEKST*
■ delete	**удалить** *udaLIT'*
■ open	**открыть** *atKRYT'*
■ close	**закрыть** *zaKRYT'*
■ save	**сохранить** *sakhraNIT'*
■ print	**напечатать** *napiCHAtat'*
■ copy	**скопировать** *skaPIravat'*
■ cut	**вырезать** *VYrezat'*
■ paste	**вставить** *FSTAvit'*

How do I connect to the internet?	**Как подключиться к сети интернет?** *KAK potklyuCHItsa k SYEti INternet?*

Who is your provider?	**Кто ваш провайдер?** *KTO VASH praVAIdyer?*
Please help me _____.	**Помогите, пожалуйста _____.** *pamaGItye paZHAlusta*
■ read my e-mail	**читать электронную почту** *chiTAT' elikTROnuyu POCHtu*
■ print a text	**печатать текст** *piCHAtat' TYEKST*
■ find a web page	**найти web страницу*** *NAIti WEB straNItsu*

* NOTE: Many words and expressions related to e-mail, addresses, and web page URLs are written with the Roman alphabet.

COMPUTER MINI-DICTIONARY

access	**выборка, доступ** *VYbarka, DOstup*
backup disk	**резервный диск** *riZERVny DISK*
browser	**браузер** *BRAUzer*
byte	**байт** *BAYT*
cable	**кабель** *KAbel'*
CD	**компактный диск** *kamPAKTny DISK*
chat room	**комната для беседы** *KOmnata dlya biSYEdy*
click	**щёлкать** *SCHYOLkat'*
computer programmer	**программист** *pragraMIST*
connect	**подключаться** *patklyuCHAtsa*

copy	**копировать**	*kaPIravat'*
CPU	**центральный процессор**	*tsinTRAL'ny praTSEsar*
crash	**зависать**	*zaviSAT'*
crashed	**полетел**	*paliTYEL*
cursor	**курсор**	*KURsar*
cut	**вырезать**	*VYrezat'*
database	**база данных**	*BAza DAnykh*
data	**данные**	*DAniye*
decoding	**рашировка**	*rashiROFka*
delete	**удалить**	*udaLIT'*
disk	**диск**	*DISK*
disk drive	**дисковод**	*diskaVOT*
diskette	**дискета**	*diSKYEta*
document	**документ**	*dakuMYENT*
download	**загружать**	*zagruZHAT'*
e-mail	**электронная почта**	*elikTROnaya POCHta*
enter	**водить**	*vaDIT'*
file	**файл**	*FAYL*
flash card	**флэш-карта**	*FLESH-KARta*
folder	**папка**	*PAPka*
font	**шрифт**	*SHRIFT*
graphics	**графика**	*GRAfika*
hard drive	**жёсткий диск**	*ZHOSki DISK*

icon	**икона** *iKOna*
inkjet printer	**струйный принтер** *STRUYny PRINter*
insert	**вставлять** *fstaVLYAT'*
Internet	**Интернет** *intirNYET*
joystick	**джойстик** *DHOYstik*
key	**клавиша** *klaVIsha*
keyboard	**клавиатура** *klaviaTUra*
laptop	**ноутбук** *NOUTbuk*
laser printer	**лазерный принтер** *LAzirny PRINter*
link	**ссылка** *SSYLka*
memory	**память** *Pamit'*
modem	**модем** *MOdem*
monitor	**монитор** *MOnitar*
motherboard	**материнская плата** *matiRINskaya PLAta*
mouse	**мышь** *MYSH*
network	**сеть** *SYET'*
online	**подключённый** *patklyuCHYOny*
open	**открывать** *atkryVAT'*
operating system	**оперативная система** *apiraTIVnaya siSTYEma*
paste	**вставлять** *fstaVLYAT'*
print	**напечатать** *napiCHAtat'*
printer	**принтер** *PRINter*

processor	**процессор** *praTSEsar*
program	**программа** *praGRAma*
save	**сохранять** *sakhraNYAT'*
scanner	**сканнер** *SKAner*
screen	**экран** *eKRAN*
search engine	**поисковая система** *paIskavaya sisTYEma*
server	**сервер** *SYERver*
site	**веб-сайт** *vyeb-SAYT*
software	**програмное обеспечение** *praGRAMnaya abispiCHEniye*
speed	**скорость** *SKOrast'*
spell checker	**проверка правописания** *praVYERka pravapiSAniye*
symbol	**символ** *SIMval*
Thesaurus	**словарь синонимов** *slaVAR' sinaNImaf*
turn off	**отключать/выключать** *atklyuCHAT'/vyklyuCHAT'*
turn on	**включать** *fklyuCHAT'*
upload	**помещать** *pamiSCHAT'*
website	**веб-сайт/веб-узел** *VYEB-SAYT/VYEB'Uzel*
wireless	**безпроводная связь** *bisPROvadnaya SVYAS'*
wireless card	**безпроводный адаптер** *bisPROvadny aDAPtir*

INTERNET SITES

The Internet provides access to many useful sites, for travel and tourism, and for information in general. Any list can only be a beginning, but here are some of my favorites. Some sites offer information in English as well as Russian. Look for the little British or American flag, or the indication английский. Sometimes you can add «/en» after the main address to see if an English version exists.

SEARCH ENGINES

Rambler	*www.rambler.ru*
Google	*www.google.ru*

USEFUL TOOLS

English-Russian dictionary	*www.rambler.ru/dict/*
weather	*www.pogoda.ru*
maps	*www.nakarte.ru*
restaurants	*www.restoran.ru*
theaters	*www.teatr.ru*
events	*www.afisha.ru*
the metro	*www.metro.ru*
Where Russia	*www.whererussia.com*
Russia Today	*www.russiatoday.ru*
Moscow Times	*www.themoscowtimes.com*
St. Petersburg Times	*www.sptimes.ru*
Anywhere Russian keyboard	*http://ourworld.compuserve.com/ homepages/PaulGor/screen_e.htm*

PLACES OF INTEREST

Moscow	*www.moskva.ru*
St. Petersburg	*www.saint-petersburg.com*

The Kremlin	*www.kreml.ru*
The Hermitage	*www.hermitage.ru*
The Bolshoi Theater	*www.bolshoi.ru*
The Mariinsky Theater	*www.mariinsky.ru*
The Mussorgsky Theater	*www.mikhailovsky.ru*

GETTING AROUND

Russian Embassy	*www.russianembassy.org*
Russian railroads	*www.eng.rzd.ru*
Aeroflot	*www.aeroflot.ru/eng*
Russian hotels	*www.hotels.ru*

GENERAL INFORMATION

Since Russians use the twenty-four hour clock, the PM hours are designated by the numbers thirteen to twenty-four.

TELLING TIME

What time is it?	**Который сейчас час?** *kaTOry siyCHAS CHAS*
One o'clock.	**Час.** *CHAS*
Two o'clock.	**Два часа.** *DVA chiSA*
Three o'clock.	**Три часа.** *TRI chiSA*
Four o'clock.	**Четыре часа.** *chiTYRrye chiSA*
Five o'clock.	**Пять часов.** *PYAT" chiSOF*
Six o'clock.	**Шесть часов.** *SHEST" chiSOF*
Seven o'clock.	**Семь часов.** *SYEM' chiSOF*
Eight o'clock.	**Восемь часов.** *VOsim' chiSOF*
Nine o'clock.	**Девять часов.** *DYEvit' chiSOF*
Ten o'clock.	**Десять часов.** *DYEsit' chiSOF*
Eleven o'clock.	**Одиннадцать часов.** *aDInatsat' chiSOF*
Twelve o'clock.	**Двенадцать часов.** *dviNAtsat' chiSOF*

One o'clock PM.	**Тринадцать часов.** *triNAtsat' chiSOF*
Noon.	**Полдень.** *POLdyen'*
Midnight.	**Полночь.** *POLnach*

Once an hour has begun, Russians look forward to the next hour. Thus, 1:05 is "five minutes of the second hour."

1:05	**пять минут второго** *PYAT miNUT ftaROva*
2:10	**десять минут третьего** *DYEsit' miNUT TRYET'yiva*
a quarter past three	**четверть четвёртого** *CHETvirt' chitVYORtava*
4:20	**двадцать минут пятого** *DVAtsat' miNUT PYAtava*
5:25	**двадцать пять минут шестого** *DVAtsat' PYAT" miNUT shiSTOva*
half past six	**половина седьмого** *palaVIna sid'MOva*

After the half hour Russians count backwards from the *next* hour; thus 7:35 is eight minus twenty-five minutes.

7:35	**без двадцати пяти восемь** *byez dvatsaTI piTI VOsim'*
8:40	**без двадцати девять** *byez dvatsaTI DYEvit'*
9:45	**без четверти десять** *byes CHETvirti DYEsit'*
10:50	**без десяти одиннадцать** *byez disiTI aDInatsat'*
11:55	**без пяти двенадцать** *byes piTI dviNAtsat'*

EXPRESSIONS OF TIME

When?	**Когда?** *kagDA*
At what time?	**В котором часу?** *f kaTOram chiSU*
at five o'clock	**в пять часов** *f PYAT" chiSOF*
in an hour	**через час** *CHEris CHAS*
before two	**до двух** *da DVUKH*
after six	**после шести** *POslye shiSTI*
about seven	**около семи** *Okala siMI*
by eight	**к восьми** *k vas' MI*
From what time?	**С какого времени?** *s kaKOva VRYEmini*
Until what time?	**До какого времени?** *da kaKOva VRYEmini*

per hour	**за час**	*za CHAS*
an hour ago	**час назад**	*CHAS naZAT*
late	**поздно**	*POZna*
early	**рано**	*RAna*
on time	**вовремя**	*VOvrimya*
in the morning	**утром**	*Utram*
in the afternoon	**днём**	*DNYOM*
in the evening	**вечером**	*VYEchiram*
around the clock	**круглосуточно**	*kruglaSUtachna*
a second	**секунда**	*siKUNda*
Just a minute!	**Минуточку!**	*miNUtachku*
Right away!	**Сейчас!**	*siyCHAS*

DAYS

What day is today?	**Какой сегодня день?** *kaKOY siVODnya DYEN'*
Today is _____.	**Сегодня _____.** *siVODnya*
■ Monday	**понедельник** *paniDYEL'nik*
■ Tuesday	**вторник** *FTORnik*
■ Wednesday	**среда** *sriDA*
■ Thursday	**четверг** *chitVERK*
■ Friday	**пятница** *PYATnitsa*
■ Saturday	**суббота** *suBOta*
■ Sunday	**воскресенье** *vaskriSYEn'ye*
today	**сегодня** *siVODnya*

yesterday	вчера	*fchiRA*
tomorrow	завтра	*ZAFtra*
the day after tomorrow	послезавтра	*pasliZAFtra*
the day before yesterday	позавчера	*pazafchiRA*
on Wednesday	в среду	*f SRYEdu*
a week from Tuesday	во вторник через неделю	*va FTORnik CHEris niDYElyu*
a day	день	*DYEN'*
a week	неделя	*niDYElya*
a month	месяц	*MYEsits*
a year	год	*GOT*
a working day	рабочий день	*raBOchi DYEN'*
a day off	выходной день	*vykhadNOY DYEN'*
a holiday	праздник	*PRAZnik*

MONTHS

January	январь	*yanVAR'*
February	февраль	*fiVRAL'*
March	март	*MART*
April	апрель	*aPRYEL'*
May	май	*MAY*
June	июнь	*iYUN'*
July	июль	*iYUL'*

August	**август** *AVgust*
September	**сентябрь** *sinTYABR'*
October	**октябрь** *akTYABR'*
November	**ноябрь** *naYABR'*
December	**декабрь** *diKABR'*

DATES

What's today's date?	**Какое сегодня число?** *kaKOye siVODnya chiSLO*
The fifth of May.	**Пятое мая.** *PYAtaya MAya*
When did it happen?	**Когда это случилось?** *kagDA Eta sluCHIlas'*
On June 1, 1991.	**Первого июня, девяноста первого года.** *PYERvava iYUnaya diviNOSta PYERvava GOda*

SEASONS

in the spring	**весной** *viSNOY*
in the summer	**летом** *LYEtam*
in the fall	**осенью** *Osin'yu*
in the winter	**зимой** *ziMOY*
every summer	**каждое лето** *KAZHdaye LYEta*
last year	**в прошлом году** *f PROSHlam gaDU*
next year	**в будущем году** *v BUdushim gaDU*

WEATHER

How is the weather today?	**Какая сегодня ногода?** *kaKAya siVODnya paGOda*
The weather today is _____.	**Сегодня погода _____.** *siVODnya paGOda*
■ good	**хорошая** *khaROshaya*
■ bad	**плохая** *plaKHAya*
What splendid weather!	**Какая прекрасная погода!** *kaKAya priKRASnaya paGOda*
Today it's _____.	**Сегодня _____.** *siVODnya*
■ hot	**жарко** *ZHARka*
■ warm	**тепло** *tiPLO*
■ cold	**холодно** *KHOladna*
■ cool	**прохладно** *praKHLADna*
The sun is shining.	**Светит солнце.** *SVYEtit SONtsa*
The wind is blowing.	**Дует ветер.** *DUyit VYEtir*
It's raining.	**Идёт дождь.** *iDYOT DOSH*
It's snowing.	**Идёт снег.** *iDYOT SNYEK*

TEMPERATURE CONVERSIONS

To change degrees Fahrenheit to Centigrade, subtract 32 and multiply by $\frac{5}{9}$.

$$41°F - 32 = 9 \times \frac{5}{9} = 5°C$$

To convert from Centigrade to Fahrenheit, multiply by ⁵/₉ and add 32.

$$10°C \times {}^9\!/\!_5 = 18 + 32 = 50°F$$

To get an approximate temperature quickly, take the degrees Fahrenheit, subtract 30 and divide by 2, or, take the degrees Centigrade, multiply by 2, and add 30.

Most seasoned travelers know a few temperatures for reference.

DEGREES	
FAHRENHEIT	CELSIUS
212	100
98.6	37
86	30
77	25
68	20
50	10
32	0
14	−10
−4	−20
−22	−30
−40	−40

It is small consolation that at minus 40 degrees, Fahrenheit and Centigrade temperatures are identical.

OFFICIAL HOLIDAYS

January 1—New Year's Day	**1 января Новый год**
January 7—Russian Orthodox Christmas	**7 января Рождество Христово**
February 23—Day of the Defender of the Fatherland	**23 февраля День защитника Отечества**

March 8—International Women's Day	**8 марта Международный женский день**
May 1—May Day Workers' Day	**1 мая Праздник весны и труда**
May 9—Victory Day	**9 мая День победы**
June 12—Day of Russia	**12 июня День России**
November 4—Day of National Unity	**4 ноября День народного единства**

Happy birthday!	**С днём рождения!** *z DNYOM raZHDYEniya*
Happy holiday!	**С праздником!** *s PRAZnikam*
Happy New Year!	**С Новым годом!** *s NOvym GOdam*

The Russian Orthodox Church still observes Christmas and Easter according to the pre-revolutionary calendar.

Merry Christmas! (with the birth of Christ)	**С Рождеством Христовым!** *s razhdiSTVOM khriSTOvym*
Happy Easter! (Christ is risen)	**Христос воскресе!** *khriSTOS vaSKRYEs'ye*

RUSSIA AND ITS NEIGHBORS

Until 1991 there were fifteen republics in what was then known as the Soviet Union (**Советский Союз** *saVYETski saYUS*), officially the Union of Soviet Socialist Republics, abbreviated in Russian as **СССР** (*ES-ES-ES-ER*). There are now fifteen independent countries, with several of them belonging to a loose Confederation of Independent States (CIS), abbreviated **СНГ** (**Содружество Независимых Государств** *saDRUzhestva nyezaVIsimykh gasuDARTSF*). The official name of what we call "Russia" is the Russian Federation (**Российская Федерация** *raSIskaya fidiRAtsiya*) with its capital in Moscow (**Москва** *maskVA*).

Armenia (capital, Yerevan)	**Армения (Ереван)**
Azerbaijan (Baku)	**Азербайджан (Баку)**
Belarus (Minsk)	**Беларусь (Минск)**
Estonia (Tallinn)	**Эстония (Таллинн)**
Georgia (Tbilisi)	**Грузия (Тбилиси)**
Kazakhstan (Almaty)	**Казахстан (Алма-Ата)**
Kyrgyzstan (Bishkek)	**Кыргызстан (Бишкек)**
Latvia (Riga)	**Латвия (Рига)**
Lithuania (Vilnius)	**Литва (Вильнюс)**
Moldova (Chisinau)	**Молдова (Кишинёв)**
Russia (Moscow)	**Россия (Москва)**
Tajikistan (Dushanbe)	**Таджикистан (Душанбе)**
Turkmenistan (Ashgabat)	**Туркменистан (Ашхабад)**
Ukraine (Kiev)	**Украина (Киев)**
Uzbekistan (Tashkent)	**Узбекистан (Ташкент)**

Only since 1991 have Russians distinguished between citizenship and nationality. A citizen of the Russian Federation says:

| I'm a Russian citizen. | **Я россиянин.** *(m)* *YA rasiYAnin* |
| | **Я россиянка.** *(f)* *YA rasiYANka* |

But to speak of his or her nationality he or she says:

I'm a Russian.	**Я русский.** *(m)* *YA RUski*
	Я русская. *(f)* *YA RUskaya*
I'm an Estonian.	**Я эстонец.** *(m)* *YA eSTOnits*
	Я эстонка. *(f)* *YA eSTONka*
I'm a Ukrainian.	**Я украинец.** *(m)* *YA ukraInits*
	Я украинка. *(f)* *YA ukraINka*

Using the same principles, you can identify yourself.

I'm American.	**Я американец.** *(m)*
	YA amiriKAnits
	Я американка. *(f)*
	YA amiriKANka
I'm Australian.	**Я австралиец.** *(m)*
	YA afstraLIyits
	Я австралийка. *(f)*
	YA afstraLIYka
I'm British.	**Я англичанин.** *(m)*
	YA angliCHAnin
	Я англичанка. *(f)*
	YA angliCHANka
I'm Canadian.	**Я канадец.** *(m)* *YA kaNAdits*
	Я канадка. *(f)* *YA kaNATka*

COUNTRIES AND NATIONALITIES

Where are you from?	**Откуда вы?** *otKUda VY*
I'm from _____ (plus genitive case).	**Я из _____.** *YA IS*
Africa	**Африка** *AFrika*
Asia	**Азия** *Aziya*
Australia	**Австралия** *afSTRAliya*
Europe	**Европа** *yiVROpa*
America	**Америка** *aMYErika*
Austria	**Австрия** *AFstriya*
Belgium	**Бельгия** *BYEL'giya*
Canada	**Канада** *kaNAda*
China	**Китай** *kiTAY*
England	**Англия** *ANgliya*
France	**Франция** *FRANtsiya*
Germany	**Германия** *girMAniya*
Greece	**Греция** *GRYEtsiya*
Hungary	**Венгрия** *VYENgriya*
India	**Индия** *INdiya*
Ireland	**Ирландия** *irLANdiya*
Israel	**Израиль** *izraIL'*
Italy	**Италия** *iTAliya*

Japan	**Япония** *yaPOniya*	
Norway	**Норвегия** *narVYEgiya*	
Poland	**Польша** *POL'sha*	
Portugal	**Португалия** *partuGAliya*	
Russia	**Россия** *raSIya*	
Scotland	**Шотландия** *shatLANdiya*	
Spain	**Испания** *iSPAniya*	
Sweden	**Швеция** *SHVEtsiya*	
Switzerland	**Швейцария** *shviyTSAriya*	
the United States	**Соединённые Штаты** *sayidiNYOniye SHTAty*	

DIRECTIONS

north	**север** *SYEvir*	
south	**юг** *YUK*	
east	**восток** *vaSTOK*	
west	**запад** *ZApat*	

IMPORTANT SIGNS

Вверх	*VVYERKH*	Up
Вниз	*VNIS*	Down
Вход	*FKHOT*	Entrance

Выход	*VYkhat*	Exit
Женщины	*ZHENshiny*	Women
Заказано	*zaKAzana*	Reserved
Закрыто	*zaKRYta*	Closed
Занято	*ZAnita*	Occupied
Запасный выход	*zaPASny VYkhat*	Emergency Exit
Идите	*iDItye*	Go
К себе	*k siBYE*	Pull
Касса	*KAsa*	Cashier
Лифт	*LIFT*	Elevator
Мест нет	*MYEST NYET*	No Vacancies (no places)
Мужчины	*mushCHIny*	Men
На себя	*na siBYA*	(Pull) to oneself
Не курить	*NYE kuRIT"*	No Smoking
Не трогать	*NYE TROgat'*	Don't Touch
Остановка автобуса	*astaNOFka aFTObusa*	Bus Stop
Осторожно	*astaROZHna*	Caution
От себя	*at siBYA*	Push
Открыто	*atKRYta*	Open
Перерыв	*piriRYF*	On Break
Стойте	*STOYtye*	Wait
Туалет	*tuaLYET*	Toilet

ABBREVIATIONS

АН	Академия Наук	Academy of Sciences
АЭС	атомная электростанция	atomic power station
АО	акционерное общество	joint stock company
ГАИ	Государственная автомобильная инспекция	State Automobile Inspection
ГУМ	Государственный универсальный магазин	State Department Store
ГЭС	гидроэлектрическая станция	hydroelectric station
ин.	иностранный	foreign
и т.д.	и так далее	et cetera (etc.)
и т.п.	и тому подобное	and so forth
к.	копейка	kopeck
кг.	килограмм	kilogram
КП	Коммунистическая партия	Communist Party
гр.	гражданин *(m)*	citizen
гр-ка	гражданка *(f)*	citizen
МГУ	Московский государственный университет	Moscow State University
мл.	младший	junior
мм.	миллиметр	millimeter
пк	персональный компьютер	PC—personal computer
р.	рубль	ruble
РФ	Российская Федерация	Russian Federation
СНГ	Содружество Независимых Государтсв	Confederation of Independent States
ст.	старший	senior
ст.	станция	station
стр.	страница	page
США		USA
ц.	цена	price
ч.	час	o'clock
шт.	штука	an item

METRIC CONVERSIONS

If you are not used to the metric system, you'll need the following tables and conversion charts during your visit to Russia.

SOME CONVENIENT ROUGH EQUIVALENTS

These are rough approximations, but they'll help you to "think metric" when you don't have a pocket calculator handy.

3 километра   (kilometers) = 2 miles
30 грамм   (grams) = 1 ounce
100 грамм   (grams) = 3.5 ounces
1 килограмм   (kilogram) = 2 pounds
1 литр   (liter) = 1 quart
1 гектар   (hectare) = 1 acre

CENTIMETERS/INCHES

It is usually unnecessary to make exact conversions from inches to the metric system, but to give you an approximate idea of how they compare, we give the following guide.

To convert **сантиметры** *santiMYEtry* (centimeters) to **дюймы** *DYUYmy* (inches), multiply by 0.39.

To convert inches (**дюймы**) to centimeters (**сантиметры**), multiply by 2.54.

Сантиметры

Дюймы

METERS/FEET

1 метр (meter) = **39.37 дюймов** (inches)
1 фут (foot) = **0.3 метр** (meter)
1 метр (meter) = **3.28 фута** (feet)
1 ярд (yard) = **0.9 метр** (meter)
1 метр (meter) = **1.09 ярд** (yard)

How tall are you in meters? See for yourself.

Футы/ДЮймы (FEET/INCHES)	Метры/Сантиметры (METERS/CENTIMETERS)
5	1.52
5 1	1.545
5 2	1.57
5 3	1.595
5 4	1.62
5 5	1.645
5 6	1.68
5 7	1.705
5 8	1.73
5 9	1.755
5 10	1.78
5 11	1.805
6	1.83
6 1	1.855

WHEN YOU WEIGH YOURSELF

1 килограмм (kilogram) = **2.2 фунта** (pounds)
1 фунт (pound) = **0.45 килограмма** (kilogram)

Килограммы KILOGRAMS	Фунты POUNDS
40	88
45	99
50	110
55	121
60	132
65	143
70	154
75	165
80	176
85	187
90	198
95	209
100	220

LIQUID MEASUREMENTS

1 литр (liter) = **1.06 кварта** (quart)
4 литра (liters) = **1.06 галлон** (gallon)

For quick approximate conversion, multiply the number of gallons (**галлоны**) by 4 to get liters (**литры**). Divide the number of **литры** (liters) by 4 to get **галлоны** (gallons).

EMERGENCY TELEPHONE NUMBERS

All emergencies	**Единый номер 112**
Fire	**Пожарная охрана 01**
Police	**Милиция 02**
Medical care	**Скорая помощь 03**
Gas leaks	**Газ 04**

MINI-DICTIONARY FOR BUSINESS TRAVELERS

amount	сумма	*SUma*
appraise	оценивать	*aTSEnivat'*
authorize	уполномочивать	*upalnaMOchivat'*
authorized edition	авторизованное издание	*avtariZOvanaye izDAniye*
bank/debit card	банковская карта	*BANkafskaya KARta*
bill	счёт	*SHOT*
bill of exchange	вексель	*VYEKsil'*
bill of lading	коносамент	*kanasaMYENT*
bill of sale	товарный чек	*taVARny CHEK*
business operation	дело	*DYEla*
buy	купить	*kuPIT'*
cash payment	наличный расчёт	*naLICHny raSHOT*
cash a check	получить деньги по чеку	*paluCHIT' DYEN'gi pa CHEku*
certified check	расчётный чек	*raSHOTny CHEK*
chamber of commerce	торговая палата	*tarGOvaya paLAta*
compensation for damages	возмещение убытков	*vazmiSHEniye uBYTkaf*
competition	конкуренция	*kankuRYENtsiya*
competitive price	конкурентоспо- собная цена	*kankurintaspa- SOBnaya tsiNA*

contract	контракт	*kanTRAKT*
contractual obligations	контрактные обязательства	*kanTRAKTniye abiZAtil'stva*
controlling interest	контрольный пакет акций	*kanTROL'ny paKYET AKtsi*
co-owner	совладелец	*savlaDYElits*
co-partner	партнёр	*partNYOR*
delivery	поставка	*paSTAFka*
down payment	первоначальный платёж	*pirvanaCHAL'ny plaTYOSH*
(payment) due	подлежит оплате	*padliZHYT' aPLAtye*
enterprise	предприятие	*pritpriYAtiye*
expedite delivery	продвинуть поставку	*praDVInut' paSTAFku*
expenses	затраты / расходы	*zaTRAty / rasKHOdy*
goods	товары	*taVAry*
hard currency	валюта	*vaLYUta*
infringement of patent rights	нарушение патентных прав	*naruSHEniye paTYENTnykh PRAF*
installment	рассрочка	*raSROCHka*
insurance	страхование	*strakhaVAniye*
international law	международное право	*mizhdunaROD-naye PRAva*
lawful possessions	законное имущество	*zaKOnaye iMUshistva*

lawsuit	судебный процесс	*suDYEBny praTSES*
lawyer	адвокат	*advaKAT*
letter of credit	аккредитив	*akridiTIF*
mail-order business	посылочная фирма	*paSYlachnaya FIRma*
manager	директор / заведующий	*diRYEKtar / zaVYEdushi*
market value (price)	рыночная цена	*RYnachnaya tsiNA*
overdue	просроченный	*praSROchiny*
payment	платёж	*plaTYOSH*
partial payment	частичный платёж	*chiSTICHny plaTYOSH*
price	цена	*tsiNA*
property	имущество	*iMUshistva*
purchasing agent	покупательный агент	*pakuPAtil'ny aGYENT*
put on the market	поставить на рынок	*paSTAvit' na RYnak*
retail price	розничная цена	*ROZnichnaya tsiNA*
sale	продажа	*praDAzha*
sales tax	налог на полупки	*naLOK na paKUPki*
to sell	продавать	*pradaVAT'*
to send	послать	*paSLAT'*
to send back	возвращать	*vazvraSHAT'*

to send COD	послать наложенным платежом	*paSLAT" naLOzhinym platiZHOM*
shipment	отправка / отгрузка	*atPRAFka / adGRUSka*
tax	налог	*naLOK*
tax-exempt	освобождённый от налогов	*asvabazhDYOny at naLOgaf*
trade	торговля	*tarGOvlya*
transact business	вести дела	*viSTI diLA*
transfer	перевод	*piriVOT*
transportation charges	плата на транспорт / на перевозку	*PLAta na TRANSport / na piriVOSku*
via	через	*CHEris*
yield a profit	приносить прибыль	*prinaSIT" PRIbyl'*

Travel Tips Many cities, which only a few short years ago could offer only very modest accommodations, have entered the twenty-first century with a flair of their own. Don't be afraid to extend your travels beyond Moscow and St. Petersburg to visit any of a dozen other cities. Historians will love Vladimir, Suzdal, Yaroslavl, Rostov, and Nizhny Novogorod. The more adventuresome might head to Siberia to visit Irkutsk and travel to Lake Baikal, a world wonder in its own right. These cities now have first-class hotels, lots of restaurants and cafes, and most importantly the inhabitants haven't grown used to foreigners. They are wonderful hosts, eager to show the best their cities and regions can offer.

QUICK GRAMMAR GUIDE

Russian is an inflected language. Nouns, pronouns, modifiers, and verbs change their forms to convey different meanings. Normally, the lexical meaning of the word is in the root, the beginning part of a word. The grammatical meaning is contained in the different endings.

NOUNS

Russian nouns are classed according to their gender, number, and case. They can be masculine, feminine, or neuter. Gender is a grammatical category not necessarily coinciding with biological reality. Masculine nouns usually end in a consonant. Feminine nouns often end in **-a** or **-я**. Neuter nouns generally end in **-o** or **-e**.

Russian nouns can be singular or plural in each of the six cases: nominative, accusative, genitive, prepositional, dative, and instrumental. (Tip: It suffices in most situations to know the nominative and accusative cases.)

MASCULINE NOUNS

SINGULAR	HARD CONSONANTS	SOFT CONSONANTS
Nominative	журнал	портфель
Accusative	журнал	портфель
Genitive	журнала	портфеля
Prepositional	журнале	портфеле
Dative	журналу	портфелю
Instrumental	журналом	портфелем
PLURAL		
Nominative	журналы	портфели
Accusative	журналы	портфели
Genitive	журналов	портфелей
Prepositional	журналах	портфелях
Dative	журналам	портфелям
Instrumental	журналами	портфелями

The accusative singular and plural forms for Russian animate (i.e. persons and animals) masculine nouns are the same as the genitive case forms.

NEUTER NOUNS

SINGULAR	ENDING IN -o	ENDING IN -e
Nominative	письмо	здание
Accusative	письмо	здание
Genitive	письма	здания
Prepositional	письме	здании
Dative	письму	зданию
Instrumental	письмом	зданием
PLURAL		
Nominative	письма	здания
Accusative	письма	здания
Genitive	писем	зданий
Prepositional	письмах	зданиях
Dative	письмам	зданиям
Instrumental	письмами	зданиями

FEMININE NOUNS

SINGULAR	ENDING IN -a	ENDING IN -я
Nominative	телеграмма	тётя
Accusative	телеграмму	тётю
Genitive	телеграммы	тёти
Prepositional	телеграмме	тёте
Dative	телеграмме	тёте
Instrumental	телеграммой	тётей
PLURAL		
Nominative	телеграммы	тёти
Accusative	телеграммы	тётей
Genitive	телеграмм	тётей
Prepositional	телеграммах	тётях
Dative	телеграммам	тётям
Instrumental	телеграммами	тётями

The accusative plural forms for Russian animate (i.e. persons) feminine nouns are the same as the genitive case plural forms. Some Russian feminine nouns end in the soft sign **-ь**, and a few neuter nouns end in **-я**. In both instances the nominative and accusative cases are identical.

You may see some variations of the above endings caused by spelling rules in Russian. The three key rules are

"8" rule: After these eight letters (**г, к, х, ж, ч, ш, щ, ц**) you may not write the letters **я** or **ю**, but must replace them with **а** or **у**.

"7" rule: After these seven letters (**г, к, х, ж, ч, ш, щ**) you may not write the letter **ы**, but must write **и**.

"5" rule: After these five letters (**ж, ч, ш, щ, ц**) you may write the letter **о** only if it is accented. When it is not accented, you replace the expected **о** with the letter **е**.

PRONOUNS

Pronouns replace, or stand in for, nouns. They also have gender, number, and case. The following personal pronouns are important for travelers.

SINGULAR	I	YOU	HE (IT)	SHE
Nom.	я	ты	он (оно)	она
Acc.	меня	тебя	его	её
Gen.	меня	тебя	его	её
Prep.	мне	тебе	нём	ней
Dat.	мне	тебе	ему	ей
Instr.	мной	тобой	им	ей

PLURAL	WE	YOU	THEY
Nom.	мы	вы	они
Acc.	нас	вас	их
Gen.	нас	вас	их
Prep.	нас	вас	них
Dat.	нам	вам	им
Instr.	нами	вами	ими

	WHO?	WHAT?
Nom.	кто	что
Acc.	кого	что
Gen.	кого	чего
Prep.	ком	чём
Dat.	кому	чему
Inst.	кем	чем

ADJECTIVES/POSSESSIVE MODIFIERS

Modifiers in Russian agree with the noun in gender, number, and case. Knowing the spelling rule will help you figure out these endings. (Hint: When the ending of the noun changes, the ending of the modifier is also likely to change.)

	Masculine	SINGULAR Neuter	Feminine	PLURAL All Genders
Nom.	новый	новое	новая	новые
Acc.	новый	новое	новую	новые
Gen.	нового	нового	новой	новых
Prep.	новом	новом	новой	новых
Dat.	новому	новому	новой	новым
Instr.	новым	новым	новой	новыми
Nom.	мой	моё	моя	мои
Acc.	мой	моё	мою	мои
Gen.	моего	моего	моей	моих
Prep.	моём	моём	моей	моих
Dat.	моему	моему	моей	моим
Instr.	моим	моим	моей	моими
Nom.	наш	наше	наша	наши
Acc.	наш	наше	нашу	наши
Gen.	нашего	нашего	нашей	наших
Prep.	нашем	нашем	нашей	наших
Dat.	нашему	нашему	нашей	нашим
Instr.	нашим	нашим	нашей	нашими

ADVERBS

Russian adverbs do not change their form. Most are readily identifiable by the endings **-о/-е** or **-и**. Some examples are

quickly	**быстро**
slowly	**медленно**
of course	**конечно**
automatically	**автоматически**

To make the comparative adverbs (quicker, slower, etc.) you change the **-о** into **-ее**

quicker	**быстрее**
slower	**медленнее**

To make the comparative of adverbs ending in **-и** you add **более** (more) or **менее** (less) before the word.

more automatically	**более автоматически**
less practically	**менее практически**

VERBS

The dictionary form of most verbs (the infinitive) ends in **-ть**. All Russian verbs have aspect, a grammatical category rendered in other ways in English. Russian aspect can be perfective or imperfective and reflects a Russian's way of looking at the world.

THE PAST TENSE
The past tense is formed by replacing the **-ть** of the infinitive form with **-л** for the masculine singular or adding

-ла for the feminine singular, **-ло** for the neuter singular, or **-ли** for all plurals.

TO SELL	ПРОДАВАТЬ
I was selling.	**Я продавал.**
Masha was selling.	**Маша продавала.**
We, You, They sold.	**Мы, Вы, Они продавали.**

TO BUY	КУПИТЬ
Ivan bought.	**Иван купил.**
Irina bought.	**Ирина купила.**
We, You, They bought.	**Мы, Вы, Они купили.**

IMPERFECTIVE PRESENT/ PERFECTIVE FUTURE

Russian verbs belong to one of two conjugations (verb classes). The final consonants in both conjugations are the same: only the vowels **e** or **и** change to indicate that a verb belongs to the first or second conjugation. If the verb is imperfective, the conjugated form is in the present tense. The conjugated form of a perfective verb signifies the future.

FIRST CONJUGATION		SECOND CONJUGATION	
TO WORK	РАБОТАТЬ	TO SPEAK WITH	ПОГОВОРИТЬ
I work.	**Я работаю.**	I'll speak.	**Я поговорю.**
You work.	**Ты работаешь.**	You'll speak.	**Ты поговоришь.**
He works.	**Он работает.**	She'll speak.	**Она поговорит.**
We work.	**Мы работаем.**	We'll speak.	**Мы поговорим.**
You work.	**Вы работаете.**	You'll speak.	**Вы поговорите.**
They work.	**Они работают.**	They'll speak.	**Они поговорят.**

THE IMPERFECTIVE FUTURE

To form the future of imperfective verbs, add the future forms of the verb "to be" **быть** to the imperfective infinitive.

TO BE	БЫТЬ	TO WORK	РАБОТАТЬ
I will be	я буду	I will be working.	Я буду работать.
you will be	ты будешь	You will be working.	Ты будешь работать.
she will be	она будет	He will be working.	Он будет работать.
we will be	мы будем	We will be working.	Мы будем работать.
you will be	бы будете	You will be working.	Вы будете работать.
they will be	они будут	They will be working.	Они будут работать.

COMMANDS

Most commands will be easily identifiable. Almost all have the ending **-айте/-яйте** or **-ите.**

Listen!	**Слушайте!**
Repeat!	**Повторяйте!**
Look!	**Смотрите!**
Help!	**Помогите!**
Go away!	**Отойдите!**

QUESTIONS

Most questions in Russian can be formed by using one of the interrogative pronouns (question words).

Who?	**Кто?**	*KTO*
What?	**Что?**	*SHTO*
Where?	**Где?**	*GDYE*
Where to?	**Куда?**	*kuDA*
When?	**Когда?**	*kagDA*
Why?	**Почему?**	*pachiMU*
How?	**Как?**	*KAK*
How much?	**Сколько?**	*SKOL'ka*

In a sentence without an interrogative, Russians use a rising tone on the word in question.

| Are you working <u>on Saturday</u>? | **Вы работаете <u>в субботу</u>?** |
| Do you want <u>to go</u>? | **Вы хотите <u>пойти</u>?** |

NEGATIONS

Form the negative by placing **не** before the verb or any other word you wish to negate.

| I don't speak Ukrainian. | **Я не говорю по-украински.** |
| No, not that one. | **Нет, не это.** |

You can always use the famous Russian "NO"—**НЕТ** for emphasis.

WORD ORDER

In general, Russian word order is freer than English. A basic rule is that any new information and consequently the most important facts are found at the end of the sentence.

PREPOSITIONS

Most prepositions are not accented in speech but are pronounced together with the following word. The list below should be helpful.

about	о	*a*
according to	по	*pa*
across	через	*CHEris*
after	после	*POslye*
among	среди	*sriDI*
around	вокруг	*vaKRUK*
at	у	*u*
before	до / перед	*da / PYErit*
behind	за	*za*
between	между	*MYEZHdu*
down	вниз	*VNIS*
during	во время	*va VRYEmya*
except	кроме	*KROmye*
for	для	*dlya*
from	из / с / от	*is / s / at*
in	в	*v*
in front of	перед	*PYErit*
inside	внутри	*vnuTRI*
on	на	*na*
on top	над	*nat*
opposite	напротив	*naPROtif*
outside	вне	*vnye*

through	через	CHEris
to	в / на	v / na
toward	к	k
under	под	pat
until	до	da
with	с	s
without	без	byes

Travel Tips Russians love winter and impatiently await its arrival. Dress warmly and wear waterproof shoes or boots because the distances between buildings are great and the streets and sidewalks tend to be slushy from October through May. You might purchase a fur hat with ear flaps (**ушанка** *uSHANka*) as a practical addition to your wardrobe and a great souvenir of your visit.

READY REFERENCE KEY

Here are some phrases and words from the book that you are likely to use often. For a more extensive list of phrases, refer to the appropriate chapter in the book.

SIMPLE WORDS AND PHRASES

| Do you speak English? | **Вы говорите по-английски?** |
| | *VY gavaRItye pa-anGLIYski* |

| I speak a little Russian. | **Я говорю немного по-русски.** |
| | *YA gavaRYU niMNOga pa-RUski* |

| Do you understand? | **Вы понимаете?**   *VY paniMAyitye* |

| I understand. | **Я понимаю.**   *YA paniMAyu* |

| I don't understand. | **Я не понимаю.**   *YA NYE paniMAyu* |

| How do you say _____ in Russian? | **Как _____ по-русски?** |
| | *KAK pa-RUski* |

| Please repeat. | **Повторите, пожалуйста.** |
| | *paftaRItye paZHAlusta* |

BEING POLITE

| Hello. | **Здравствуйте.**   *ZDRASTvuytye* |

| Yes. | **Да.**   *DA* |

| No. | **Нет.**   *NYET* |

Please.	**Пожалуйста.** *paZHAlusta*
Thank you.	**Спасибо.** *spaSIba*
Excuse me!	**Извините!** *izviNItye*
That's all right.	**Хорошо.** *kharaSHO*
It doesn't matter.	**Ничего.** *nichiVO*
Good-bye.	**До свидания.** *da sviDAniya*

BASIC NEEDS

What is it?	**Что это?** *SHTO Eta*
When?	**Когда?** *kagDA*
Where?	**Где?** *GDYE*
Where to?	**Куда?** *kuDA*
■ to the right	**направо** *naPRAva*
■ to the left	**налево** *naLYEva*
■ straight ahead	**прямо** *PRYAma*
How much does it cost?	**Сколько стоит?** *SKOL'ka STOit*
I'd like _____.	**Мне хочется _____.** *MNYE KHOchitsa*
Please bring me _____.	**Принесите мне, пожалуйста _____.** *priniSItye MNYE paZHAlusta*
Please show me _____.	**Покажите мне, пожалуйста _____.** *pakaZHYtye MNYE paZHAlusta*

ENGLISH-RUSSIAN DICTIONARY

Accented syllables are indicated by capital letters in the italicized phonetic transcription. Verbs are identified according to their aspects: (**i**) imperfective; (**p**) perfective. Nouns that end in the soft sign "**ь**" are either (**m**) masculine or (**f**) feminine; neuter nouns that do not end in **o** or **e** are indicated by an (**n**). All definitions reflect only the usage(s) actually presented in the chapters of this book. To avoid confusion the abbreviations (**adj**) for adjective and (**adv**) for adverb are used.

A

abdomen живот *zhiVOT*

able мочь (i) *MOCH*

about о / об *O / OP*

above над *NAT*

abscess нарыв *naRYF*

accept принимать (i) *priniMAT'*

accepted, acceptable принято *PRInita*

accommodations размещение *razmiSCHYEniye*

according to по *PO*

account счёт *SHYOT*

accumulate набраться (p) *naBRAtsa*

ace (cards) туз *TUS*

achievement достижение *dastiZHEniye*

get acquainted познакомиться (p) *paznaKOmitsa*

across через *CHEris*

active действующий *DYEYSTvuyushi*

adapter адаптер *aDAPtir*

address адрес *Adris*

adhesive tape пластырь (m) *plaSTYR'*

administrator администратор *adminiSTRAtar*

advance: in advance заранее *zaRAniye*

Africa Африка *Afrika*

after после *POslye*

afternoon: in the afternoon днём *DNYOM;* **good afternoon.** добрый день. *DObry DYEN'*

again вновь *VNOF'*

ago назад *naZAT*

ahead: straight ahead прямо *PRYAma*

aid помощь (f) *POmash*

air conditioning кондиционер *konditsiaNYER*

air mattress надувной матрац *naduvNOY maTRATS*

aircraft самолёт *samaLYOT*

airmail letter авиаписьмо *aviapiS'MO*

airport аэропорт *aeraPORT*

aisle проход *praKHOT*

alarm clock будильник *buDIL'nik*

alcohol спирт *SPIRT*

all (everything) всё *FSYO*

all (everyone) все *FSYE*

allergy аллергия *alirGIya*

allow (may I) разрешить (p) *razriSHYT*

almonds миндаль (m) *minDAL'*

almost чуть *CHUT'*

alone (m) один *aDIN*

alone (f) одна *aDNA*

already уже *uZHE*

also также *TAGzhe*

amalgam амальгама *amal'GAma*

amber янтарь (m) *yanTAR'*

ambulance скорая помощь *SKOraya POmash*

America Америка *aMYErika*

American (m) американец *amiriKAnits*

American (f) американка *amiriKANka*

American американскний *amiriKANski*

amethyst аметист *amiTIST*

among среди *sriDI*

amount сумма *SUma*

and и / а *I / A*

ankle лодышка *laDYSHka*

anniversary годовщина *gadafSHIna*

another другой *druGOY*

another (more) ещё *yiSHO*

antacid щёлочь (f) *SHOlach*

antique store комиссионный магазин *kamisiOny magaZIN*

antiseptic антисептик *antiSYEPtik*

anyone кто-нибудь *KTO-nibut'*

apartment квартира *kvarTIra*

appetizer закуска *zaKUSka*

apple яблоко *YABlaka*

application анкета *anKYEta*

make an appointment (sign up) записаться (p) *zapiSAtsa*

appraise оценивать (i) *aTSEnivat'*

approach подойти (p) *padayTI*

apricot абрикос *abriKOS*

April апрель (m) *aPRYEL'*

aquamarine аквамарин *akvamaRIN*

area code код города *KOT GOrada*

arm рука *ruKA*

around вокруг *vaKRUK*

around the clock круглосуточно *kruglaSUtachna*

arrival заезд *zaYEST*

arrival прибытие *priBYtiye*

arrive прибывать (i) *pribyVAT'*

art искусство *isKUSTva*

artichoke артишок *artiSHOK*

artist художник *khuDOZHnik*

ASA ГОСТ *GOST*

ashtray пепельница *PYEpil'nitsa*

ask спрашивать (i) *SPRAshivat'*

asparagus спаржа *SPARzha*

aspirin аспирин *aspiRIN*

assortment ассорти (n) *asarTI*

Astoria Астория *aSTOriya*

at у *U*

ATM (automatic teller machine) банкомат *bankaMAT*

attack приступ *PRIstup*

attorney адвокат *advaKAT*

attraction достопримечательность (f) *dastaprimiCHAtil'nast'*

auburn каштановый *kaSHTAnavy*

August август *AVgust*

Australia Австралия *afSTRAliya*

Australian (m) австралиец *afstraLIyets*

Australian (f) австралийка *afstraLIYka*

author автор *AFtar*

authorized авторизованный *aftariZOvany*

automatic автоматический *aftamaTIchiski*

auto repair автосалон *Afta-saLON*

average средний *SRYEDni*

awful ужасно *uZHASna*

B

back спина *spiNA*

back (in the back) сзади *ZAdi*

backwards назад *naZAT*

bad плохой *plaKHOY*

baggage багаж *baGASH;* **check baggage** сдать в багаж *ZDAT' v baGASH*

baggage claim check багажная бирка *baGAZHnaya BIRka*

baked печёный *piCHOny*

bakery булочная *BUlachnaya*

balcony балкон *balKON*

ball мяч *MYACH*

ballet балет *baLYET*

banana банан *baNAN*

bandage бинт *BINT*

bangs чёлка *CHOLka*

bank банк *BANK*

bank/debit card банковская карта *BANkafskaya KARta*

banker банкир *banKIR*

bar бар *BAR*

bar (of soap, etc.) кусок *kuSOK*

barber shop парикмахерская *parikMAkhirskaya*

basketball баскетбол *baskitBOL*

bathhouse баня *BAnya*

bathing suit купальник *kuPAL'nik*

bathing trunks плавки *PLAFki*

bathroom туалет *tuaLYET*

bathtub ванна *VAna*

battery батарея *bataRYEya*

battery (car) аккумулятор *akumuLAYtar*

be быть (i) *BYT'*

beach пляж *PLYASH*

beads бусы *BUsy*

beans фасоль (f) *faSOL'*

beard борода *baraDA*

beautiful красивый *kraSIvy*

beauty parlor женский салон *ZHENski saLON*

bed кровать (f) *kraVAT'*

beef Stroganoff беф-строганов *bif-STROganaf*

beer пиво *PIva;* **bottled beer** пиво бутылочное *PIva buTYlachnaya;* **draught beer** пиво разливное *PIva razLIVnaya*

beets свёкла *SVYOkla*

beet soup борщ *BORSH*

before до / перед *DO / PYErit*

beg просить (i) *praSIT'*

begin начинать(ся) (i) *nachiNAtsa*

beginning (starting time) начало *naCHAla*

behind за *ZA*

bellboy швейцар *shviyTSAR*

belt пояс *POyas,* ремень (m) *riMYEN'*

best лучший *LUchshy*

better лучше *LUche*

between между *MYEZHdu*

beverage напиток *naPItak*

big большой *bal'SHOY*

bill (check) чек *CHEK*

bill (paper currency) купюра *kuPYUra*

billion миллиард *miliART*

bindings крепления *kriPLYEniya*

bird птица *PTItsa*

birthday день рождения *DYEN' razhDYEniya;* **Happy Birthday!** С днём рождения! *z DNYOM razhDYEniya*

bishop (chess) слон *SLON*

black чёрный *CHORny*

blank form бланк *BLANK*

blanket одеяло *adiYAla*

bleeding кровотечение *kravatiCHEniye*

blender сокавыжиматель (m) *sakavyzhiMAtil'*

blind (f) слепая *slyePAya*

blind (m) слепой *slyePOY*

bliny блины *bliNY*

blond белокурый *bilaKUry*

blood кровь (f) *KROF'*

blouse блузка *BLUSka*

blow дуть (i) *DUT'*

blown glass художественное стекло *khuDOzhistvinaye stiKLO*

blue: dark blue синий *SIni;* **light blue** голубой *galuBOY*

blues блюз *BLYUS*

board доска *daSKA*

boarding pass посадочный талон *paSAdachny taLON*

boat лодка *LOTka,* теплоход *tiplaKHOT*

bobby pin шпилька *SHPILka*

body тело *TYEla*

boiled варёный *vaRYOny*

boiling water кипяток *kipiTOK*

Bolshoi Theater Большой театр *bal'SHOY tiATR*

bolt (fastener) болт *BOLT*

Bon voyage! Счастливого пути! *shastLIvava puTI*

bone кость (f) *KOST'*

book книга *KNIga*

bookstore книжный магазин *KNIZHny magaZIN*

booth кабина *kaBIna*

boot сапог *saPOK*

Boris Godunov Борис Годунов *baRIS gaduNOF*

borrow брать взаймы *BRAT' vzayMI*

bottle бутылка *buTYLka*

bottom дно *DNO*

bouillon бульон *buL'YON*

box ящик *YAshik,* коробка *kaROPka*

box (packet) пакет *paKYET*

box (loge) ложа *LOzha*

boxing бокс *BOKS*

bra бюстгальтер *byustGAL'tir*

bracelet браслет *braSLYET*

brake тормоз *TORmas*

brand марка *MARka*

bread хлеб *KHLYEP*

break (recess) перерыв *piriRYF*

break сломать (p) *slaMAT'*

breakfast завтрак *ZAFtrak*

breast грудь (f) *GRUT'*

breathe дышать (i) *dySHAT'*

bridge мост *MOST*

briefcase портфель (m) *partFYEL'*

bring принести (p) *priniSTI*

British (m) англичанин *angliCHAnin*

British (f) англичанка *angliCHANka*

British (English) английский *anGLIYski*

broken bone перелом *piriLOM*

brooch брошь (f) *BROSH*

brook ручей *ruCHEY*

brother брат *BRAT*

brown коричневый *kaRICHnivy*

bruise ушиб *uSHYP*

brunette брюнетка *bryuNYETka*

brush щётка *SHOTka*

buckwheat гречка *GRECHka*

buffet, snack bar буфет *buFYET*

builder строитель (m) *straItil'*

building здание *ZDAniye*

bulb лампочка *LAMpachka*

bumper бампер *BAMpir*

bun (hairdo) пучок *puCHOK*

bunch of twigs веник *VYEnik*

bureau (office) бюро *byuRO*
burn ожог *aZHOK*
burn oneself обвариться (p) *obvaRItsa*
bus автобус *aFTObus*
business бизнес *BIZnis*
business lunch бизнес-ланч *BIZnis LANCH*
businessman бизнесмен *biznisMYEN*
but а / но *A / NO*
butane gas газ *GAS*
butcher shop магазин "Мясо" *magaZIN MYAsa*
butter масло *MAsla*
button пуговица *PUgavitsa*
buy купить (p) *kuPIT'*

C

cabbage капуста *kaPUsta*
cabbage soup щи *SHI*
cabin каюта *kaYUta*
cable television кабельное телевидение *KAbil'nayi tiliVIdiniye*
cafe кафе *kaFYEY*
cafeteria столовая *staLOvaya*
cake торт *TORT*
call (summon) позвать (p) *paZVAT'*
call (telephone) позвонить (p) *pazvaNIT'*
camera фотоаппарат *fotaapaRAT*
can банка *BANka*
can мочь (i) *MOCH*; **I can** я могу *YA maGU*; **you can** ты можешь *TY MOzhish*; **he/she can** он/она может *ON/aNA MOzhit*; **we can** мы можем *MY MOzhim*; **you can** вы можете *VY MOzhitye*; **they can** они могут *aNI MOgut*
Canada Канада *kaNAda*
Canadian (m) канадец *kaNAdits*

Canadian (f) канадка *kaNATka*
Canadian канадский *kaNATski*
candy конфета *kanFYEta*
cane палка *PALka*
cap шапочка *SHApachka*
capital капитал *kapiTAL*
cappucino капочино *kapaCHEEna*
car автомобиль (m) *aftamaBIL'*, машина *maSHYna*
car wash автомойка *aftaMOYka*
carat карат *kaRAT*
carburetor карбюратор *karbyuRAtar*
card карта *KARta*
carefully осторожно *astaROZHna*
carp карп *KARP*
carrots морковь (f) *marKOF'*
carry понести (p) *paniSTI*
cart тележка *tiLYESHka*
carved object резьба *riz'BA*
cash наличные (деньги) *naLICHniye (DYEN'gi)*
cash register кассовой аппарат *kasaVOY apaRAT*
cashier касса *KAsa*
casino казино *kaziNO*
cassette кассета *kyaSYEta*
cassette recorder магнитофон *magnitaFON*
category категория *katiGOriya*
cathedral собор *saBOR*
Catholic католический *kataLIchiski*
cauliflower цветная капуста *tsvitNAya kaPUsta*
caution! опасность! (f) *aPASnast'*
caviar икра *iKRA*; **black caviar** зернистая икра *zirNIStaya iKRA*; **red caviar** кетовая икра *KYEtavaya iKRA*

CD (compact disc)
  компактный диск
  kamPAKTny DISK
cell phone мобильник
  maBIL'nik
cellular phone сотовый
  телефон *SOtavy tiliFON*
cemetery кладбище
  KLADbishe
center середина *siriDIna*
centimeter сантиметр
  santiMYETR
central центральный
  tsinTRAL'ny
century век *VYEK*
ceramics керамика *kiRAmika*
cereal (cold) крупа *kruPA*
cereal (warm) каша *KAsha*
certified letter ценное
  письмо *TSEnaye piS'MO*
chain цепочка *tsiPOCHka*
chaise longue шезлонг
  shizLONG
champagne шампанское
  shamPANskaye
change размен *razMYEN*
change разменять (i)
  razmiNYAT'
changing room примерочная
  кабина *priMYErachnaya
  kaBIna*
charge the battery зарядить
  аккумулятор *zariDIT'
  akumuLYAtar*
charm (jewelry) брелок
  briLOK
chassis шасси (n) *shaSI*
cheap, inexpensive дешёвый
  diSHOvy
cheaper, less expensive
  подешевле *padiSHEvlye*
check (bill) чек *CHEK*
check проверить (p)
  praVYErit'
Check! Шах! *SHAKH*
checkbook чековая книжка
  CHYEkavaya KNISHka

checked в шашечку
  f SHAshichku
checkers шашки *SHASHki*
check-in регистрация
  rigiSTRAtsiya
Checkmate! Мат! *MAT*
check-out time расчётный
  час *rasSHOTny CHAS*
checkroom камера хранения
  KAmira khraNYEniya
cheek щека *shiKA*
Cheers! На здоровье! *na
  zdaROv'ye*
cheese сыр *SYR*
cherry вишня *VISHnya*
chess шахматы *SHAKHmaty*
chest cold бронхит *branKHIT*
chestnut каштан *kaSHTAN*
chew жевать (i) *zhiVAT'*
chewing tobacco махорка
  maKHORka
chicken курица *KUritsa*,
  цыплёнок *tsyPLYOnak*
chiffon шифон *shiFON*
children дети *DYEti*
chills озноб *aZNOP*
Chinese Китайский *kiTAYski*
chocolate шоколадный
  shakaLADny
chop/cutlet отбивная котлета
  atbivNAya katLYEta
Christ the Saviour Cathedral
  Храм Христа Спасителя
  KHRAM khriSTA spaSItilya
church церковь (f) *TSERkaf*
cigarette сигарета *sigaRYEta*
cigar сигар *siGAR*
Cinderella Золушка *ZOlushka*
circle кольцо *kal'TSO*
circle (theater) ярус *YArus*
circus цирк *TSYRK*
**CIS (Confederation of
  Independent States)**
  СНГ *ES-EN-GE*
citizen (m) гражданин
  grazhdaNIN
citizen (f) гражданка
  grazhDANka

city город *GOrat*

city tour экскурсия по городу *ekSKURsiya pa GOradu*

class класс *KLAS;* **economy class** туристический класс *turiSTIchiski KLAS*

classical классический *klaSIchiski*

clean почистить (p) *paCHIStit'*

cleaned убран *Ubran*

cleansing cream крем для очистки кожи *KRYEM dlya aCHISTki KOzhi*

clear сброс *ZBROS*

clinic поликлиника *paliKLInika*

clock часы *chiSY*

close закрывать(ся) (i) *zakryVAt(sa),* закрыть(ся) (p) *zaKRYt(sa)*

closeout sale распродажа *raspraDAzha*

closed закрыто *zaKRYta*

clothing одежда *aDYEZHda*

clubs (cards) трефы *TRYEfy*

clutch pedal сцепление *tsiPLYEniye*

coat пальто *pal'TO*

coatroom гардероб *gardiROP*

Coca-Cola Кока-кола *KOka-Kola*

cocktails коктейли *kakTYEYli*

cocoa (hot chocolate) какао *kaKAo*

cod треска *triSKA*

coffee кофе (m) *KOfye*

coffeemaker кофеварка *kafeVARka*

cognac коньяк *kaN'YAK*

cold (in the head) насморк *NASmark*

cold холодный *khaLODny*

colleague коллега *kaLYEga*

collect (telegram) доплатно *daPLATna*

collection сборник *ZBORnik*

collector's stamps коллекционные марки *kaliktsiOniye MARki*

cologne одеколон *adikaLON*

color цвет *TSVYET*

color(ed) цветной *tsvitNOY*

color rinse окраска *aKRASka*

comb расчёска *rasCHOSka*

comb зачёсывать (i) *zaCHOsyvat'*

come прийти (p) *priyTI*

comedy комедия *kaMYEdiya*

comment примечание *primiCHAniye*

committee комитет *kamiTYET*

communist коммунистический *kamuniSTIchiski*

company фирма *FIRma*

compartment купе *kuPYE*

competition конкуренция *kankuRYENtsiya*

completely совсем *saFSYEM*

computer (adj) компьютерный *kamP'YUtirny*

computer (n) компьютер *kamPYUter*

comrade товарищ *taVArish*

concert концерт *kanTSERT*

conductor (musical) дирижёр *diriZHOR*

Confederation of Independent States Содружество Независимых Государств *saDRUzhestva nyezaVIsimykh gasuDARTSF*

confirm подтвердить (p) *patvirDIT'*

connect to the internet подключиться к сети интернет *potklyuCHItsa k SYEti intirNYET*

constipation запор *zaPOR*

consular officer сотрудник консульства *saTRUDnik KONsul'stva*

contact lens контактная линза *kanTAKTnaya LINza*

contact person контактное лицо *kanTAKTnaye liTSO*

contract контракт *kanTRAKT*

control контроль (m) *kanTROL'*

conventional units у.е.

conversation разговор *razgaVOR*

cookie печенье *piCHEn'ye*

cool прохладный *praKHLADny*

cop милиционер *militsiaNYER*

copy скопировать *skaPIravat'*

cord шнур *SHNUR*

corduroy рубчатый вельвет *RUPchaty vil'VYET*

correct правильный *PRAvil'ny*

correspondent корреспондент *karispanDYENT*

cosmonaut космонавт *kasmaNAFT*

cosmos космос *KOSmas*

cost стоить (i) *STOit'*

cot раскладушка *rasklaDUSHka*

cotton вата *VAta*

cotton fabric хлопчатобумажная ткань *khlapchatabuMAZHnaya TKAN'*

cough кашель (m) *KAshil'*

cough покашлять (p) *paKASHlit'*

cough drops таблетки от кашля *taBLYETki at KASHlya*

cough syrup микстура от кашля *mikSTUra at KASHlya*

count посчитать (p) *pashiTAT'*

country страна *straNA*

countryside деревня *diRYEVnya*

coupon, ticket талон *taLON*

course (currency exchange rate) курс *KURS*

cover charge входной билет *FKHODny biLYET*

CPU (central processing unit) системный блок *siSTYEMny BLOK*

crab краб *KRAP*

cramp судорога *SUdaraga*

crazy: are you crazy? вы с ума сошли? *VY s uMA saSHLI*

cream сливки *SLIFki;* **whipped cream** взбитые сливки *VZBItiye SLIFki*

cream cheese творог *tvaROK*

credit card кредитная карточка *kriDITnaya KARtachka*

cross-country skis беговые лыжи *bigaVIye LYzhi*

crossing (pedestrian) переход *piriKHOT*

crossing (vehicular) переезд *piriYEST*

crown (dental) коронка *kaRONka*

cruise круиз *kruIS*

crutches костыли *kostyLI*

crystal хрусталь (m) *khruSTAL'*

cucumber огурец *aguRYETS*

cuisine кухня *KUKHnya*

cupcake кекс *KYEKS*

curls кудри *KUdri*

currants смородина *smaROdina*

currency (foreign—freely convertible) валюта *vaLYUta*

currency exchange обмен валюты *abMYEN vaLYUty*

currency exchange point обменный пункт *abMYEny PUNKT*

curve поворот *pavaROT*

customs declaration
декларация *diklaRAtsiya*
cut порез *paRYES*
cut (p) вырезать *VYrezat'*
cut oneself порезаться (p)
paRYEzatsa
cuticle scissors маникюрные
ножницы *maniKYURniye*
NOZHnitsy
cutlet котлета *katLYEta*

D

dacha (country home) дача
DAcha
dance танцевать (i) *tantsiVAT'*
dangerous опасный *aPASny*
dark (adj) тёмный *TYOMny*
darkly (adv) темно *timNO*
darker потемнее
patimNYEye
darn it! чёрт возьми! *CHORT*
vaz'MI
date дата *DAta*
date (calendar) число
chiSLO
date (fruit) финик *FInik*
daughter дочка *DOCHka*,
дочь (f) *DOCH*
day день (m) *DYEN'*
dead end тупик *tuPIK*
deaf (f) глухая *gluKHAya*
deaf (m) глухой *gluKHOY*
deal (cards) сдавать (i)
zdaVAT'
December декабрь (m)
diKABR'
deck of cards колода *kaLOda*
declaration декларация
diklaRAtsiya
declare декларировать (i)
diklaRIravat'
deeply глубоко *glubaKO*
degree (of temperature)
градус *GRAdus*
delete, pull (a tooth)
удалить (p) *udaLIT'*

delivery доставка *daSTAFka*,
поставка *paSTAFka*
deluxe люкс *LYUKS*
dental зубной *zubNOY*
dentist зубной врач *zubNOY*
VRACH
denture зубной протез
zubNOY praTYES
deodorant дезодорант
dizadaRANT
depart отправляться (i)
atpraVLYAtsa, уезжать (i)
uyiZHAT'
department store универмаг
univirMAK
departure выезд *Vyyist*
departure отправление
atpraVLYEniya
deposit (security) залог
zaLOK
deposit slip приходный ордер
priKHODny ORdir; **make a**
deposit выдать вклад
VYdat' FKLAT
desk стол *STOL*
desktop рабочий стол
raBOchi STOL
desktop computer
настольный компьютер
naSTOL'ny kamPYUter
dessert сладкое *SLATkaye*
destination направление
napraVLYEniye
detour объезд *aBYEST*
develop (film) проявлять (i)
prayiVLYAT'
devil чёрт *CHORT*
dial набирать (i) *nabiRAT'*
diamond бриллиант *briliANT*
diamonds (cards) бубны
BUBny
diaper пелёнка *piLYONka*
diarrhea понос *paNOS*
dictionary словарь (m)
slaVAR'
digital watch электронные
часы *elikTROniye chiSY*
dinner ужин *Uzhin*

diplomat   дипломат *diplaMAT*

direction   направление *napravLYEniye*

directional signal
сигнальный огонь *sigNAL'ny aGON'*

disabled   инвалид *invaLIT*

disc, disk   диск *DISK*

disconnect   разъединить (р) *razyidiNIT*

discotheque   дискотека *diskaTYEka*

discount   льготный *L'GOTny*

discount   скидка *SKITka;*
discount card   скитная карта *SKITnaya KARta*

dish   блюдо *BLYUda*

dislocated   вывыхнут *VYvykhnut*

disposable diapers   бумажная пелёнка *buMAZHnaya piLYONka*

disturb   беспокоить *bispoKOyit'*

dizzy: I'm dizzy   голова кружится *galaVA KRUzhitsa*

do   сделать (р) *ZDYElat'*

dock   пристань (f) *PRIstan'*

doctor   врач *VRACH*

dollar   доллар *DOlar*

Domodedovo airport
Домодедово *damaDYEdava*

door   дверь (f) *DVYER'*

double bed   двуспальная кровать *dvuSPAL'naya kraVAT'*

down   вниз *VNIS*

downhill skis   горные лыжи *GORniye LYzhi*

downtown   центр *TSENTR*

drama   драма *DRAma*

drama (tragedy)   трагедия *traGYEdiya*

dress   платье *PLAt'ye*

dress (oneself)   одеваться (i) *adiVAtsa*

drink   пить (i) *PIT'*,   выпить (р) *VYpit'*

drive by   заехать (р) *zaYEkhat'*

driver   водитель (m) *vaDItil'*

driver's license   водительские права *vaDItil'skiye praVA*

drop (n)   капля *KAplya*

drop   уронить (р) *uraNIT*

drugstore   аптека *apTYEka*

dry   сухой *suKHOY*

dry cleaner's   химчистка *khimCHISTka*

dry cleaning   чистка *CHISTka*

duck   утка *UTka*

during   во время *va VRYEmya*

duty (customs)   пошлина *POSHlina*

E

each   каждый *KAZHdy*

ear   ухо *Ukha*

ear drops   ушные капли *ushNIye KApli*

early   рано *RAna*

earring   серьга *sir'GA*

east   восток *vaSTOK*

easy   лёгкий *LYOki*

edition   издание *iZDAniye*

egg   яйцо *yayTSO;*   **hard-boiled egg**   яйцо вкрутую *yayTSO fkruTUyu;*   **soft-boiled egg**   яйцо всмятку *yayTSO FSMYATki*

eggplant   баклажан *baklaZHAN*

eight   восемь *VOsim'*

eight hundred   восемьсот *vasim'SOT*

eighteen   восемнадцать *vasimNAtsat'*

eighth   восьмой *vaS'MOY*

eighty   восемьдесят *VOsim'disit*

elbow   локоть (m) *LOkat'*

elderly   пожилой *pazhiLOY*

electrical   электрический *elikTRIchiski*

electronic электронный *elikTROni*

elevator лифт *LIFT*

eleven одиннадцать *aDInatsat'*

embassy посольство *paSOL'stva*

e-mail электронная почта *elikTROnaya POCHta*

emerald изумруд *izumRUT*

emergency exit запасный выход *zaPASny VYkhat*

end конец *kaNETS*

end кончать(ся) (i) *kanCHAtsa*

engagement/wedding ring обручальное кольцо *abruCHAL'naye kal'TSO*

England Англия *ANgliya*

English английский *anGLIYski*

enlarge (be) увеличить (p) *uviLIchit'*

enough (be) хватить (p) *KHVAtit'*

enter, come in входить (i) *fkhaDIT'*

enter, insert ввод *VVOT*

enter text вводить текст *vaDIT TYEKST*

enterprise предприятие *pridpriYAtiye*

entirely совсем *saFSYEM*

entrance вход *FKHOT*

entrance ticket, cover charge входной билет *fkhadNOY biLYET*

entry въезд *VYEST*

envelope конверт *kanVYERT*

eraser ластик *LAStik*

err ошибиться (p) *ashiBItsa*

escort проводить (i) *pravaDIT'*

etc., et cetera и т. д., и так далее *I TAK DAliye*

Eugene Onegin Евгений Онегин *yivGYEni aNYEgin*

even out подравнять (p) *padravNYAT'*

evening вечер *VYEchir;* **in the evening** вечером *VYEchiram;* **good evening!** добрый вечер! *DObry VYEchir;* **evening dress** вечернее платье *viCHERniye PLAt'i*

everyone все *FSYE*

everything всё *FSYO*

except кроме *KROmye*

exchange обменять (i) *abmiNYAT';* заменять (i) *zamiNYAT'*

exchange rate обменный курс *abMYEny KURS*

excursion экскурсия *ekSKURsiya*

excuse извинить (p) *izviNIT';* **excuse me!** извините! *izviNItye*

exhaust pipe выхлопная трубка *vykhlapNAya TRUPka*

exhibition выставка *VYstafka*

exit выход *VYkhat*

exit выходить (i) *vykhaDIT',* выйти (p) *VYti*

expected ожидаемый *azhiDAimy*

expenses затраты *zaTRAty,* расходы *rasKHOdy*

expensive дорогой *daraGOY;* **more expensive** подороже *padaROzhe*

exposure кадр *KADR*

extension cord удлинитель (m) *udliNItil'*

extra лишний *LISHni*

extra (spare) запасный *zaPASny*

eye глаз *GLAS*

eye drops глазные капли *glazNIye KApli*

eyebrow бровь (f) *BROF'*

F

fabric ткань (f) *TKAN'*

face лицо *liTSO*

fall осень (f) *Osin'*; **in the fall** осенью *Osin'yu*

fall упасть (p) *uPAST"*

false tooth вставной зуб *fstavNOY ZUP*

family семья *siM'YA*

family name фамилия *faMIliya*

fan вентилятор *vintiLYAtar*

fan belt ремень вентилятора *riMYEN' vintiLYAtara*

far далеко *daliKO*

farewell! прощайте! *praSHAYtye*

fast быстрый *BYStry*

father отец *aTYETS*

faucet смеситель (m) *smiSItil'*

fax факс *FAKS*; телефакс *tiliFAKS*

February февраль (m) *fiVRAL'*

fee плата *PLAta*

feed кормить (i) *karMIT"*

feel чувствовать себя (i) *CHUSTvavat' siBYA*

felt войлок *VOYlak*

fender решётка *riSHOTka*

fever жар *ZHAR*; **I have a fever** у меня температура *u miNYA timpiraTUra*

few несколько *NYEskal'ka*

field поле *POlye*

fifteen пятнадцать *pitNAtsat'*

fifth пятый *PYAty*

fifty пятьдесят *pidiSYAT*

fig фига *FIga*

figure skates фигурные коньки *fiGURniye kan'KI*

file файл *FAIL*

filet of sturgeon балык *baLYK*

filling (dental) пломба *PLOMba*

film (photographic) плёнка *PLYONka*

filter фильтр *FIL'TR*

find найти (p) *nayTI*

finger палец *PAlits*

fingernail ноготь (m) *NOgat'*

fire пожар *paZHAR*

first первый *PYERvy*

fish рыба *RYba*

fish рыбный (adj) *RYBny*

five пять *PYAT*

five hundred пятьсот *pit'SOT*

fix чинить (i) *chiNIT"*, починить (p) *pachiNIT'*

flannel фланель (f) *flaNYEL'*

flash вспышка *FSPYSHka*

flashlight фонарь (m) *faNAR'*

flight полёт *paLYOT*

flints кремни *krimNI*

floor этаж *eTASH*

flowers цветы *tsviTY*

fold сложить *slaZHYT'*

folder папка *PAPka*

folk народ *naROT*

folk music народная музыка *naRODnaya MUzyka*

food блюдо *BLYUda*; еда *yiDA*

food court ресторанный дворик *ristaRAny DVOrik*

fool дурак *duRAK*

foot ступня *stupNYA*

for для *DLYA*

foreign иностранный *inaSTRAny*

forest лес *LYES*

fork вилка *VILka*

form форма *FORma*

fortress крепость (f) *KRYEpast'*

forty сорок *SOrak*

four четыре *chiTYrye*

four hundred четыреста *chiTYrista*

foursome четверо *CHETvira*

fourteen четырнадцать *chiTYRnatsat'*

fourth четвёртый *chitVYORty*

fox лиса *liSA*

frame (for glasses) оправа *aPRAva*

free (vacant) свободный *svaBODny*

fresh свежий *SVYEzhi*

Friday пятница *PYATnitsa*

fried жареный *ZHAriny*

friend друг *DRUK*

from из *IS*, от *OT*, с *S*

front (in front) перед *PYErit*, спереди *SPYEridi*

fruits фрукты *FRUKTy*

fuel pump бензонасос *binzanaSOS*

fund фонд *FONT*

fur (n) мех *MYEKH*

fur (adj) меховой *mikhaVOY*

future будущий *BUdushi*

G

gabardine габардин *gabarDIN*

gains доходы *daKHOdy*

gallery галерея *galiRYEya*

gallon галлон *gaLON*

garden сад *SAT*

garlic чеснок *chiSNOK*

gas (butane) газ *GAS*

gas station заправка *zaPRAfka*

gasoline бензин *binZIN*

gas tank бензобак *binzaBAK*

gauze (sanitary) napkin марлевая салфетка *MARlivaya salFYETka*

gear скорость (f) *SKOrast'*

gear shift сцепление *tsiPLYEniye*

general delivery до востребования *da vasTRYEbavaniya*

Georgian грузинский *gruZINski*

get off выйти (р) *VYti*

get to проехать (р) *praYEkhat'*

gift подарок *paDArak*

gift certificate подарочный сертификат *paDArachny sertifiKAT*

gift wrapping упаковка подарков *upaKOFka paDArok*

gin джин *DZHIN*

give дать (р) *DAT'*

glass стакан *staKAN*

glasses очки *achKI*

gloss гланц *GLANTS*

glove перчатка *pirCHATka*

glue клей *KLYEY*

go by foot идти (i) *iTI*

go by vehicle ехать (i) *YEkhat'*

gold золото *ZOlata*

gold(en) золотой *zalaTOY*

gold-plated позолоченый *pazaLOchiny*

good хороший *khaROshi*

good-bye! до свидания! *da sviDAniya*

good luck! удачи! *uDAchi*

goodness: my goodness! боже мой! *BOzhe MOY*

goods, items товары *taVAry*

goose гусь (m) *GUS'*

gram грамм *GRAM*

grape виноград *vinaGRAT*

grapefruit грейпфрут *GRYEYPfrut*

gray серый *SYEry*

grease смазать (р) *SMAzat'*

great великий *viLIki*

green зелёный *ziLYOny*

grill гриль (m) *GRIL'*

grilled обжаренный *abZHAriny*

group группа *GRUpa*

guest (m) гость *GOST'*

guest card карта гостя *KARta gaSTYA*

guidebook путеводитель (m) *putivaDItil'*

GUM ГУМ *GUM*
gum десна *diSNA*
gymnastics гимнастика
  gimNAstika

H

hair волос *vaLOS*
haircut стрижка *STRISHka;*
  have a haircut постричься
  (р) *paSTRICHtsa*
hairdo причёска
  priCHOSka
hair dryer фен *FYEN*
hair spray лак для волос
  LAK dlya vaLOS
half половина *palaVIna*
hall зал *ZAL*
ham ветчина *vichiNA*
hammer молоток
  malaTOK
hand кисть (f) *KIST'*
hand brake ручной тормоз
  ruchNOY TORmas
handkerchief носовой платок
  nasaVOY plaTOK
handle ручка *RUCHka*
hanger вешалка *VYEshalka;*
  плечик *PLYEchik*
happen случиться (р)
  sluCHItsa
hard disk жёсткий диск
  ZHOski DISK
hat шапка *SHAPka*
have/there is есть *YEST'*
hay fever сенная лихорадка
  SYEnaya likhaRATka
he он *ON*
head голова *galaVA*
headache головная боль
  galavNAya BOL'
headlight фара *FAra*
health здоровье *zdaROv'ye*
hearing aid слуховой аппарат
  slukhaVOY apaRAT
heart сердце *SYERtse*
heart attack сердечный

приступ *sirDYECHny
  PRIstup*
hearts (cards) черви *CHERvi*
hectare гектар *gikTAR*
heel каблук *kaBLUK*
height рост *ROST*
hello! здрабствуйте!
  ZDRASTvuytye
help помочь (р) *paMOCH*
here здесь *ZDYES*
here it is вот оно *VOT aNO*
herring селёдка *siLYOTka*
herringbone ёлочка
  YOlachka
hi! привет! *priVYET*
high высокий *vySOki*
hill холм *KHOLM*
hip бедро *biDRO*
history история *iSTOriya*
hockey хоккей *khaKYEY*
hockey skates хоккейные
  коньки *khaKYEYniye kan'KI*
holiday праздник *PRAZnik*
home / house дом *DOM*
at home дома *DOma*
(to) home домой *daMOY*
hood капот *kaPOT*
horn гудок *guDOK*
hospital больница *bal'NItsa*
hospitality гостеприимство
  gastipriIMstva
hot (spicy) острый *Ostry*
hot (temperature) жаркий
  ZHARki
hot (object) горячий
  gaRYAchi
hotel гостиница *gaSTInitsa*
hour час *CHAS*
household хозяйственный
  khaZYAYSTviny
how как *KAK*
how many, how much
  сколько *SKOL'ka*
humor юмор *YUmar*
hundred сто *STO*
hungry (m) голоден *GOladin*
hungry (f) голодна *galaDNA*
hurry спешить (i) *spiSHYT'*

hurt болеть (i) *baLYET'*; **it**
  hurts болит *baLIT*; **that**
  hurts больно *BOL'na*
husband муж *MUSH*

I

I я *YA*
ice лёд *LYOT*
ice skates коньки *kan'KI*
if если *YEsli*
ignition зажигание
  zazhiGAniye
imam имам *iMAM*
in в *V*
inch дюйм *DYUYM*
(be) included входить (i)
  fkhaDIT'
inexpensive дешёвый
  diSHOvy
infection инфекция
  inFYEKtsiya
information информация
  infarMAtsiya
initial первоначальный
  pirvanaCHAL'ny
inside внутри *vnuTRI*
insole стелька *STYEL'ka*
insomnia бессоница
  biSOnitsa
inspection инспекция
  inSPYEKtsiya
institute институт *instiTUT*
instrument инструмент
  instruMYENT
insurance страхование
  strakhaVAniye
interest rate процент
  praTSENT
intermission антракт
  anTRAKT
international международный
  mizhdunaRODny
internet интернет *intirNET*
interpreter переводчик
  piriVOTchik
into в *V*

Intourist Интурист
  intuRIST
introduce (oneself)
  представить(ся) (p)
  pritSTAvit'/pritSTAvitsa
investment инвестиция
  inviSTItsiya
invite пригласить (p)
  priglaSIT'
iodine йод *YOT*
Irish coffee Айриш-кофе
  AYrish-KOfye
ironing глажка *GLASHka*
Italian итальянский
  itaLYANski
item штука *SHTUka*
ivory слоновая кость
  slaNOvaya KOST'

J

jack (car) домкрат *damKRAT*
jack (cards) валет *vaLYET*
jacket пиджак *pidZHAK*
jade нефрит *niFRIT*
January январь (m) *yinVAR'*
jasper яшма *YASHma*
jazz джаз *DZHAS*
jeans джинсы *DZHYNsy*
jelly варенье *vaRYEn'ye*
jewelry store ювелирный
  магазин *yuviLIRny
  magaZIN*
juice сок *SOK*
julienne жульен *zhuL'YEN*
July июль (m) *iYUL'*
June июнь (m) *iYUN'*
junior младший *MLADshi*
just in case (string bag)
  авоська *aVOS'ka*

K

key ключ *KLYUCH*
keyboard клавиатура
  klaviaTUra

key card (pass) пропуск *PROpusk*

"key lady" дежурная *diZHURnaya*

kidney soup рассольник *raSOL'nik*

kilo(gram) кило (грамм) *kiLO / kilaGRAM*

kilometer километр *kilaMYETR*

king король (m) *kaROL'*

kiosk киоск *kiOSK*

kitchen кухня *KUKHnya*

kiwi киви *KIvi*

knee колено *kaLYEna*

knife нож *NOSH*

knight (chess) офицер *afiTSER*

knock over сбить (p) *ZBIT'*

know знать (i) *ZNAT'*

know how уметь (i) *uMYET'*

kopeck копейка *kaPYEYka*

Kremlin Кремль (m) *KRYEML'*

kvass квас *KVAS*

L

lace кружева *kruzhiVA*

ladies' женский *ZHENski*

lake озеро *Ozira*

lamb баранина *baRAnina*

lame (f) хромая *khraMAya*

lame (m) хромой *khraMOY*

lamp лампа *LAMpa*

land приплывать (i) *priplyVAT'*

language язык *yiZYK*

lapel pin значок *znaCHOK*

laptop computer ноутбук *NOTbuk*

large крупный *KRUPny*

larger больше *BOL'she*

last длиться (i) *DLItsa*

late поздно *POZna*

(be) late опаздывать (i) *aPAZdyvat'*

later позже *POzhe*

latte латте *LAte*

laundromat прачечная самообслуживания *PRAchichnaya samaapSLUzhivaniya*

laundry прачечная *PRAchichnaya*

lawyer адвокат *advaKAT*

laxative слабительное *slaBItil'naye*

leak протекать (i) *pratiKAT'*

lean прислоняться (i) *prislaNYAtsa*

leather кожа *KOzha*

leave, depart отправляться (i) *atpraVLYAtsa*

leave (something) оставить (p) *aSTAvit'*

left левый *LYEvy*; **to the left** налево *naLYEva*; **on the left** слева *SLYEva*

leg нога *naGA*

lemon лимон *liMON*

lend давать взаймы *daVAT' vzayMI*; одолжить (p) *adalZHYT'*

length длинна *dliNA*

length (duration) продолжительность *pradal'ZHItil'nast'*

Lenin Ленин *LYEnin*

Leningrad Ленинград *lininGRAT*

lens (eyeglass) стекло *stiKLO*

lens (contact) контактная линза *kanTAKTnaya LINza*

less меньше *MYEN'she*

let (allow) пусть *PUST'*

let in пускать (i) *puSKAT'*

letter письмо *piS'MO*

lettuce салат *saLAT*

library библиотека *bibliaTYEka*

lie (in bed) лежать (i) *liZHAT'*

lie down ложиться (i) *laZHYtsa*, лечь (p) *LYECH*

lifeguard   спасатель (m)
spaSAtil'
light   светлый *SVYETly*
lighter   зажигалка
zazhiGALka
like, be pleasing to
нравиться *NRAvitsa*
like, love   любить (i) *lyuBIT'*
I'd like   мне хочется *MNYE
KHOchitsa*
lined paper   бумага в линейку
buMAga v liNYEYku
linen   полотно *palatNO*
linen towel, sheet   простыня
praSTYnya
lip   губа *GUba*
lipstick   губная помада
gubNAya paMAda
liqueur   ликёр *liKYOR*
list   список *SPIsak*
listen   слушать (i) *SLUshat'*
liter   литр *LITR*
little   немного *niMNOga*,
мало *MAla*
live   живой *zhiVOY*
liver   печень (f) *PYEchin'*
loaf   батон *baTON*
lobster   омар *aMAR*
long   длинный *DLIny*
(a) long time   долго *DOLga*
long-distance call
междугородный разговор
*mizhdugaRODny
razgaVOR*
look   смотреть (i) *smaTRYET'*
look at   взглянуть (p)
vzgliNUT'
lose   потерять(ся) (p)
patiRYAtsa
lose a game   проиграть (p)
praiGRAT'
losses   убытки *uBYTki*
lost luggage   розыск багажа
ROzysk
lotion   крем *KRYEM*, лосьон
laS'YON
loud   громко *GROMka*
lousy   плохо *PLOkha*

love   любить (i) *lyuBIT'*
lunch   обед *aBYET*

M

magazine   журнал *zhurNAL*
magnesia   магнезия
magNYEziya
magnetic   магнитический
magniTIchiski
mail   почта *POCHta*
mailbox   почтовый ящик
pachTOvy YAshik
main   главный *GLAVny*
maitre d'hotel   метрдотель
(m) *mitradaTYEL'*
make   сделать (p) *ZDYElat'*
make-up   мэйк-ап *meyk-AP*
make up (a room)   убрать (p)
uBRAT'
malachite   малахит
malaKHIT
Maly Theater   Малый театр
MAly tiATR
man   мужчина *mushCHIna;*
young man   молодой
человек *malaDOY
chilaVYEK*
manager   заведующий
zaVYEduyushi
Manezh   Манеж *maNYESH*
manicure   маникюр
maniKYUR
many, much   много *MNOga;*
how many?   сколько?
SKOL'ka
map   план *PLAN*
March   март *MART*
Mariinsky Theater
Мариинский театр
maRIinskiy tiATR
market   рынок *RYnak*
marmot   сурок *suROK*
**married: are you married? (of
a man)**   вы женаты? *VY
zhiNAty;* **are you married?
(of a woman)**   вы
замужем? *VY ZAmuzhim*

mascara тушь для ресниц *TUSH dlya risNITS*

massage массаж *maSASH*

matches спички *SPICHki*

material, fabric ткань (f) *TKAN'*

matte матовый *MAtavy*

matter дело *DYEla*

mattress матрац *maTRATS*

mausoleum мавзолей *mavzaLYEY*

maximum максимальный *maksiMAL'ny*

may (one) можно *MOZHna*

maybe может быть *MOzhit BYT'*

mayonnaise майонез *mayaNYES*

mead медовуха *midaVUkha*

mean значить (i) *ZNAchit'*

meat мясо *MYAsa*

meat мясной (adj) *miSNOY*

medicine лекарство *liKARSTva*

medium средний *SRYEDni*

meeting встреча *FSTRYEcha*

melon дыня *DYnya*

memory память (f) *PAmit'*

men's мужской *mushSKOY*

menthol ментол *minTOL*

menu меню *miNYU*

message сообщение *saapSCHYEniye*

meter метр *MYETR*

Metro метро *miTRO*

mezzanine бельэтаж *bileTASH*

microwave oven микроволновая печь *mikraVOL'naya PYECH'*

midnight полночь (f) *POLnach*

migration card миграционная карта *migratsiOnaya KARta*

mild слабый *SLAby*

milk молоко *malaKO*

millimeter миллиметр *miliMYETR*

million миллион *miliON*

mind ум *UM*

mine, my мой, моя, моё, мои *MOY, maYA, maYO, maI*

mineral water минеральная вода *miniRAL'naya vaDA*

minimal минимальный *miniMAL'ny*

minister пастор *PAStar*

minivan route taxi маршрутка *marSHRUTka;* маршрутное такси *marSHRUTnaya taKSI*

mink норка *NORka*

mint мята *MYAta*

Mint Монетный двор *maNYETny DVOR*

minute минута *miNUta;* **just a minute!** минуточку! *miNUtachku*

mirror зеркало *ZYERkala*

Miss, Mrs. госпожа *gaspaZHA*

Miss! девушка! *DYEvushka*

Mister господин *gaspaDIN*

mitten рукавица *rukaVItsa*

mixture микстура *mikSTUra*

mocha мокка *MOka*

modem модем *MOdem*

modern современный *savriMYEny*

monastery монастырь (m) *manaSTYR'*

Monday понедельник *paniDYEL'nik*

money деньги *DYEN'gi*

money order денежный перевод *DYEnizhny piriVOT*

monitor монитор *MOnitar*

month месяц *MYEsits*

monument памятник *PAmitnik*

more больше *BOL'she*

morning утро *Utra;* **in the morning** утром *Utram;* **good morning** доброе утро *DObraye Utra*

mortgage ипотека *ipaTYEka*

Moscow Москва *maskVA*

mosque мечеть (f) *miCHET'*
mother мать (f) *MAT'*
mountain гора *gaRA*
mouse мышь *MYSH*
mouth рот *ROT*
mouthwash зубной эликсир *zubNOY elikSIR*
movie фильм *FIL'M*
MP3 player МП3 плеер *EM PI TRI PLYEir*
much много *MNOga*
muffin кекс *KYEKS*
museum музей *muZYEY*
mushroom гриб *GRIP*
music музыка *MUzyka*
musical мюзикл *MYUzikl*
musical музыкальный *muzyKAL'ny*
Mussorgsky Theater Театр Мусоргского *tiATR MUsorgskava*
must надо *NAda*
mustache усы *uSY*
mustard горчица *garCHItsa*
mustard plaster горчичник *garCHICHnik*
myself (m) сам *SAM*
myself (f) сама *saMA*
mystery (film, novel) детектив *ditikTIF*

N

nail clippers кусачки *kuSACHki*
nail file пилка *PILka*
nail polish remover ацетон *atsiTON*
name: first name имя (n) *Imya;* **patronymic** отчество *Ochistva;* **family name** фамилия *faMIliya;* **my name is** меня зовут *miNYA zaVUT;* **what is your name?** как вас зовут? *KAK VAS zaVUT*
napkin салфетка *salFYETka*

narrow (too tight) тесны *tiSNY*
nationality национальность (f) *natsiaNAL'nast'*
nausea тошнота *tashnaTA*
near близко *BLISka*
nearby поблизости *paBLIzasti*
nearest ближайший *bliZHAYshi*
necessary нужно *NUZHna*
neck шея *SHEya*
necklace ожерелье *azhiRYEl'ye*
need: I need мне нужен *MNYE NUzhin;* мне нужна *MNYE nuzhNA;* мне нужно *MNYE NUZHna;* мне нужны *MNYE nuzhNY*
needle иголка *iGOLka*
nested doll матрёшка *maTRYOSHka*
never никогда *nikagDA*
Nevsky Невский *NYEfski*
new новый *NOvy*
newspaper газета *gaZYEta*
newsstand разетный киоск *gaZYETny kiOSK*
next следующий *SLYEduyushi*
night ночь (f) *NOCH;* **good night!** спокойной ночи! *spaKOYnay NOchi*
nightclub ночной клуб *nachNOY KLUP*
nightgown ночная рубашка *nachNAya ruBASHka*
nine девять *DYEvit'*
nine hundred девятьсот *divit'SOT*
nineteen девятнадцать *divitNAtsat'*
ninety девяносто *diviNOSta*
ninth девятый *diVYAty*
no нет *NYET*
noisy шумно *SHUMna*
nonprescription безрецептный *bizriTSEPTny*

non-smoking некуряший *nikuRYAshi*

nonsense ерунда *yirunDA*

noodles лапша *lapSHA*

noodle soup суп-лапша *SUP-lapSHA*

noon полдень (m) *POLdin'*

no one никто *niKTO*

normal нормальный *narMAL'ny*

north север *SYEvir*

nose нос *NOS*

not не *NYE*

notebook тетрадь (f) *tiTRAT''*

nothing ничего *nichiVO*

novel роман *raMAN*

November ноябрь (m) *naYABR'*

now сейчас *siCHAS*

number номер *NOmir*, число *chiSLO*

nurse медсестра *mitsiSTRA*

nut гайка *GAYka*

nut (food) орех *aRYEKH*

The Nutcracker Щелкунчик *schilKUNchik*

nylon нейлон *niyLON*

O

oatmeal овсянный *aFSYAny*

oats овёс *aVYOS*

obligation обязательство *abiZAtil'stva*

occupied занято *ZAnita*

o'clock (hour) час *CHAS*

October октябрь (m) *akTYABR'*

of course конечно *kaNYESHna*

office канцелярский *kantsiLYARski*

often часто *CHASta*

oil масло *MAsla*

ointment мазь (f) *MAS'*

Old Arbat Старый Арбат *STAry arBAT*

on на *NA*

once раз *RAS*

oncoming встречный *FSTRYECHny*

one (m) один *aDIN*

one (f) одна *aDNA*

oneself себе, себя *siBYE, siBYA*

one-room (apartment) однокомнатная *adnaKOMnatnaya*

onion лук *LUK*

only только *TOL'ka*

on time вовремя *VOvrimya*

onto на *NA*

onyx оникс *Oniks*

open открывать(ся) (i) *atkryVAtsa*, открыть(ся) (p) *atKRYtsa*

opened открыто *atKRYta*

opera опера *Opira*

opera glasses бинокль (m) *biNOKL'*

operetta оперетта *apiRYEta*

opposite напротив *naPROtif*

optician оптика *OPtika*

or или *Ili*

orange (n) апельсин *apil'SIN*

orange (adj) апельсиновый *apil'SInavy*

orchestra seat партер *parTYER*

order заказ *zaKAS*

order порядок *paRYAdak*

order заказывать (i) *zaKAzyvat'*, заказать (p) *zakaZAT'*

Orthodox православный *pravaSLAVny*

ouch! ой! *OY*

our наш, наша, наше, наши *NASH, NAsha, NAshe, NAshi*

outside вне *VNYE*

overheat перегреваться (i) *pirigriVAtsa*

oversized/overweight негабаритный *nigabaRITny*

owe: I owe (m) я должен *YA DOLzhin;* **I owe (f)** я должна *YA dalzhNA;* **You owe** Вы должны *VY dalzhNY*

Р

pack пачка *PACHka*
package посылка *paSYLka*
packet пакет *paKYET*
page страница *straNItsa*
paid parking платная парковка *PLATnaya parKOfska*
pair пара *PAra*
pajamas пижама *piZHAma*
palace дворец *dvaRYETS*
Palace of Congresses Дворец съездов *dvaRYETS SYEZdaf*
pancake блин *BLIN*
pancake house блинная *BLInaya*
panties трусики *TRUsiki*
pants брюки *BRYUki*
pantyhose колготки *kalGOTki*
paper (n) бумага *buMAga*
paper (adj) бумажный *buMAZHny*
paper clip скрепка *SKRYEPka*
paprika паприка *Paprika*
pardon простить (i) *praSTIT'*
pardon прощение *praSCHYEniye*
pardon me! простите! *praSTItye*
park парк *PARK*
parking стоянка *staYANka*
part часть (f) *CHAST'*
part (in the hair) пробор *praBOR*
partial частичный *chaSTICHny*
Partizan metro station Партизанская *partiZANskaya*
partner партнёр *partNYOR*

party (political) партия *PARtiya*
pass by проходить (i) *prakhaDIT'*
passenger пассажир *pasaZHYR*
passing обгон *abGON*
passport паспорт *PASpart*
past прошлый *PROshly*
paste паста *PASta*
paste (p) вставить *FSTAvit'*
pastry пирожное *piROZHnaye;* пирожок *piraZHOK*
path дорожка *daROSHka,* путь (m) *PUT',* тропинка *traPINka*
patronymic отчество *Ochistva*
pawn (chess) пешка *PYESHka*
pay платить (i) *plaTIT'*
pay telephone телефон-афтомат *tiliFON-aftaMAT*
payment оплата *aPLAta,* плата *PLAta,* платёж *plaTYOSH*
peach персик *PYERsik*
pear груша *GRUsha*
pearl жемчуг *ZHEMchuk*
peas горох *gaROKH*
pedestrian пешеходный *pishiKHODny*
pelmeni (Siberian dumplings) пельмени *pil'MYEni*
pen ручка *RUCHka*
pencil карандаш *karanDASH*
penicillin пеницилин *pinitsiLIN*
people's народный *naRODny*
pepper перец *PYErits*
Pepsi Пепси *PEPsi*
performance спектакль (m) *spikTAKL'*
perfume духи *duKHI*
permanent химическая завивка *khiMIchiskaya zaVIFka*

person to person на человека *na chilaVYEka*

personal личный *LICHny*

personal computer персональный компьютер *persaNAL'ni kamPYUter*

Petersburg Петербург *pitirBURK*

pharmacy аптека *apTYEka*

pheasant фасан *faSAN*

phone позвонить (p) *pazvaNIT'*

photograph фотографировать (i) *fatagraFIravat'*

phrasebook разговорник *razgaVORnik*

pick up (drive by) заехать (p) *zaYEkhat'*

picture картина *karTIna*

picture (photo) фотография *fataGRAfiya*

pie пирог *piROK*

piece (chess) фигура *fiGUra*

pike/perch судак *suDAK*

pillow подушка *paDUSHka*

pin булавка *buLAFka*

PIN number код *KOT*

pinch жать (i) *ZHAT'*

pineapple ананас *anaNAS*

pink розовый *ROzavy*

pipe трубка *TRUPka*

pipe tobacco трубочный табак *TRUbachny taBAK*

place место *MYESta*

plaid в клетку *f KLYETku*

plans планы *PLAny*

plant растение *raSTYEniye*

plate тарелка *taRYELka*

platform платформа *platFORma*

platinum платина *PLAtina*

play играть (i) *iGRAT'*

please пожалуйста *paZHAlusta*

pleasing приятно *priYATna*

pleasure удовольствие *udaVOL'stviye*; **with pleasure** с удовольствием *s udaVOL'stviyim*

pliers плоскогубцы *plaskaGUPtsy*

plug розетка *raZYETka*

plum слива *SLIva*

pocket (adj) карманный *karMAny*

pocketbook сумка *SUMka*

poetry стихотворение *stikhatvaRYEniye*

point пункт *PUNKT*

pole палка *PALka*

police милиция *miLItsiya*

polka dot горошек *gaROshik*

polo shirt футболка *fudBOLka*

polyclinic поликлиника *paliKLInika*

polyester полиэфир *palieFIR*

pomegranate гранат *graNAT*

pond пруд *PRUT*

pony tail хвост *KHVOST*

pop поп *POP*

poplin поплин *paPLIN*

popular популярный *papuLYARny*

porcelain фарфоровый *farFOravy*

pork свиной *sviNOY*

portable computer переносный компьютер *piriNOSny kamPYUter*

porter носильщик *naSIL'shik*

post office почта *POCHta*

postcard открытка *atKRYTka*

poster плакат *plaKAT*

potatoes картофель (m) *karTOfil'*; картошка *karTOshka*

pound фунт *FUNT*

powder пудра *PUdra*

practically практически *prakTIchiski*

prefer предпочитать (i) *pritpachiTAT'*

premium премия *PRYEmiya*

prescription рецепт *riTSEPT*

press гладить (i) *GLAdit'*

pressing глажение *GLAzhiniye*

price цена *tsiNA*

priest священник *sviSHEnik*

print напечатать *napiCHAtat'*

printed matter бандероль (f) *bandiROL'*

printer принтер *PRINter*

private taxi частник *CHASnik*

problem проблема *praBLYEma*

process процесс *praTSES*

profession профессия *praFYEsiya*

profit прибыль (f) *PRIbyl'*

program программка *praGRAMka*

prohibited запрещено *zaprishiNO*

Protestant протестантский *pratiSTANTski*

provider провайдер *praVAIdyer*

Pulkovo Airport Пулково *PULkava*

pull! (toward oneself) к себе *k siBYE*

pull (a tooth) удалить (p) *udaLIT'*

pull-out couch раскладной диван *raskladNOY diVAN*

pump насос *naSOS*

pumpkin тыква *TYKva*

punch (a ticket) пробить (p) *praBIT'*

purchase покупка *paKUPka*

push нажать (p) *naZHAT'*

push! (away from oneself) от себя *at siBYA*

put, place положить (p) *palaZHYT'*, поставить (p) *paSTAvit'*

Q

quality качество *KAchistva*

quantity (number) количество *kaliCHYEstva*

quart кварта *KVARta*

quarter четверть (f) *CHETvirt'*

quartz кварцовый *KVARtsavy*

queen королева *karaLYEva*

queen (cards) дама *DAma*

Queen of Spades Пиковая дама *PIkavaya DAma*

quiet! тише! *TIshe*

R

rabbi раввин *raVIN*

rabbit кролик *KROlik*

radiator радиатор *radiAtar*

radio радио *RAdio*

radish редиска *riDISka*

ragout рагу *raGU*

railroad железнодорожный *zhiliznadaROZHny*

rain дождь (m) *DOSH*

raincoat куртка *KURTka*; плащ *PLASH*

raisin изюм *iZYUM*

raspberries малина *maLIna*

rayon вискоза *viSKOza*

razor бритва *BRITva*

razor blade лезвие *LYEZviye*

reach (get to) попасть (p) *paPAST'*

ready готово *gaTOva*

rear задний *ZADni*

rear orchestra амфитеатр *amfitiATR*

receipt квитанция *kviTANtsiya*

receive, pick up получить (p) *paluCHIT'*

reception room приёмная *priYOMnaya*

recommend рекомендовать (i) *rikamindaVAT'*

record пластинка *plaSTINka*

record player проигрыватель (m) *praIgryvatil'*

red красный *KRASny*

Red Square Красная площадь *KRASnaya PLOshat'*

refrigerator холодильник
khalaDIL'nik
regards! привет! *priVYET*
registered letter заказное
письмо *zakazNOye piS'MO*
**registration (check-in
counter)** регистрация
rigiSTRAtsiya
remembrance на память *na
PAmit'*
rent взять на прокат *VZYAT'
na praKAT*
rental прокат *praKAT*
repair чинить (i) *chiNIT'*,
починить (p) *pachiNIT'*
repairs ремонт *riMONT*;
auto repair shop
автосервис *aftaSYERvis*
repeat повторить (p)
paftaRIT'
replace заменить (p)
zamiNIT'
republic республика
riSPUblika
request заявка *zaYAFka*
request просить (i) *praSIT'*
reservation бронирование
braNIravaniye
reserve забронировать (p)
zabraNIravat'
reserved заказано *zaKAzana*
restaurant ресторан
ristaRAN
restriction ограничение
agraniCHEniye
restroom (men's) мужской
туалет *mushSKOY tuaLYET*;
(ladies') женский туалет
ZHENsky tuaLYET
retail price розничная цена
ROZnichnaya tsiNA
return обратный *aBRATny*;
there and back туда и
обратно *tuDA I aBRATna*
return восвращать(ся) (i)
vazvraSHAtsa, вернуть(ся)
(p) *virNUtsa*

revolution революция
rivaLYUtsiya
rib ребро *riBRO*
rice рис *RIS*
ride проезд *praYEST*
right правый *PRAvy*; **to the
right** направо *naPRAva*;
on the right справа
SPRAva
right of way преимущество
priiMUshistva
ring кольцо *kal'TSO*
ring (theater) ярус *YArus*
river река *riKA*
road дорога *daROga*
road map автодорожная карта
aftadaROZHnaya KARta
roast beef ростбиф *rastBIF*
robe халат *khaLAT*
rock рок *ROK*
roll булочка *BUlachka*
roll (of something) рулон
ruLON
rook (chess) ладья *laD'YA*
room (hotel) номер *NOmir*
rouge румяна *ruMYAna*
row ряд *RYAT*
rubber band резинка
riZINka
ruble рубль (m) *RUBL'*
ruby рубин *ruBIN*
ruler линейка *liNYEka*
rum ром *ROM*
Russia Россия *raSIya*
Russian российский
raSIski
Russian (m) русский *RUski*
Russian (f) русская
RUskaya
Russian citizen (f) россиянка
rasiYANka
Russian citizen (m)
россиянин *rasiYAnin*
Russian Federation
Российская Федерация
raSIskaya fidiRAtsiya
rye ржаной *rzhaNOY*
rye рожь (f) *ROSH*

S

sable соболь (m) *SObal'*

saccharin сахарин *sakhaRIN*

safe сейф *SYEYF*

sail away отплывать (i) *atplyVAT'*

salad салат *saLAT*

salami колбаса *kalbaSA*

sale продажа *praDAzha*

sale items товары по сниженным ценам *taVAry pa SNIzhinym tsiNAM*

salmon сёмга *SYOMga*

salt соль (f) *SOL'*

sample попробовать (p) *paPRObavat'*

sandwich бутерброд *butirBROT*

sanitary napkins гигиенические салфетки *gigiiNIchiskiye salFYETki*

sapphire сапфир *sapFIR*

sateen сатин *saTIN*

satin атлас *atLAS*

Saturday суббота *suBOta*

sauce соуса *SOUsa*

sauerkraut квашенная капуста *KVAshinaya kaPUSta*

sauna сауна *SAUna*

save сохранить *sakhraNIT'*

say сказать (p) *skaZAT'*

scanner сканер *SKAner*

scarf шарф *SHARF*

schedule расписание *raspiSAniye*

schnitzel шницель (m) *SHNItsil'*

science наука *naUka*

science fiction научно-популярный *naUCHna-papuLYARny*

scissors ножницы *NOZHnitsy*

score счёт *SHOT*

Scotch tape скотч *SKOTCH*

scrambled eggs яичница-болтунья *yaICHnitsa-balTUn'ya*

screw винтик *VINtik*

screwdriver отвёртка *atVYORTka*

sea море *MOrye*

seasickness морская болезнь *marSKAya baLYEZN'*

seasoning приправа *priPRAva*

seat место *MYESta*

second (sixtieth part of a minute) секунда *siKUNda*

second второй *ftaROY*

section отдел *aDYEL*

security безопасность (f) *bizaPASnast'*

security охрана *aKHRAna*

sedative успокаивающее *uspaKAivayushiye*

see смотреть (i) *smaTRYET'*

seem казаться (i) *kaZAtsa*

self сам *SAM*

sell продавать (i) *pradaVAT'*

semi-dry полусухое *palusuKHOye*

send послать (p) *paSLAT'*

senior старший *STARshi*

separately отдельно *aDYEL'na*

September сентябрь (m) *sinTYABR'*

seriously серьёзно *siR'YOZna*

service обслуживание *apSLUzhivaniye*

service bureau бюро обслуживания *byuRO apSLUzhivaniya*

service (religious) служба *SLUZHba*

service station бензоколонка *binzakaLONka*

set (hairdo) укладка *uKLATka*

seven семь *SYEM'*

seven hundred семьсот *sim'SOT*

seventeen семнадцать *simNAtsat'*

seventh седьмой *sid'MOY*

seventy семьдесят *SYEM'disit*

sew пришить (p) *priSHYT"*

shadow тень (f) *TYEN'*

shame: what a shame! как жаль! *KAK ZHAL'*

shampoo шампунь (m) *shamPUN'*

sharpener точилка *taCHILka*

shave побриться (p) *paBRItsa*

she она *aNA*

sheepskin овчина *afCHIna*

Sheremetyevo Airport Шереметьево *shiriMYEt'iva*

shift (gear) сцепление *tsiPLYEniye*

shine светить (i) *SVYEtit'*

shipment отправка *atPRAFka*

shirt рубашка *ruBASHka*, сорочка *saROCHka*

shish kebab шашлык *shaSHLYK*

shoelace шнурок *shnuROK*

shoes обувь (f) *Obuf'*; **men's shoes** ботинки *baTINki*; **women's shoes** туфли *TUfli*

shop, store магазин *magaZIN*

shopping mall торговый комплекс *tarGOvy KOMpliks*

short короткий *kaROTki*

shorts шорты *SHORty*

shoulder плечо *pliCHO*

show варьете *var'yiTE*

show шоу *SHO*

shower душ *DUSH*

shuffle перетасовать (p) *piriTAsavat'*

shut up (keep silent) молчать (i) *malCHAT"*

sick: I feel sick я заболел *YA zabaLYEL*

sickness болезнь (f) *baLYEZN'*

side сторона *staraNA*

side бок *BOK*

sideburn височка *viSOCHka*

sign расписаться (p) *raspiSAtsa*

signal сигнальный *sigNAL'ny*

signature подпись *POTpis'*

sign language немая азбука *neMAya AZbuka*

silk шёлк *SHOLK*

silver серебро *siriBRO*

silver (adj) серебряный *siRYEbriny*

sing петь (i) *PYET"*

single bed односпальная кровать *adnaSPAL'naya kraVAT"*

single ticket единый билет *yiDIny biLYET*

sink умывальник *umyVAL'nik*

sister сестра *siSTRA*

sit сидеть (i) *siDYET"*, посидеть (p) *pasiDYET"*

six шесть *SHEST'*

six hundred шестьсот *shist'SOT*

sixteen шестнадцать *shistNAtsat'*

sixth шестой *shiSTOY*

sixty шестьдесят *shizdiSYAT*

size размер *razMYER*

skate кататься на коньках *kaTAtsa na kan'KAKH*

skates коньки *kan'KI*

ski кататься на лыжах *kaTAtsa na LYzhakh*

skin кожа *KOzha*

skirt юбка *YUPka*

skis лыжи *LYzhi*

slacks штаны *shtaNY*

sled санки *SANki*

Sleeping Beauty Спящая красавица *SPYAschaya kraSAvitsa*

sleeping pills снотворное *snaTVORnaye*

sleeve рукав *ruKAF*

slide слайд *SLAYT*

slip (ladies') комбинация *kambiNAtsiya*

slipper тапочка *TApachka*

slippery скользкий *SKOL'ski*

slow медленный *MYEdliny*

slower медленнее *MYEdliniye*

small мелький *MYEL'ki*

smaller меньше *MYEN'she*

smart-card смарт-карта *SMART KARta*

smile улыбаться (i) *ulyBAtsa*

smoke курить (i) *kuRIT'*, закурить (p) *zakuRIT'*

smoking курящий *kuRYAshi*

smorgasbord шведский стол *SHVYETski STOL*

snack bar закусочная *zaKUsachnaya*

snow снег *SNYEK*

so так *TAK*

soap мыло *MYla*

soccer футбол *fudBOL*

socialist социалистический *satsialiSTIchiski*

sock носок *naSOK*

soft мягкий *MYAki*

soft drink лимонад *limaNAT*

sole (shoe) подмётка *padMYOTka*

solid-color однотонное *adnaTOnaye*

solyanka (fish or meat soup) солянка *saLYANka*

someone кто-нибудь *KTO-nibut'*

something что-нибудь *SHTO-nibut'*

son сын *SYN*

soon скоро *SKOra*

sore throat ангина *anGIna*

soup суп *SUP*

sour cream сметана *smiTAna*

south юг *YUK*

souvenir сувенир *suviNIR*

Soviet советский *saVYETski*

space космос *KOSmas*

spades (cards) пики *PIki*

spare part запчасть (f) *zapCHAST'*

spark plug свеча *sviCHA*

speak говорить (i) *gavaRIT'*, поговорить (p) *pagavaRIT'*

special особый *aSOby*

special delivery письмо с доставкой *piS'MO z daSTAFkay*

specialty (of the house) фирменное блюдо *FIRminaye BLYUda*

speed скорость (f) *SKOrast'*

spin кружиться (i) *kruZHYtsa*

spinach шпинат *shpiNAT*

splendid прекрасный *priKRASny*

sponge мочалка *maCHALka*

spoon ложка *LOSHka*

sporting goods спорттовары *sparttaVAry*

spot пятно *pitNO*

spring весна *viSNA*; **in the spring** весной *viSNOY*

square площадь (f) *PLOshat'*; **Red Square** Красная площадь *KRASnaya PLOshat'*

St. Petersburg Санкт Петербург *SANKT pitirBURK*

stadium стадион *stadiON*

stage сцена *TSEna*

stainless steel нержавейка *nirzhaVYEYka*

stamp марка *MARka*

stand стоять (i) *staYAT'*; **taxi stand** стоянка такси *staYANka taKSI*

stand up вставать (i) *fstaVAT'*

starched накрахмаленный *nakrakhMAliny*

starting time начало *naCHAla*

state (one of the United States) штат *SHTAT*

state государственный *gasuDARSTviny*

station станция *STANtsiya*

station (railroad) вокзал *vagZAL*

station-to-station на номер *na NOmir*

St. Basil's Cathedral Храм Басилия Блаженного/ Покровский собор *KHRAM vaSIliya blaZHEnava/ paKROFski saBOR*

steak бифштекс *bifSHTYEKS*

steal украсть (p) *uKRAST'*

steam room парильня *paRIL'nya*

steering wheel руль (m) *RUL'*, рулевое колесо *ruliVOye kaliSO*

stem (of a watch) головка *gaLOFka*

stewed тушёный *tuSHOny*

stewed fruit компот *kamPOT*

stocking чулок *chuLOK*

stomach желудок *zhiLUdak*; **upset stomach** желудочное расстройство *zhiLUdachnaye raSTROYSTva*

stone камень (f) *KAmin'*

stop! стоп! *STOP*

stop (bus, trolley) остановка *astaNOFka*

stop (restrain) задержать (p) *zadirZHAT'*

stop (halt) остановиться (p) *astanaVItsa*

store магазин *magaZIN*

story (tale) рассказ *raSKAS*

straight прямой *priMOY*; **straight ahead** прямо *PRYAma*

strawberries клубника *klubNIka*

street улица *Ulitsa*

striking (extravagant) экстравагантное *ekstravaGANTnaye*

string шпагат *shpaGAT*

string beans стручковая фасоль *struchKOvaya faSOL'*

stripe полоска *paLOSka*

strong крепкий *KRYEPki*

student студент *stuDYENT*

stuffed cabbage голубцы *galupTSY*

sturgeon осетрина *asiTRIna*

sturgeon soup солянка *saLYANka*

stylish модный *MODny*

subway метро *miTRO*

such такой *taKOY*

suede замша *zamSHA*

sugar сахар *SAkhar*

suit костюм *kaSTYUM*

suitcase чемодан *chimaDAN*

summer лето *LYEta*; **in the summer** летом *LYEtam*

sun солнце *SONtse*

sunburn солнечный ожог *SOLnichny aZHOK*

Sunday воскресенье *vaskriSYEn'ye*

sunglasses солнечные очки *SOLnichniye achKI*

suntan загар *zaGAR*

suntan lotion крем от загара *KRYEM at zaGAra*

super! классно! *KLAsna*

super: you're super! молодец! *malaDYETS*

supermarket гастроном *gastraNOM*

supplies товары *taVAry*

suppository свеча *sviCHA*

Swan Lake Лебединое озеро *libiDInaye Ozira*

sweater свитер *SVItir*

sweet сладкий *SLATki*

swelling опухоль (f) *Opukhal'*

swim купаться (i) *kuPAtsa*, плавать (i) *PLAvat'*

swimming pool бассейн *baSYEYN*

switch выключатель (m) *vyklyuCHAtil'*
swollen вздут *VZDUT*
synagogue синагога *sinaGOga*
system система *siSTYEma*

T

table стол *STOL*, столик *STOlik*
taillight задняя фара *ZADniya FAra*
tailor ателье мод *atiL'YE MOT*
take, get взять (p) *VZYAT'*
take (escort) проводить (i) *pravaDIT'*
take (medicine) принимать (i) *priniMAT'*
take (transport by vehicle) отвезти (p) *atviSTI*
takeout вынос *Vynas*
talcum тальк *TAL'K*
tall высокий *vySOki*
tampon тампон *tamPON*
tangerine мандарин *mandaRIN*
tape лента *LYENta*, плёнка *PLYONka*
tax налог *naLOK*
taxi такси (n) *taKSI*
taxi stand стоянка такси *staYANka taKSI*
tea чай *CHAY*
teacher преподаватель (m) *pripadaVAtil'*
telegram телеграмма *tiliGRAma*
telephone телефон *tiliFON*
telephone booth телефонная кабина *tiliFOnaya kaBIna*; **pay telephone** телефон-афтомат *tiliFON-aftaMAT*
telephone call разговор *razgaVOR*
telephone card телефонная карта *tiliFOnaya KARta*

telephone receiver трубка *TRUPka*
television телевизор *tiliVIzar*
telex телекс *TYEliks*
temperature температура *timpiraTUra*
temporary временный *VRYEminy*
ten десять *DYEsit'*
tennis теннис *TYEnis*
tenth десятый *diSYAty*
tequila текила *tiKIla*
terrible страшный *STRASHny*
terrycloth махровая ткань *maKHROvaya TKAN'*
text текст *TYEKST*
Thai тайский *TAYski*
thank you спасибо *spaSIba*
that one то *TO*
that's fine ладно *Ladna*
theater театр *tiATR*
their их *IKH*
there там *TAM*, туда *tuDA*
thermometer термометр *tirMOmitr*
they они *aNI*
thing вещь (f) *VYESH*
think думать (i) *DUmat'*
third третий *TRYEti*
thirsty: I'm thirsty мне хочется пить *MNYE KHOchitsa PIT'*
thirteen тринадцать *triNATsat'*
thirty тридцать *TRItsat'*
this это *Eta*
thousand тысяча *TYsicha*
three три *TRI*
three hundred триста *TRISta*
threesome трое *TROye*
throat горло *GORla*
through через *CHEris*
thumbtack кнопка *KNOPka*
Thursday четверг *chitVYERK*
thus так *TAK*
ticket билет *biLYET*

ticket punch компостер
kamPOStir

tie галстук *GALstuk*

tighten подвернуть (p)
padvirNUT'

time время (n) *VRYEmya;*
how long (how much time)
сколько времени *SKOL'ka
VRYEmini*

tint тон *TON*

tire шина *SHYna;* **the tire is
flat** спустила шина
SPUStila SHYna

tired (m) устал *uSTAL*

tired (f) устала *uSTAla*

tissue салфетка *salFYETka*

title название *naZVAniye*

to в *V,* на *NA*

toaster тостер *TOStir*

tobacco табак *taBAK*

today сегодня *siVODnya*

toenail ноготь (m) *NOgat'*

together вместе *VMYEStye*

toilet унитаз *uniTAS*

toilet paper туалетная
бумажка *tuaLYETnaya
buMAZHka*

toiletries shop парфюмерия
parfyuMYEriya

token жетон *zhiTON*

tomato помидор *pamiDOR*

tomorrow завтра *ZAFtra*

tongue язык *yiZYK*

tonight сегодня вечером
siVODnya VYEchiram

too (excessively) слишком
SLISHkam

tooth зуб *ZUP*

toothache зубная боль
zubNAya BOL'

toothbrush зубная щётка
zubNAya SHOTka

toothpaste зубная паста
zubNAya PASta

top: from the top сверху
SVYERkhu; **on top** над
NAT

topaz топаз *taPAS*

touch-up поправка *paPRAFka*

tour тур *TUR*

tourist (n) турист *tuRIST*

tourist (adj) туристический
turiSTIchiski

tourmaline турмалин
turmaLIN

toward к *K*

towel полотенце *palaTYENtse*

tower башня *BASHnya*

toy игрушка *iGRUSHka*

trade торговля *tarGOvlya*

traffic движение *dviZHEniye*

traffic jam пробка *PROPka*

train поезд *POyist*

train car вагон *vaGON*

tram/trolleycar трамвай
tramVAY

transfer перевод *piriVOT,*
переход *piriKHOT*

transfer передать (p)
piriDAT, пересесть (p)
piriSYEST'

transformer трансформатор
transfarMAtar

translation перевод *piriVOT*

transmission (auto)
переключение скоростей
*piriklyuCHEniye
skaraSTYEY*

transportation перевозка
piriVOSka, транспорт
TRANSpart

traveler's check дорожный
чек *daROZHny CHEK*

tree дерево *DYEriva*

trim подстричь (p)
padSTRICH'

trip поездка *paYEska;*
проезд *praYEST*

trolleybus троллейбус
traLYEYbus

trout форель (m) *faRYEL'*

trunk (of a car) багажник
baGAZHnik

try on примерить (p)
priMYErit'

tsar царь (m) *TSAR'*

Tuesday вторник *FTORnik*
tuna тунец *tuNYETS*
turkey индейка *inDYEYka*
turn (in a line) очередь (f) *Ochirit'*
turn оборот *abaROT*
turn повернуть (p) *pavirNUT'*
turnip репька *RYEP'ka*
turquoise бирюза *biRYUza*
tweezers щипчики *SHIPchiki*
twelve двенадцать *dviNAtsat'*
twenty двадцать *DVAtsat'*
twigs веник *VYEnik*
twisted растянут *raSTYAnut*
two два *DVA*
twosome двое *DVOye*
two hundred двести *DVYESti*
two-room (apartment) двукомнатная *dvuKOMnatnaya*
typewriter пишущая машина *PIshushaya maSHYna*

U

ugh! фу! *FU*
umbrella зонт *ZONT*
under под *POT*
underpants (men's) трусы *truSY*
undershirt майка *MAYka*
understand понимать (i) *paniMAT'*
underwear нижнее бельё *NIZHnie biL'YO*
undress раздеться (p) *razDYEtsa*
union союз *saYUS*
United States Соединённые Штаты *sayidiNYOniye SHTAty*
university университет *univirsiTYET*
until до *DO*
until later! пока! *paKA*

up вверх *VVYERKH*
upset stomach желудочное расстройство *zhiLUdachnaye raSTROYSTva*
urgently срочно *SROCHna*
USA США *SA SHA A*
use использоваться (i) *isPOL'zavatsa*
USSR СССР *ES ES ES ER*
U-turn разворот *razvaROT*
Uzbek узбекский *uzBYEkski*

V

vacancy: no vacancy мест нет *MYEST NYET*
valley долина *daLIna*
valuable ценный *TSEny*
valuables ценные вещи *TSEniye VYEshi*
value (market) рыночная цена *RYnachnaya tsiNA*
van микроавтобус *mikraaFTObus*
vanilla сливочное *SLIvachnaye*
VCR видео-магнитофон *VIdio-magnitaFON*
veal телятина *tiLYAtina*
vegetables овощи *Ovashi*
vegetarian вегетарианский *vigitariANsky*
velvet бархат *BARkhat*
velveteen вельвет *vil'VYET*
Vernissage Вернисаж *virniSASH*
very очень *Ochin'*
(the) very самый *SAmy*
victory победа *paBYEda*
view вид *VIT*
village село *siLO*
vinegar уксус *UKsus*
visa виза *VIza*
vitamin витамин *vitaMIN*
Vnukovo Airport Внуково *VNYkava*
vodka водка *VOTka*

vodka glass рюмка *RYUMka*
voice голос *GOlas*
voucher ваучер *VAUchir*
voyage: Bon voyage!
Счастливого пути!
shastLIvava puTI

W

waist талия *TAliya*
wait ждать (i) *ZHDAT'*,
подождать (p) *padaZHDAT'*
waiter официант *afitsiANT*
waiter! молодой человек!
malaDOY chilaVYEK
waitress официантка
afitsiANTka
waitress! девушка!
DYEvushka
wake разбудить (p)
razbuDIT'
walk ходить (i) *khaDIT'*
walker ходунки *khadunKI*
wallet бумажник
buMAZHnik
want хотеть (i) *khaTYET'*;
I want я хочу *YA
khaCHU*; **you want** ты
хочешь *TY KHOchish*;
he/she wants он/она хочет
ON/aNA KHOchit; **we want**
мы хотим *MY khaTIM*; **you
want** вы хотите *VY
khaTItye*; **they want** они
хотят *aNI khaTYAT*
war война *vayNA*
warm тёплый *TYOply*
warmth тепло *tiPLO*
wash, washing (of clothes)
стирка *STIRka*
wash (clothes) стирать (i)
stiRAT'
wash (shampoo) мытьё
myT'YO
wash (give a shampoo)
помыть голову *paMYT'
GOlavu*
washbasin тазик *TAzik*

washing machine стиральная
машина *stiRAL'naya
maSHYna*
wash and wear немнущаяся
ткань *niMNUshayasya
TKAN'*
watch часы *chiSY*
water вода *vaDA*
watermelon арбуз *arBUS*
wave волна *valNA*
we мы *MY*
weak слабый *SLAby*
weakness слабость (f)
SLAbast'
weather погода *paGOda*
web page Web страница *WEB
straNItsa*
wedding ring обручальное
кольцо *abruCHAL'naye
kal'TSO*
Wednesday среда *sriDA*
week неделя *niDYElya*
well! ну! *NU*
west запад *ZApat*
what что *SHTO*
what for зачем *zaCHYEM*
wheat пшеница *pshiNItsa*
wheel колесо *kaliSO*
wheelchair инвалидное
кресло *invaLIDnaye
KRESla*
when когда *kagDA*
where где *GDYE*
where from откуда *atKUda*
where to, which way куда
kuDA
which какой *kaKOY*,
который *kaTOry*
whipped взбитый *VZBIty*
whipped cream взбитые
сливки *VZBItiye SLIFki*
white белый *BYEly*
who кто *KTO*
whose чей, чья, чьё, чьи
CHEY, CHYA, CHYO, CHI
why почему *pachiMU*
wide широкий *shiROki*
wife жена *zhiNA*

will be быть (i) *BYT'*; **I will be** я буду *YA BUdu*; **you will be** ты будешь *TY BUdish*; **he/she will be** он/она будет *ON/aNA BUdit*; **we will be** мы будем *MY BUdim*; **you will be** вы будете *VY BUditye*; **they will be** они будут *aNI BUdut*

win выиграть (p) *VYigrat'*

wind ветер *VYEtir*

wind (a watch) заводить (i) *zavaDIT*

window окно *akNO*; окошко *aKOshka*

windshield ветровое стекло *vitraVOye stiKLO*

windshield wiper стеклочиститель (m) *stiklachiSTItil'*

wine вино *viNO*

wineglass бокал *baKAL*

winter зима *ziMA*; **in the winter** зимой *ziMOY*

wish желать (i) *zhiLAT'*

with с *S*

withdrawal slip расходный ордер *rasKHODny ORdir*; **make a withdrawal** принять вклад *priNYAT' FKLAT*

without без *BYES*

wolf волк *VOLK*

woman женщина *ZHENshina*

women's женский *ZHENski*

wonderful замечательно *zamiCHAtil'na*

wool шерсть (f) *SHERST'*

word слово *SLOva*

work работать (f) *raBOtat'*

worker, working рабочий *raBOchi*

worse хуже *KHUzhe*

would бы *BY*

wound рана *RAna*

wrap завернуть (p) *zavirNUT'*

wraparound накидка *naKITka*

wrench гаечный ключ *GAyichny KLYUCH*

wrist запястье *zaPYASt'ye*

wristwatch наручные часы *naRUCHniye chiSY*

write писать (i) *piSAT*, написать (p) *napiSAT'*; **write down** записать (p) *zapiSAT'*; **write out** выписать (p) *VYpisat'*

writer писатель *piSAtil'*

writing pad блокнот *blakNOT*

writing paper бумага для писем *buMAga dlya PIsim*

wrong: you've reached a wrong number вы не туда попали *VY NYE tuDA paPAli*; **something wrong** проблема *praBLYEma*

Y

yard ярд *YART*

year год *GOT*

yellow жёлтый *ZHOLty*

yes да *DA*

yesterday вчера *fchiRA*

yet уже *uZHE*

yield уступить (p) *ustuPIT'*

yogurt кефир *kiFIR*

you ты, вы *TY, VY*

young молодой *malaDOY*

young man! молодой человек! *malaDOY chilaVYEK*

your твой, твоя, твоё, твои *TVOY, tvaYA, tvaYO, tvaI*, ваш, ваша, ваше, ваши *VASH, VAsha, VAshe, VAshi*

Z

zero нуль (m) *NUL'*

zoo зоопарк *zaaPARK*

RUSSIAN-ENGLISH DICTIONARY

А

а and, but

абонементная книжка book of tickets

абрикос apricot

август August

авиаписьмо airmail letter

авоська "just in case" (string bag)

австралиец (m) Australian

австралийка (f) Australian

Австралия Australia

автобус bus

автодорожная карта road map

автоматически automatically

автоматический automatic

автомобиль (m) car

автомойка car wash

автор author

авторизованный authorized

автосалон auto repair

автосервис auto repair shop

адаптер adapter

адвокат lawyer

администратор administrator

адрес address

Азия Asia

Айриш-кофе Irish coffee

аквамарин aquamarine

аккумулятор car battery

аллергия allergy

амальгама amalgam filling

Америка America

американец (m) American

американка (f) American

американский American

аметист amethyst

амфитеатр rear orchestra

ананас pineapple

ангина sore throat

английский English

англичанин (m) British (Englishman)

англичанка (f) British (Englishwoman)

Англия England

антисептик antiseptic

анкета application

антракт intermission

апельсин orange

апельсиновый (adj) orange

апрель (m) April

аптека pharmacy, drugstore

артишок artichoke

арбуз watermelon

аспирин aspirin

ассорти (n) assortment

Астория Astoria

ателье мод tailor

атлас satin

Африка Africa

ацетон nail polish remover

аэропорт airport

Б

багаж baggage

багажная бирка baggage claim check

багажник trunk (of a car)

баклажан eggplant

балет ballet

балкон balcony

балык filet of sturgeon

бампер bumper

банан banana

бандероль (f) printed matter

банк bank

банка can, jar

банкир banker

банковская карта bank/debit card

банкомат ATM (automatic teller machine)
баня bathhouse
бар bar
баранина lamb
бархат velvet
баскетбол basketball
бассейн swimming pool
батерейка, батерея battery
батон loaf
башня tower
беговые лыжи cross-country skis
бедро hip
без without
безопасность (f) security
безрецептный nonprescription
белокурый blond
белый white
бельэтаж mezzanine
бензин gasoline
бензобак gas tank
бензоколонка service station
бензонасос fuel pump
беспокоить disturb
бессоница insomnia
беф-строганов beef Stroganoff
библиотека library
бизнес business
бизнес-ланч business lunch
бизнесмен businessman
билет ticket
бинокль (m) opera glasses
бинт bandage
бирка claim check
бирюза turquoise
бифштекс steak
бланк blank form
ближайший nearest
близко near
блин pancake/bliny
блинная pancake house
блокнот writing pad
блузка blouse
блюдо dish, food
блюз blues
бог god
Боже мой! My goodness!

бок side
бокал wineglass
бокс boxing
более more
болезнь (f) sickness
болеть (i) ache; **болит** it hurts
болт bolt (fastener)
боль (f) pain, ache
больница hospital
больно painful, it hurts
больше more, larger
большой large
Большой театр Bolshoi Theater
Борис Годунов Boris Godunov
борода beard
борщ beet soup
ботинки men's shoes
браслет bracelet
брат brother
брать взаймы borrow
брелок charm
бриллиант diamond
бритва razor
бритьё a shave
бровь (f) eyebrow
бронирование reservation
бронхит chest cold
брошь (f) brooch
брюки pants
брюнетка brunette
бубны diamonds (cards)
будильник alarm clock
будущий future; **в будущем году** next year
булавка pin
булочка roll
булочная bakery
бульон bouillon
бумага paper
бумажник wallet
бумажный (adj) paper
бусы beads
бутерброд sandwich
бутылка bottle
буфет buffet, snack bar

бы would
бывать (i) to be
быстрый fast
быть (i) to be, will be; **я буду** I will be; **ты будешь** you will be; **он/она будет** he/she will be; **мы будем** we will be; **вы будете** you will be; **они будут** they will be
бюро bureau
бюро обслуживания service bureau
бюстгальтер bra

В

в in, into, to
вагон train car
валет jack (cards)
валюта foreign currency
ванна bathtub
варёный boiled
варенье jelly
варьете show
вата cotton
ваучер voucher
ваш, ваша, ваше, ваши your
вверх up
ввод enter
веер fan
век century
великий great (too big)
вельвет velveteen
веник bunch of twigs
вентилятор auto fan
Вернисаж Vernissage
вернуть(ся) (p) return
весна spring; **весной** in the spring
ветер wind
ветровое стекло windshield
ветчина ham
вечер evening; **вечером** in the evening
вечернее платье evening dress
вешалка hanger

вещь (f) thing
взбитый whipped
взглянуть (p) look at
вздут swollen
взять (p) take, get
вид view
видео-магнитофон VCR
виза visa
вилка fork
вино wine
виноград grape(s)
виноградный (adj) grape
винтик screw
виски whiskey
вискоза rayon
височка sideburn
витамин vitamin
вишня cherry
вклад deposit
вместе together
вне outside
вниз down
Внуково Vnukovo
внутри inside
во время during
вовремя on time
вода water
водитель (m) driver
водительские права driver's license
водка vodka
возвращать(ся) (i) return
возраст age
войлок felt
война war
вокзал (railroad) station
вокруг around
волк wolf
волна wave
волос hair
восемнадцать eighteen
восемь eight
восемьдесят eighty
восемьсот eight hundred
воскресенье Sunday
восток east

востребование   demand; **до востребования**   general delivery
восьмой   eighth
вот   here is
врач   doctor
временный   temporary
время (n)   time
сколько времени   how long, how much time
все   everyone
всё   everything
вспышка   flash
вставать (i)   stand up
вставить (p)   paste, put in
вставной зуб   false tooth
встреча   meeting
встречный   oncoming
вторник   Tuesday
второй   second
вход   entrance
входить (i)   enter; **входить в стоимость**   included in the price
входной билет   entrance ticket, cover charge
вчера   yesterday
въезд   entry
вы   you (plural and polite singular)
вывыхнут   dislocated
выдать вклад   make a deposit
выезд   departure
вызвать (p)   call for, summon
выиграть (p)   win
выйти (p)   exit, get out
выключатель (m)   switch
вылетать (i)   fly away
вынос   takeout
выписать (p)   write out
выпить (p)   drink
вырезать (p)   cut
высокий   high, tall
выставка   exhibition
выхлопная трубка   exhaust pipe
выход   exit
выходить (i)   exit, get out
выходной день   day off

Г

габардин   gabardine
гаечный ключ   wrench
газ   butane gas
газета   newspaper
газетный киоск   newsstand
гайка   nut
галерея   gallery
галлон   gallon
галстук   tie
гардероб   coatroom
гастроном   supermarket
где   where
гектар   hectare
гигиенические салфетки   sanitary napkins
гимнастика   gymnastics
главный   main
гладить (i)   press
глажение   pressing
глажка   ironing
глаз   eye
гланц   gloss
глубоко   deeply
глухая (f)   deaf
глухой (m)   deaf
говорить (i)   speak
год   year
годовщина   anniversary
гол   goal
голландский   Dutch
голова   head
головка   stem of a watch
головной   head; **головная боль**   headache
голоден (m), голодна (f)   hungry
голубой   light blue
голубцы   stuffed cabbage
горло   throat
гора   mountain
горные лыжи   downhill skis
город   city
горох   peas
горошек   polka dot
горчица   mustard

горчичник mustard plaster
горячий hot
господин Mister
госпожа Miss, Mrs.
ГОСТ ASA (film speed)
гостеприимство hospitality
гостиница hotel
гость (m) guest
государственный state
готово ready
градус degree (of temperature)
гражданин (m), гражданка (f) citizen
грамм gram
гранат pomegranate
грейпфрут grapefruit
гриб mushroom
гриль (m) grill
громко loudly
громче louder
грудь (f) breast
грузинский Georgian
груша pear
губа lip
губка sponge
губная помада lipstick
гудок horn
гусь (m) goose

Д

да yes
давать взаймы lend
далее farther
далеко far
дама queen (cards)
дата date
дать (p) give
дача dacha (country house)
два (m), две (f) two
двадцать twenty
двенадцать twelve
дверь (f) door
двести two hundred
движение traffic
двое twosome
дворец palace

Дворец съездов Palace of Congresses
двухкомнатная two-room (apartment)
двуспальная кровать double bed
двушка two-kopeck coin
девушка young girl, miss (to waitress)
девяносто ninety
девятнадцать nineteen
девятый ninth
девять nine
девятьсот nine hundred
дежурная "key lady"
дезодорант deodorant
действующий active
декабрь (m) December
декларация customs declaration
декларировать (i) declare
дело matter, business
денежный fiscal, money; **денежный перевод** money order
день (m) day; **днём** in the afternoon
деньги money
деревня countryside
деревья trees
десна gum
десятый tenth
десять ten
детектив mystery (film, novel)
дети children
детский children's
дешёвый cheap, inexpensive
джаз jazz
джин gin
джинсы jeans
диета diet
дипломат diplomat
директор director
дирижёр musical conductor
диск disc, disk
дискотека discotheque
длина length
длинный long

длиться (i)   last
для   for
до   before, until
добрый   good; доброе утро
   good morning; добрый вечер
   good evening; добрый день
   good afternoon
дождь (m)   rain; идёт дождь
   it's raining
долго   a long time
должен (m), должна (f)
   I must, I owe
долина   valley
доллар   dollar
дом   home; дома   at home;
   домой   (to) home
домкрат   auto jack
Домодедово   Domodedovo
доплатно   collect (telegram)
дорога   road, path, way
дорогой   dear, expensive
дорожка   path
дорожный чек   traveler's
   check
доска   board
доставка   delivery; письмо с
   доставкой   special delivery
   letter
достижение   achievement
достопримечательность (f)
   attraction
доходы   gains
дочка   daughter
дочь (f)   daughter
драма   drama
друг   friend
другой   another
дуть (i)   blow
думать (i)   think
дурак   fool
духи   perfume
душ   shower
дыня   melon
дышать (i)   breathe
дюйм   inch

Е–Ё

Евгений Онегин   Eugene
   Onegin
Европа   Europe
еда   food
единый билет   single ticket
ёлочка   herringbone
ерунда   nonsense
если   if
есть (i)   there is
ехать (i)   go (by vehicle)
ещё   another, more

Ж

жаль   it's a pity; как жаль
   what a shame
жар   fever
жареный   fried
жаркий   hot (temperature)
жать (i)   pinch; они жмут
   they pinch
ждать (i)   wait
жевать (i)   chew
желать (i)   wish
железнодорожный переезд
   railroad crossing
жёлтый   yellow
желудок   stomach
желудочное расстройство
   upset stomach
жемчуг   pearl
жена   wife
женат   married (of a man)
женский   ladies', women's
женский салон   beauty parlor
женщина   woman
жесткий диск   hard disk
жетон   token
живой   live
живот   abdomen
жульен   julienne
журнал   magazine

З

за behind
заболеть (р) fall ill
забронировать (р) reserve
заведующий manager
завернуть (р) wrap
завивка a permanent
заводить (i) wind (a watch)
заводиться (i) turn over (car)
завтра tomorrow
завтрак breakfast
загар sunburn
задержать (р) stop, restrain
задний rear, tail
заезд arrival
заехать (р) pick up, drive by
зажигалка lighter
зажигание ignition
заказ order
заказано reserved
заказать (р) order
заказное письмо registered
  letter
заказывать (i) order
заколка bobby pin
закрывать(ся) (i) close
закрыто closed
закрыть(ся) (р) close
закурить (р) smoke
закуска appetizer
закусочная snack bar
зал hall
залог security deposit
заменять exchange
заменить (р) replace
замечательно wonderful
замужем married (of a woman)
замша suede
занято occupied
запад west
запасный emergency, spare
запасный выход emergency
  exit
записать(ся) (р) write down,
  register
запор constipation

заправка gas station
запрещено prohibited
запчасть (f) spare part
запястье wrist
заранее in advance
зарядить (р) charge (the car
  battery)
затраты expenses
заушник eyeglass arm
зачем? what for?
зачёсывать (i) comb
заявка request
звать (i) call; **меня зовут**
  my name is; **как вас зовут?**
  what is your name?
здание building
здесь here
здоровье health; **На здоровье!**
  Cheers! (to your health).
Здравствуйте! Hello!
зелёный green
зеркало mirror
зернистая икра black caviar
зима winter; **зимой** in the
  winter
знать (i) know
значить (i) mean
значок lapel pin
золото gold
золотой gold(en)
Золушка Cinderella
зонт umbrella
зоопарк zoo
зуб tooth
зубной dental
зубная боль toothache
зубной врач dentist
зубной протез denture
зубной эликсир mouthwash

И

и and
иголка needle
играть (i) play
игрушка toy
идти (i) go (by foot); **идите!**
  go!

из from
извинить (p) excuse;
извините! excuse me!
издание edition
изделия goods
изумруд emerald
изюм raisin
икра caviar; **зернистая икра**
black caviar; **кетовая икра**
red caviar
или or
имам imam
имущество property
имя (n) first name
инвалид disabled
инвалидное кресло
wheelchair
инвестиция investment
индейка turkey
иностранный foreign
инспекция inspection
институт institute
инструмент instrument
интернет internet
Интурист Intourist
ипотека mortgage
инфекция infection
информация information
искусство art
использоваться (i) use
история history
итальянский Italian
июль (m) July
июнь (m) June

Й

йод iodine

К

к toward
кабельное телевидение cable
television
кабина cabin
каблук heel
кадр exposure (film)

каждый each, every
казаться (i) seem
казино casino
как how
какао cocoa, hot chocolate
какой which
камень (f) stone
камера хранения checkroom
Канада Canada
канадец (m) Canadian
канадка (f) Canadian
канадский Canadian
канцелярский office,
stationery
капитал capital
капля drop; **ушные капли**
ear drops; **глазные капли**
eye drops
капот hood
капочино cappuccino
капуста cabbage
карандаш pencil
карат carat
карбюратор carburetor
карманный pocket
карп carp
карта card, map
карта гостя guest card
картина picture
картофель (m) potatoes
картошка potato(es)
касса cashier
кассета cassette
кассовой аппарат cash
register
кататься (i) ride; **кататься**
на коньках go ice skating;
кататься на лыжах go
skiing; **кататься на санках**
go sledding
категория category
католический Catholic
кафе cafe
качество quality
каша warm cereal
кашель (m) cough
каштан chestnut
каштановый auburn

каюта cabin
кварта quart
квартира apartment
кварцовый quartz
квас kvass
крашенная капуста
    sauerkraut
квитанция receipt
кекс cupcake, muffin
керамика ceramics
кефир yogurt-like beverage
киви kiwi
кило, килограмм kilo(gram)
километр kilometer
киоск kiosk; газетный киоск
    newspaper stand
кипяток boiling water
кисть (f) hand
китайский Chinese
клавиатура keyboard
кладбище cemetery
класс class
классический classical
классно! super!
класть (i) put down; не
    кладите трубку! don't
    hang up!
клей glue
клетка plaid
клеющая лента Scotch tape
клубника strawberries
ключ key
книга book
книжный магазин bookstore
кнопка thumbtack
когда when
код PIN number
код города area code
кожа skin, leather
Кока-кола Coca-Cola
коктейли cocktails
колбаса salami
колготки pantyhose
колено knee
колесо wheel, tire
количество number (quantity)
коллега (m & f) colleague
коллекционный collector's

колода deck of cards
кольцо ring, circle
комбинация ladies' slip
комедия comedy
комиссионый магазин
    antique store
комитет committee
компактный диск CD
    (compact disc)
компостер ticket punch
компот stewed fruit
компьютер (n) computer
компьютерный (adj)
    computer
конверт envelope
кондитерская pastry shop
кондиционер air conditioning
конец end
конечно of course
конкуренция competition
конституция constitution
контактная линза contact
    lens
контактное лицо contact
    person
контракт contract
контроль (m) control
конфета candy
концерт concert
кончать(ся) (i) end
коньки ice skates
коньяк cognac
копейка kopeck
коридор corridor, lane
коричневый brown
кормить (i) feed, serve food
коробка box
королева queen
король (m) king
коронка dental crown
короткий short
корреспондент correspondent
космонавт cosmonaut
космос cosmos, space
костёл Catholic church
костыли crutches
кость (f) bone
костюм suit

котлета cutlet
который who, what, which
кофе (m) coffee
кофеварка coffeemaker
краб crab
красивый beautiful
Красная площадь Red Square
красный red
кредитная карточка credit card
крем cream, lotion
Кремль (m) Kremlin
кремни flints
крепкий strong
крепления bindings
крепость (f) fortress
кровать (f) bed
кровотечение bleeding
кровь (f) blood
кролик rabbit
кроме except
круглосуточно around the clock
кружева lace
кружиться (i) spin; **голова кружится** I'm dizzy
круиз cruise
крупа cold cereal
крупный large
кто who
кто-нибудь anyone
куда where to, which way
кудри curls
купальник bathing suit
купаться (i) swim
купе compartment
купить (p) buy
купюра bill (paper currency)
курить (i) smoke; **не курить** no smoking
курица chicken
курс course (currency exchange rate)
куртка raincoat
курящий smoking, smoker; **для курящих** smoking section
кусачки nail clippers

кусок piece, bar (of soap, etc.)
кухня cuisine; kitchen

Л

ладно that's fine
ладья rook (chess)
лак для волос hair spray
лампа lamp
лампочка bulb
лапша noodles
ластик eraser
латте latte
Лебединое озеро Swan Lake
левый left
лёгкий easy, light
лёковой автомобиль passenger car
лежать (i) lie (in bed)
лезвие razor blade
лекарство medicine; **рецептное лекарство** prescription medicine; **безрецептное лекарство** nonprescription medicine
Ленин Lenin
Ленинград Leningrad
лента tape, film
лес forest
лето summer; **летом** in the summer
лечь (p) lie down; **лечь в больницу** go to the hospital
ли if, whether
ликёр liqueur
лимон lemon
лимонад soft drink
линейка ruler; **бумага в линейку** lined paper
линза lens
линия line
лиса fox
литр liter
лифт elevator
лихорадка fever; **сенная лихорадка** hay fever
лицо face
личный personal

лишний   extra
лодка   boat
лодышка   ankle
ложа   box, loge
ложиться (i)   lie down
ложка   spoon
локоть (m)   elbow
лосьон   face lotion
лук   onion
лучше   better
лучший   best
лыжи   skis
льготный   discount
любить (i)   like, love
люкс   deluxe

M

мавзолей   mausoleum
магазин   store, shop
магнезия   magnesia
магнитический   magnetic
магнитофон   cassette recorder
мазь (f)   ointment
май   May
майка   undershirt
майонез   mayonnaise
максимальный   maximum
мал, мала, малы   too small
малахит   malachite
маленький   little, small
малина   raspberries
мало   a little
мандарин   tangerine
маникюр   manicure
маникюрные ножницы
     cuticle scissors
Мариинский театр   Mariinsky
     Theater
марка   stamp, brand
марлевый   gauze; марлевая
     салфетка   gauze (sanitary)
     napkin
март   March
маршрутка, маршрутное
     такси   minivan route taxi
масло   butter, oil
массаж   massage

мат!   checkmate!
матовый   matte
матрац   mattress
матрёшка   nested doll
мать (f)   mother
махорка   chewing tobacco
махровая ткань   terrycloth
машина   car
медленнее   slower
медленный   slow
медовуха   mead
медсестра   nurse
между   between
междугородный   intercity;
     междугородный разговор
     long-distance call
международный   international
мелький   small
менее   less
ментол   menthol
меньше   less, smaller
меню (n)   menu
место   seat, place; мест нет
     no vacancies
месяц   month
метр   meter
метрдотель (m)   maitre d'hotel
метро   subway (metro)
мех (n)   fur
меховой (adj)   fur
мечеть (f)   mosque
миграционная карта
     migration card
микроавтобус   van
микроволновая печь
     microwave oven
микстура   mixture; микстура
     от кашля   cough syrup
милиционер   cop
милиция   police
миллиард   billion
миллиметр   millimeter
миллион   million
миндаль (m)   almonds
минеральная вода   mineral
     water
минимальный   minimal

минута minute; **минуточку!** just a minute!
младший younger, junior
много many, much
мобильник cell phone
модем modem
модный stylish, fashionable
может быть maybe, perhaps
можно may (one)
мой, моя, моё, мои mine
мокка mocha
молодец! you're super!
молодой young
молодой человек! young man! waiter!
молоко milk
молоток hammer
молчать (i) shut up (silent)
монастырь (m) monastery
Монетный двор Russia's Mint
монитор monitor
море sea
морковь (f) carrot
мороженое ice cream
морская болезнь seasickness
Москва Moscow
мост bridge
мочалка sponge
мочь (i) can, be able to; **я могу** I can; **ты можешь** you can; **он/она может** he/she can; **мы можем** we can; **вы можете** you can; **они могут** they can
МРЗ плеер MP3 player
муж husband
мужской male, men's
мужчина man
музей museum
музыка music
музыкальный musical
мундштук cigarette holder
мы we
мыло soap
мытьё (n) wash (shampoo)
мышь mouse
мэйк-ап make-up
мюзикл musical

мягкий soft
мясо meat
мясной (адй) meat
мята mint
мяч ball

Н

на on, onto, to
набирать (i) dial
набор set, collection
набраться (p) accumulate
над on top of
надо must (one)
надувной inflatable, pneumatic
нажать (p) push
назад ago, backwards
название title
найти (p) find
накидка wraparound
накрахмаленный starched
налево to the left
наличные (деньги) cash
налог tax
напечатать print
написать (p) write
напиток beverage
направление destination, direction
направо to the right
напротив opposite
народный folk (adj), people's
наручные часы wristwatch
нарушение violation
нарыв abscess
насморк cold (in the head)
насос pump
настольный компьютер desktop computer
наука science
научно-популярный science fiction
начало beginning, starting time
начинать(ся) (i) begin
наш, наша, наше, наши our
не no
Невский Nevsky

негабаритный oversized/overweight

неделя week

нейлон nylon

некурящий non-smoking; для некурящих non-smoking section

немая азбука sign language

немного a little

немнущаяся ткань wash and wear

нержавейка stainless steel

несколько few

нет no

нефрит jade

нечего nothing

нижнее бельё underwear

нижний lower; нижняя юбка half slip

никто no one

ничего nothing, never mind

но but

новый new

нога leg

ноготь (m) fingernail, toenail

нож knife

ножницы scissors

номер number, hotel room; на номер station-to-station call

норка mink

нормальный normal

нос nose

носильщик porter

носок sock

носовой платок handkerchief

ноутбук laptop computer

ночная рубашка nightgown

ночной клуб nightclub

ночь (f) night

ноябрь (m) November

нравиться like, be pleasing to

ну! well!

нужен, нужна, нужно, нужны necessary, I need

нуль (m) zero

O

о/об about

обвариться (p) burn oneself

обгон passing

обед lunch

обжаренный grilled

обмен валюты currency exchange

обменный курс exchange rate

обменять (i) exchange

оборот curve, turn

обратный return

обручальное кольцо engagement/wedding ring

обслуживаться (i) be waited on

обслуживание service

обувь (f) shoes

обхват circumference

объезд detour

объявляться (i) announce

обязательство obligation

овёс oats

овощи vegetables

овсянный oatmeal

овчина sheepskin

огонь (m) fire

ограничение restriction

огурец cucumber

одеваться (i) dress (oneself)

одежда clothing

одеколон cologne

одеяло blanket

один (m), одна (f) one

одиннадцать eleven

однокомнатная one-room (apartment)

односпальная кровать single bed

однотонный solid color

одолжить (p) lend

ожерелье necklace

ожидаемый expected

ожог a burn

озеро lake

озноб chills

ой! ouch!
окно window
около near
окошко window
октябрь (m) October
омар lobster
он he
она she
они they
оникс onyx
оно it
опаздывать (i) be late
опасность (f) caution
опасный dangerous
опера opera
оперетта operetta
оплата payment
оправа frame for eyeglasses
оптика optician
опухоль (f) swelling
орех nut
освобождённый exempt, free from
осень (f) fall; **осенью** in the fall
осетрина sturgeon
особый special
оставить (p) leave (something)
остановиться (p) stop (halt)
остановка (bus, trolley) stop
осторожно carefully
острый hot, spicy
от from
отбивная котлета chop/cutlet
отвезти (p) take (by vehicle)
отвёртка screwdriver
отдел section
отдельно separately
отец father
открывать(ся) (i) open
открытка postcard
открыто open
открыть(ся) (p) open
откуда from where
отойти (p) go away
отплывать (i) sail away
отправка shipment

отправление departure
отправлять(ся) (i) leave, depart, send
отставать (i) lag behind; **они отстают** my watch is slow
отчество patronymic
офицер knight (chess)
официант waiter
официантка waitress
охрана security
оценивать (i) appraise
очень very
очередь (f) turn in a line
очки eyeglasses
ошибиться (p) err

П

пакет box, packet
палец finger
палка cane, pole
пальто coat
памятник monument
память (f) memory; **на память** in remembrance
папка folder
паприка paprika
пара pair
парикмахерская barber shop
парильня steam room
парк park
партер orchestra (in the theater)
Партизанская Partizan metro station
партия (political) party
партнёр partner
парфюмерия toiletry shop
паспорт passport
пассажир passenger
паста paste
пастор minister (pastor)
пачка pack, package
пелёнка diaper
пельмени pelmeni, Siberian dumplings
пельменная pelmeni cafe
пеницилин penicillin

пепельница ashtray
Пепси Pepsi
первоначальный initial
первый first
перевод translation, transfer
переводчик interpreter
перевозка transportation
перегреваться (i) overheat
перед before, in front of
передать (p) transfer
переезд (vehicular) crossing
перезвонить (p) call back
переключение скоростей
    transmission;
    автоматическое
    переключение скоростей
    automatic transmission
перелом broken bone
переносный компьютер
    portable computer
перерыв break (recess)
пересесть (p) transfer
перетасовать (p) shuffle
переход transfer, (pedestrian)
    crossing
перец pepper
персик peach
персональный компьютер
    personal computer
перчатка glove
Петербург Petersburg
петь (i) sing
печёный baked
печень (f) liver
печенье cookie
пешеходный pedestrian
пешка pawn (chess)
пиво beer; пиво бутылочное
    bottled beer; пиво
    разливное draught beer
пиджак jacket
пижама pajamas
пики spades (cards)
Пиковая дама Queen of
    Spades
пилка nail file
пирог pie
пирожное pastry

пирожок pastry
писатель (m) writer
письмо letter
питательный nourishing,
    moisturizing
пить (i) drink; мне хочется
    пить I'm thirsty
пишущая машинка
    typewriter
плавать (i) swim
плавки bathing trunks
плакат poster
план map
планы plans
пластинка musical record
пластырь (m) adhesive tape
плата charge, fee, payment
платёж payment
платина platinum
платить (i) pay
платная парковка paid
    parking
платок kerchief; носовой
    платок handkerchief
платформа platform
платье dress
плащ raincoat
плёнка photographic film, tape
плечик hanger
плечо shoulder
плиссированная ткань
    permanent press
пломба dental filling
плоскогубцы pliers
плохой bad, poor
площадь (f) square
пляж beach
по according to
победа victory
поближе nearer
поблизости nearby
побольше more
побриться (p) have a shave
повернуть (p) turn
поворот curve, turn
повторить (p) repeat
повторять (i) repeat
поговорить (p) speak (with)

погода weather
под under
подарок gift
подарочный сертификат gift certificate
подвернуть (p) tighten
подешевле less expensive
подключиться (p) connect
подлиннее longer
подмётка sole of a shoe
подобный similar; **и тому подобное** and so forth
подождать (p) wait
подойти (p) approach
подороже more expensive
подпись signature
подравнять (p) even out
подстричь (p) trim
подтвердить (p) confirm
подушка pillow
поезд train
поездка trip
поехать (p) go (by vehicle); **поедем!** let's go!
пожалуйста please, you're welcome
пожар fire
Пожарная охрана Fire Department
поживать (i): как вы поживаете? how are you?
пожилой elderly
позавчера day before yesterday
позвать (p) call, summon
позвонить (p) call on the telephone
поздно late
позже later
познакомиться (p) get acquainted
позолоченый gold-plated
пойти (p) go (by foot)
пока! until later!
показать (p) show
покашлять (p) cough
покой peace (of mind)
покороче shorter

покупка purchase
пол floor
полдень (m) noon
поле field
полёт flight
поликлиника clinic
полиэфир polyester
полночь (f) midnight
половина half
положить (p) put, place
полоска stripe
полотенце towel
полотно linen
полусухое semi-dry
получить (p) receve, pick up
помада: губная помада lipstick
помидор tomato
помочь (p) help; **помогите!** help!
помощь (f) help; **скорая помощь** first aid, ambulance
помыть (p) wash
понедельник Monday
понести (p) carry
понимать (i) understand
понос diarrhea
поп pop
попасть (p) get to; **вы не туда попали** you've reached a wrong number
поплин poplin
поправка touch-up
попробовать (p) sample
популярный popular
порез a cut
порезаться (p) cut oneself
портфель (m) briefcase
порядок order; **всё в порядке** everything is in order
посадка boarding, landing of an airplane
посадочный билет boarding pass
посветлее lighter
посидеть (p) sit
послать (p) send

после after
послезавтра day after tomorrow
посмотреть (p) look
посольство embassy
поставить (p) put in
поставка delivery
постричься (p) have a haircut
посчитать (p) count, add up
посылка package
потемнее darker
потерять (p) lose
почему why
починить (p) repair
почистить (p) clean
почта post office; **Главный Почтамт** General Post Office
почтовый postal
почтовый ящик mailbox
пошлина (customs) duty
пояс belt
правый right (direction)
правильный right, correct
православный Orthodox
праздник holiday
практически practically
прачечная laundry
прачечная самообслуживания laundromat
предпочитать (i) prefer
предприятие enterprise
представить(ся) (p) introduce (oneself)
преимущество advantage, right of way
прекрасный splendid
премия premium
преподаватель (m) teacher
прибытие arrival
прибывать (i) arrive
прибыль (f) profit
привет! hi!, regards!
пригласить (p) invite
приёмная reception room, waiting room
прийти (p) arrive, come
примерить (p) try on

примерочная кабина changing room
примечание comment
принести (p) bring
принимать (i) accept, take (medicine)
приносить (i) bring
принтер printer
принято accepted, acceptable
принять вклад make a withdrawal
приплывать (i) land
приправа seasoning
прислоняться (i) lean on
пристань (f) dock
приступ attack; **сердечный приступ** heart attack
приходный ордер deposit slip
причёска hairdo
пришить (p) sew on
приятно pleasing
пробить (p) punch a ticket
пробка traffic jam
проблема problem, something wrong
пробор part (in the hair)
провайдер provider
проверить (p) check
проводить (i) take, escort
программка program
продавать (i) sell
продажа sale
продолжительность length, duration
проезд ride, trip
проездной билет trip ticket
проехать (p) get to
проиграть (p) lose a game
проигрыватель (m) record player
прокат rental; **на прокат** for rent
пропуск key card (pass)
просветить (p) X-ray
просить (i) beg, request
простить (p) pardon; **простите!** pardon me!
простыня linen towel, sheet

протез (зубной) denture
протекать (i) leak
протестантский Protestant
профессия profession
прохладный cool
проход aisle
проходить (i) pass by
процент interest rate
процесс process
прошлый past, previous; в
    прошлом году last year
прощайте! farewell!
прощение forgiveness
проявлять (i) develop film
пруд pond
прямо straight ahead
прямой straight
птица bird
пуговица button
пудра powder
Пулково Pulkovo Airport
пункт point
пускать (i) let in
пусть let, allow
путеводитель (m) guidebook
путешествие (m) trip
путь (m) way, path
пучок bun (hairdo)
пшеница wheat
пятнадцать fifteen
пятница Friday
пятно spot
пятый fifth
пять five
пятьдесят fifty
пятьсот five hundred

Р

работать (i) work
рабочий worker, working
рабочий стол desktop
раввин rabbi
рагу ragout
радиатор car radiator
радио radio
раз one time, once
разбить(ся) (p) break, shatter

разбудить (p) wake
разворот U-turn
разговор conversation,
    telephone call
разговорник phrasebook
раздеться (p) undress
    (oneself)
разливное пиво beer on tap
размен change (money)
разменять (i) change
размер size
разрешить (p) allow
разъединить (p) disconnect
рана wound
рано early
раскладной диван pull-out
    couch
раскладушка cot
расписаться (p) sign
расписание schedule
распродажа big sale
рассказ short story
рассольник kidney soup
расстройство disorder;
    желудочное расстройство
    upset stomach
растение plant
растительное масло vegetable
    oil
растянут twisted
расходный ордер withdrawal
    slip
расходы expenses
расчёска comb
расчётный час check-out time
ребро rib
революция revolution
регистрация registration,
    check-in
редиска radish
резинка rubber band
резьба carved object
рейс flight
река river
рекомендовать (i) recommend
ремень (m) belt
ремень вентилятора (m) fan
    belt

ремонт repairs
репька turnip
ресница eyelash
республика republic
ресторан restaurant
ресторанный дворик food court
рецепт prescription
рецептный отдел prescription section (pharmacy)
решётка fender
ржаной rye
рис rice
рисование drawing
рождение birth; **с днём рождения!** happy birthday!
рожь rye
розетка plug
розничная цена retail price
розовый rose, pink
розыск багажа lost luggage
рок rock
ром rum
роман novel
Российская Федерация Russian Federation
российский Russian
Россия Russia
россиянин (m) Russian citizen
россиянка (f) Russian citizen
рост height
ростбиф roast beef
рот mouth
рубашка shirt
рубин ruby
рубль (m) ruble
рубчатый вельвет corduroy
рука arm
рукав sleeve
рукавица mitten
рулевое колесо steering wheel
руль (m) steering wheel
рулон roll (of something)
румяна rouge
русский (m) Russian, Russian man
русская (f) Russian woman
ручей brook

ручка pen, door handle
ручной hand
ручной тормоз hand brake
ручные часы wristwatch
рыба fish
рыбный (adj) fish
рынок market
рыночная цена market value (price)
рычаг lever; **рычаг переключения** gear shift
рюмка vodka glass
ряд row

С

с from, with
сад garden
салат salad, lettuce
салон section on an airplane
салфетка napkin, tissue
сам self
самолёт aircraft
самообслуживание self-service
самый the very (best, least)
Санкт Петербург St. Petersburg
сантиметр centimeter
санки sled
сапог boot
сапфир sapphire
сатин sateen
сауна sauna
сахар sugar
сахарин saccharin
сбить (p) knock over
сборник collection
сброс clear
свежий fresh
свёкла beets
сверху from the top
светить (i) shine
светлый light
свеча suppository, spark plug
свидание appointment; **до свидания** good-bye
свиной pork
свитер sweater

свободный free
священник priest
сдавать (i) deal the cards, give over
сделать (p) do, make
себе, себя oneself
север north
сегодня today
седьмой seventh
сейф safe
сейчас now
секунда second (sixtieth part of a minute)
секундная стрелка second hand
селёдка herring
село village
сёмга salmon
семнадцать seventeen
семь seven
семьдесят seventy
семьсот seven hundred
семья family
сенная лихорадка hay fever
сентябрь (m) September
сердце heart
серебро silver
серебряный (adj) silver
середина center
серый gray
серьга earring
серьёзно seriously
сестра sister
сзади in the back
сигарета cigarette
сигар cigar
сигнальный огонь directional signal
сидеть (i) sit
синагога synagogue
синий dark blue
система system
системный блок CPU
сказать (p) say
сканер scanner
скидка discount
скитная карта discount card
скольский slippery

сложить fold
сколько how much, how many
скопировать copy
скорая помощь first aid, ambulance
скоро soon
скорость (f) speed, gear
скотч Scotch tape
скрепка paper clip
слабительное laxative
слабость (f) weakness
слабый weak, mild
сладкий sweet
сладкое dessert
слайд slide
слева on the left
следующий next
слепая (f) blind
слепой (m) blind
слива plum
сливки cream
сливочное creamy (vanilla)
слишком too (excessively)
словарь (m) dictionary
слово word
сломать (p) break
слон bishop (chess)
слоновая кость ivory
служба service
слуховой аппарат hearing aid
случиться (p) happen
слушать (i) listen
слышно audible
смазать (p) grease
смарт-карта smart-card
сменить (p) change, replace; **сменить масло** change the oil
смеситель faucet
сметана sour cream
смородина currants
смотреть (i) look, see, watch
СНГ CIS
снег snow; **идёт снег** it's snowing
сниженный reduced; **товары по сниженным ценам** sale items

снимите! cut the deck!
снотворное sleeping pills
соболь (m) sable
собор cathedral
советский Soviet
современный modern
совсем completely, entirely
Содружество Независимых Государтсв Confederation of Independent States
Соединённые Штаты United States
сойти (p) go out; **вы с ума сошли?** are you crazy?
сокавыжиматель (m) blender
солнечные очки sunglasses
солнечный ожог sunburn
солнце sun
соль (f) salt
солянка solyanka (fish or meat soup)
сообщение message
сорок forty
сорочка shirt
сосиска hot dog
сотовый телефон cellular phone
сотрудник консульства consular officer
соуса sauce
сохранить (p) save
социалистический socialist
союз union
спаржа asparagus
спасатель (m) lifeguard
спасибо thank you
спектакль (m) performance
спереди in the front
спешить (i) hurry; **они спешат** my watch is fast
спина back
спирт alcohol
список list
спичка match
спокойной ночи! good night!
спорттовары sporting goods
справа on the right
спрашивать (i) ask

спустить (p) descend; **спустила шина** the tire is flat
Спящая красавица Sleeping Beauty
среда Wednesday
среди among
средний average, medium
срочно urgently
СССР USSR
стадион stadium
стакан glass
станция station
стартер starter
старший elder, senior
Старый Арбат Old Arbat
стекло glass, eyeglass lens
стеклочиститель (m) windshield wiper
стелька insole
стиральная машина washing machine
стирать (i) wash clothes
стирка wash, washing (clothes)
стихотворение poetry
сто hundred
стоимость (f) cost, price
стоить (i) cost
стол desk, table
столик table
столовая cafeteria
стоп stop
сторона side
стоянка parking; **стоянка такси** taxi stand
стоять (i) stand; **стойте!** wait!
страна country
страница page
страхование insurance
страшный terrible
стрелка hand of a watch
стрижка haircut
стричь (i) cut hair
строитель (m) builder
стручковая фасоль string beans

студент student
ступня foot
суббота Saturday
сувенир souvenir
судак pike/perch
судорога cramp
сумка pocketbook
сумма amount
суп soup
сурок marmot
сухой dry
сцена stage
сцепление gear shift, clutch pedal
счастливого пути! bon voyage!
счёт account, score
США USA
сын son
сыр cheese
сюда here

Т

табак tobacco
таблетка tablet
тазик washbasin
тайский Thai
так so, thus, this way
такой such
также also
такси (n) taxi
талия waist
талон ticket, coupon
тальк talcum powder
там there
тампон tampon
танцевать (i) dance
тапочка slipper
тарелка plate
твой, твоя, твоё, твои your
творог cream cheese
театр theater
Театр оперы и балета Мусоргского Mussorgsky Opera and Ballet Theater
театральный theatrical
текила tequila
текст text

телевизор television
телеграмма telegram
тележка (baggage) cart
телекс telex
телефакс fax
телефон telephone
телефон-автомат pay telephone
телефонная кабина telephone booth
телефонная карта telephone card
тело body
телятина veal
темно (adv) darkly
тёмный (adj) dark
температура temperature
теннис tennis
тень (f) shadow
тепло warmth
тёплый warm
теплоход boat
термометр thermometer
тесны too narrow
тетрадь (f) notebook
тётя aunt
тише quieter
ткань (f) material, fabric
то that one
товарищ comrade
товары goods, items, supplies
только only
томатный tomato
тон tint
топаз topaz
торговля trade
торговый (adj) trade
торговый комплекс shopping mall
тормоз brake
торт cake
тостер toaster
точилка sharpener
тошнота nausea
трагедия tragedy (drama)
трамвай tram, trolleycar
транспорт transportation
трансформатор transformer

треска cod
третий third
трефы clubs (cards)
три three
тридцать thirty
тринадцать thirteen
триста three hundred
трогать (i) touch; не трогать
   don't touch
трое threesome
троллейбус trolleybus
тропинка path
трубка pipe, telephone
   receiver
трубочный табак pipe
   tobacco
трусики ladies' panties
трусы men's underpants
туалет bathroom, restroom
туалетная бумажка toilet
   paper
туда there
туз ace (cards)
тунец tuna
тупик dead end
тур tour, trip
турист tourist
туристический (adj) tourist;
   туристический класс
   economy class
турмалин tourmaline
туфли women's shoes
тушёный stewed
тушь (f) mascara
ты you (singular)
тыква pumpkin
тысяча thousand

удлинитель (m) extension
   cord
удовольствие pleasure; с
   удовольствием with
   pleasure
у.е. conventional units
уезжать (i) depart
ужасно awful
уже already
ужин dinner
узбекский Uzbek
укладка set (hairdo)
украсть (p) steal
украска color rinse
уксус vinegar
улыбаться (i) smile
ум mind
уметь (i) know how
умывальник sink
универмаг (универсальный
   магазин) department store
университет university
унитаз toilet
упаковка подарков gift-
   wrapping
упасть (p) fall
уронить (p) drop
успокаивающее sedative
устал (m), устала (f) tired
уступить (p) yield
усы mustache
утка duck
утро morning; утром in the
   morning
ухо ear
ушиб bruise
ушные капли ear drops

У

у at, near
убран cleaned, picked up
убрать (p) make up
убыток a loss
увеличить (p) enlarge
удалить (p) delete, pull (a
   tooth)
удачи! good luck!

Ф

файл file
факс fax
фамилия family name
фара headlight
фарфоровый porcelain
фасан pheasant
фасоль (f) beans
февраль (m) February

фен hair dryer
фига fig
фигура chess piece
фигурные коньки figure skates
фильм movie
фильтр filter
финик date (fruit)
фирма business firm
фирменное блюдо house specialty
фланель (f) flannel
фонарь (m) flashlight
фонд fund
форель (m) trout
форма form
фотоаппарат camera
фотографировать (i) photograph
фотография picture
фототовары photographic supplies
фрукты fruits
фу! ugh!
фунт pound
фут foot (measurement)
футбол soccer
футболка polo shirt

X

халат robe
хватить (p) be enough
хвост (pony) tail
химический chemical
химчистка dry cleaner's
хлеб bread
хлопчатобумажная ткань cotton fabric
ходить (i) go, walk
ходунки walker
хозяйство economy
хозяйственный household
хоккей hockey
хоккейные коньки hockey skates
холодильник refrigerator
холодный cold

холм hill
хороший good
хорошо! that's good/okay!
хотеть(ся) (i) want, like;
    я хочу I want; ты хочешь you want; он/она хочет he/she wants; мы хотим we want; вы хотите you want; они хотят they want
Храм Василия Блаженного/ Покровский собор St. Basil's Cathedral
Храм Христа Спасителя Christ the Saviour Cathedral
хрен horseradish
хромая (f) lame
хромой (m) lame
хрусталь (m) crystal
художественный artistic
художник artist
хуже worse

Ц

царь (m) tsar
цвет color
цветная капуста cauliflower
цветы flowers
цена price
ценный valuable
ценное письмо certified letter
центральный central
центр downtown
цепочка chain
церковь (f) church
цирк circus
цыплёнок chicken

Ч

чай tea
час hour, o'clock; **в котором часу?** at what time?
часовая стрелка hour hand
частичный partial
частник private taxi driver
часто often

часть (f) part
часы watch, clock
чей, чья, чьё, чьи whose
чек check, bill
чековая книжка checkbook
чёлка bangs
человек person; **на человека** person-to-person call; **молодой человек!** young man! waiter!
чемодан suitcase
черви hearts (cards)
через across, through
чёрный black
чёрт devil; **чёрт возьми!** darn it!
чеснок garlic
четверг Thursday
четверо foursome
четвёртый fourth
четверть (f) quarter
четыре four
четыреста four hundred
четырнадцать fourteen
чинить (i) repair
число number, date; **какое сегодня число?** what's today's date?
чистка dry cleaning
читать (i) read
что what
что-нибудь something
чувствовать себя (i) feel
чулок stocking
чуть almost

Ш

шампанское champagne
шампунь (m) shampoo
шапка hat
шапочка cap
шарф scarf
шасси (n) chassis
шах! check! (in chess)
шахматы chess
шашечка check; **в шашечку** checked

шашки checkers
шашлык shish kebab
шашлычная shish kebab cafe
шведский стол smorgasbord
швейцар bellboy
шезлонг chaise longue
шёлк silk
Шереметьево Sheremetyevo
шерсть (f) wool
шестнадцать sixteen
шестой sixth
шесть six
шестьдесят sixty
шестьсот six hundred
шея neck
шина car tire
широкий wide
шифон chiffon
шницель (m) schnitzel
шнур cord
шнурок shoelace
шоколадный chocolate
шорты shorts
шоу show
шпагат string
шпилька bobby pin
шпинат spinach
штаны slacks
штат state
штука item
шуба fur coat
шумно noisy

Щ

щека cheek
Щелкунчик The Nutcracker
щёлочь (f) antacid
щётка brush
щи cabbage soup
щипчики tweezers

Ъ

ъ the hard sign

Ь

ь   the soft sign

Э

экскурсионный (adj) excursion

экскурсия (n)   excursion

экскурсия по городу   city tour

экстравагантный   extravagant, striking

электрический   electrical

электронная почта   e-mail

электронный   electronic

электронные часы   digital watch

электронный билет   electronic ticket

электротовары   electrical supplies

эликсир; зубной эликсир mouthwash

Эрмитаж   Hermitage

этаж   floor

это   this, that

эхо   echo

Ю

юбка   skirt

ювелирный   jewelry

юг   south

юмор   humor

Я

я   I

яблоко (n)   apple

яблочный (adj)   apple

язык   tongue, language

яичница   omelet; **яичница-болтунья**   scrambled eggs; **яичница-глазунья**   fried eggs

яйцо   egg; **яйцо вкрутую** hard-boiled egg; **яйцо всмятку**   soft-boiled egg

январь (m)   January

янтарь (m)   amber

ярд   yard (measurement)

ярус   (theater) circle, ring

яшма   jasper

ящик   box; **почтовый ящик** mailbox

INDEX

abbreviations, 174
accidents, 146–147
adjectives, 185
adverbs, 186
airport transportation, 22–23
air travel, 50–52
alcoholic beverages, 90
appetizers, 85–86
audio equipment, 117–119

baggage, 21–22
bakery, 92
banking, 27
barber shop, 128–130
basic needs, 193
bathhouse, 132–134
beach, 76–78
beauty parlor, 130–132
beverages, 89–91
bill, settling, 91
body parts, 142–143
bookstore, 105–106
boots, 111–112
bread, 92
buses, 40–41
business traveler, mini-
    dictionary for, 178–181

cake, 93
camera repairs, 138
cardinal numbers, 13–15
cards, 75
car rentals, 60–61
cheese, 92
chess, 76
citizenship, 170
clothing, 106–109
cold cuts, 93
commands, 188
communications, 152–159
computers, 158–159

consonants, 3
countries, 171–172
countryside, 79–80
credit cards, 26–27
currency exchange, 24–25
customs, 20
Cyrillic alphabet, 1–2

dairy, 92
dates, 165
days of the week, 163–164
dentist, 147–148
dessert, 89
directions, 172
doctor, 141–142
driving a car, 56–68
dry cleaning, 134–135

eating out, 82–85
eggs, 86
electrical appliances, 113
emergencies, 11–13
English-Russian dictionary,
    194–223
entertainment, 69–80
exchange rate, 24–25
exclamations, 10–11
expressions:
    frequently used, 5–9
    time, 162–163

fabric, 110–111
faxes, 156–157
first course, 86–87
fish, 87
food:
    restaurant, 85–91
    shopping for, 92–95, 114
fruit, 94

general information, 160–181
good-byes, 101

grammar:
  adjectives/possessive
    modifiers, 185
  adverbs, 186
  commands, 188
  negations, 189
  nouns, 182–184
  prepositions, 190–191
  pronouns, 184–185
  questions, 188–189
  verbs, 186–188
  vowels, 2
  word order, 189
greetings, 96–99

the handicapped, 149–151
hard vowels, 2
holidays (official), 167–168
hotel, 30–37
household items, 114

ice cream, 95
imperfective future tense,
  188
imperfective present tense,
  187
introductions, 96–99

jewelry store, 116–117

kopecks, 26

laundry, 134–135

main course, 87–89
meat, 87–89
medical care, 141–151
menu, 85–91
metric system, 115, 175–177
metro, 38–40
milk, 92
mini-dictionary (business
  travelers), 178–181
money, 26
months of the year, 164–165
Moscow, 46–47

nationality, 170
negations, 189
newsstand, 119
night life, 74–75
nouns, 182–184
numbers, 13–17

office supplies, 123–124
optician, 148–149
ordinal numbers, 16

parking, 60
passport control, 18–20
pastry shop, 93
past tense, 186–187
perfective future tense, 187
personal care/services,
  128–138
pharmacy, 139–141
photographic equipment,
  120–121
pool, 76–78
porters, 21–22
possessive modifiers, 185
post office, 152–153
poultry, 89
prepositions, 190–191
problems, 11–13
pronouns, 184–185
pronunciation guide, 2–4

quantities, 16–17
questions, 9, 188–189

ready reference key:
  basic needs, 193
  politeness, 192–193
  simple words/phrases,
    192
religious services, 48–49
restaurants, 81–91
rubles, 18, 26
Russian language, 1
Russian-English dictionary,
  224–247
Russian Federation, 169

St. Petersburg, 47–48
salad, 86
seasonings, 93
seasons, 165
second course, 87–89
service charge, 91
services. *See* personal
    care/services
service stations, 63–64
shipboard travel, 52–53
shoe repairs, 136
shoes, 111–112
shopping, 102–127
sightseeing, 44–46
signs:
    important, 172–173
    road, 56–59
simple words/phrases, 192
socializing, 99–101
soft vowels, 3
soup, 86–87
souvenirs, 121–123
sports, 76–79
stressed syllable, 2
subway, 38–40

taxis, 42–43
telegrams, 157–158

telephone numbers
    (emergency), 177
telephones, 153–156
temperature conversions,
    166–167
theater ticket, 73–74
time, 160–163
tipping, 28, 91
tobacco, 124–125
toiletries, 125–127
train service, 54–55
trams, 40–41
travel:
    air, 50–52
    shipboard, 52–53
    train, 54–55
trolleybuses, 40–41

vegetables, 95
verbs, 186–188
video equipment, 117–119
vowels, 2

watch repairs, 136–138
weather, 166
winter sports, 78–79
word order, 189